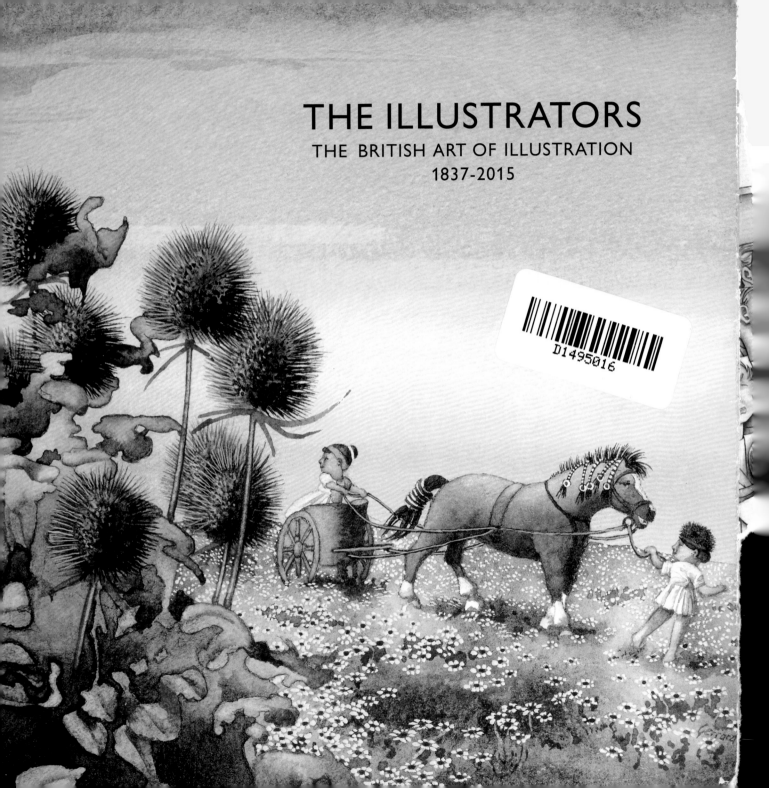

THE ILLUSTRATORS

THE BRITISH ART OF ILLUSTRATION

1837-2015

Our annual selling exhibition, the biggest event worldwide for cartoon and illustration collectors, features over 800 pictures covering the last two centuries. The exhibition is accompanied by a 350 page catalogue with over 584 images, which gives a true flavour of the show. The catalogue is available from the gallery at £20 + p&p (£5 UK, £10 Europe, £20 World).

Copyright © Chris Beetles Ltd 2015
8 & 10 Ryder Street
St James's
London SW1Y 6QB
020 7839 7551
gallery@chrisbeetles.com
www.chrisbeetles.com

ISBN 978-1-905738-71-7

Cataloguing in publication data is available from
the British Library

Written and researched by David Wootton
With contributions by Alexander Beetles
Edited by Catherine Andrews, Fiona Nickerson
and David Wootton
Design by Jeremy Brook of Graphic Ideas
Photography by Julian Huxley-Parlour
Reproduction by www.cast2create.com
Colour separation and printing by Geoff Neal
Litho Limited

Front cover: Roy Gerrard, *So into the field that night the daring twosome crept* [**392**]
Front endpaper: Arnold Roth, *It's Spring!* [**224**] [detail]
Frontispiece: William Heath Robinson, *Until the Other Children Came Home* [**136**]
Title page: Peter Cross, *Loud Speakers* [**445**]
[in a modified form]
Contents: William Heath Robinson, *Ladybirds* [**134**]
Back endpaper: Emma Chichester Clark, *Let me introduce – the friends of Mother Goose!* [**468**] [detail]
Back cover: Aubrey Beardsley, *A Damosel with Peacocks in a Garden* [**42**]

The Illustrators

*Audio guide available on request
(Special rates for groupies)*

THE BRITISH ART OF ILLUSTRATION
1837-2015

CHRIS BEETLES

8 & 10 Ryder Street, St James's, London SW1Y 6QB
020 7839 7551 gallery@chrisbeetles.com www.chrisbeetles.com

CONTENTS

4

THE
NINETEENTH
CENTURY

VICTORIAN ILLUSTRATORS AND CARTOONISTS

JOSEPH NOEL PATON
(1821-1901)

WILLIAM PURTON
(1833-1891)

JOHN LAWSON
(born 1838)

FRANK DADD
(1851-1929)

GORDON FRASER
(1859-1895)

*

JOHN TENNIEL
(1820-1914)

CHARLES KEENE
(1823-1891)

GEORGE DU MAURIER
(1834-1896)

WILLIAM RALSTON
(1841-1911)

LINLEY SAMBOURNE
(1844-1910)

PHIL MAY
(1864-1903)

JOSEPH NOEL PATON

Sir Joseph Noel Paton, RSA (1821-1901)

Joseph Noel Paton was the leading Scottish artist of the Victorian period to specialise in imaginative figure subjects, and notably fairies. In producing such masterpieces as *The Quarrel of Oberon and Titania*, he capitalised on his mimetic skills in order to represent the supernatural with great conviction.

Joseph Noel Paton was born in Dunfermline, Fife, on 13 December 1821, the second of three children of a damask designer and manufacturer. His father's interests as an antiquarian and collector provided early inspiration. (The collection, inherited by Paton, is now in the National Museum of Scotland, Edinburgh.) From his earliest years, his reading fired his imagination, and he made drawings based on tales of Celtic romance and legend, in addition to episodes from the Bible and ancient history. He developed talents for both literature and art, and would become a poet and critic as well as a painter and sculptor.

On completing his education at Dunfermline School and Dunfermline Art Academy, Paton spent three years in his father's profession, becoming director of design at Brown, Sharp & Co's sewn-muslin factory at Paisley, Strathclyde. Then, in 1842, he left Scotland for London where, in the following year, he entered the Royal Academy Schools. Though he did not take up a studentship, his time at the Schools proved important to his artistic development, for he met and befriended a younger, precocious student, John Everett Millais.

Paton's aptitude for literary subjects enabled him to work as both illustrator and painter. He contributed to Samuel Carter Hall's *The Book of British Ballads* (1842 & 1844) and Mrs Anna Maria Hall's *Midsummer Eve: A Fairy Tale of Love* (1847), two landmarks in the construction of the Victorian imagination. He also entered the competitions for the decoration of the rebuilt Houses of Parliament, a project on which the health of British history painting seemed so strongly to depend. He established his reputation in England with his two prizewinning entries, *The Spirit of Religion* (1845) and especially *The Reconciliation of Oberon and Titania* (1847). He had already exhibited his first, small version of its pendant, *The Quarrel of Oberon and Titania*, in Edinburgh in 1846, as his diploma work on becoming an associate of the Royal Scottish Academy.

Paton was invited by Millais to join the newly founded Pre-Raphaelite Brotherhood. Though sympathetic to its ideals, he declined, for he disliked London and preferred to return to Scotland. As a result, he practised and promoted its principles in the Scottish capital, recording the natural world in almost uncanny detail, and capitalising on his mimetic skills in order to convincingly represent the supernatural. This he demonstrated triumphantly with the large version of *The Quarrel of Oberon and Titania*, judged to be *the* painting of the exhibition when shown, in 1850, at the Royal Scottish Academy. He was elected a full academician in the same year.

Paton's approach to landscape painting was influenced not only by the example of the Pre-Raphaelites but by the writings of their champion, John Ruskin. Paton met Ruskin through Millais and, in 1853, attended the lectures that he gave in Edinburgh on Architecture and Painting. Soon after, he went on painting trips with his brother, the artist Waller Hugh Paton, to the Isle of Arran (1854 and 1855), possibly to Loch Lomond (1858), and later to the Continent (1861 and 1868).

By the late 1850s, Paton was as well known and admired in England as in Scotland, through his exhibits at the Royal Academy (1856-83) and his illustrations to Charles Kingsley's *The Water Babies* (1863). He was appointed Queen's Limner for Scotland in 1866, and knighted a year later.

His work as an original imaginative painter culminated in 1867, with the completion of *The Fairy Raid* and its exhibition at the Royal Academy. Five years later, he declined the invitation of Lewis Carroll to illustrate *Through the Looking-Glass and What Alice Found There*, the author's second great work of fantasy, stating that John Tenniel remained the ideal artist for the job. Instead, he devoted his remaining time to painting religious subjects in an academic manner comparable to that of his compatriot William Dyce. He died at his home in Edinburgh on 26 December 1901. Of the eleven children from his marriage to Margaret Gourlay (died 1900), his sons Frederick Noel Paton and Ronald Noel Paton also became artists.

His work is represented in the collections of the British Museum; and the Art Gallery and Museum, Kelvingrove (Glasgow) and the National Gallery of Scotland (Edinburgh).

Further reading:
Alasdair A Auld, *Fact and Fancy: Drawings and Paintings by Joseph Noel Paton, 1821-1901*, Scottish Arts Council, 1967; Alasdair A Auld, 'Paton, Sir (Joseph) Noel [Noël] (*b* Dunfermline, Fife, 1821; *d* Edinburgh, 25 Dec 1901)', Jane Turner (ed), *The Dictionary of Art*, London: Macmillan, 1996, vol 24, page 266; Nicola Bown, 'Paton, Sir Joseph Noël (1821-1901)', H C G Matthew and Brian Harrison (eds), *Oxford Dictionary of National Biography*, Oxford University Press, 2004, vol 43, pages 62-63; Francina Irwin (ed), M H Noel-Paton and J P Campbell, *Noel Paton, 1821-1901*, Edinburgh: The Ramsay Head Press, 1990

01 FAIRIES
Signed with initial 'I' and dated 1876
Oil on board
5 ½ x 4 inches

WILLIAM PURTON
The Rev William Purton (1833-1891)

Having grown up among artists, the Reverend William Purton became an amateur draughtsman of some skill and flair. This is demonstrated by both the caricatures in his published volume, *The Dunce's Dessert* (1861), and his unpublished drawings for Tennyson's *Idylls of the King* (1864).

William Purton was born in Hampstead, Middlesex, on 4 February 1833, the elder surviving son of William Purton of the Woodhouse, Hopton Wafers, Cleobury Mortimer, Shropshire, and his wife and cousin, Sarah Cooper of Hampstead. His grandfather was William Purton of Faintree Hall, Shropshire.

Purton grew up in an artistic atmosphere, as his father was an amateur artist, and one of John Constable's circle of friends in Hampstead during the last years of his life.

Like his grandfather and father before him, Purton went up to Trinity College, Oxford, in 1851, and gained a BA in Mathematics in 1855, and an MA in 1858. He was ordained deacon by the Bishop of Hereford in 1856, and priest by the same Bishop in the following year. He commenced his ministerial duties, in 1856, as curate of St Leonard's, Bridgnorth, Shropshire (his uncle, John Purton, being the rector of nearby Oldbury). Three years later, he married Mary Hamilton Mackenzie, the second daughter of the late Duncan Mackenzie, of Merklands, County Perth.

As a young curate, Purton published two books that he had produced while he was a student, and which indicate his Classical interests: *The Dunce's Dessert; or Horatian Trifles and Homeric Cream* (1861) and *Gradus ad Homerum; or, The A B C D of Homer: a heteroclite translation of the 1st 4 books of the Iliad into English heroics* (1862). The former comprises his one claim to fame as an illustrator, consisting as it does of a series of comic images suggested by Greek and Latin quotations. Some of the images clearly caricature his Oxford contemporaries, while others represent Classical characters in a hand that suggests John Leech reworking John Flaxman.

Purton made his drawings for the first set of Alfred Tennyson's *Idylls of the King* in 1864, a year after his appointment as Vicar of Stottesdon, Cleobury Mortimer. He responded to Tennyson's phenomenally popular poem in a style that cleverly emulates the intentionally stiff Medievalism of, for instance, Daniel Maclise and Paolo Priolo (the second of which had illustrated a special edition of the first set of *Idylls of the King* for the Art Union of London in 1862). While it is not known whether the drawings were intended for publication, he did publish *Philocalia: Elementary essays on natural, poetic and picturesque beauty* in the same year.

Purton contributed to the religious debates of the day, becoming a priest-associate of the Society of St John the Evangelist, the Anglican religious

order that was founded in Cowley, Oxford, in 1866. In 1870, he became Vicar of St Anne's, Willenhall, Staffordshire, and soon published two theological volumes that caused minor controversy in the press: *A Rational and Scriptural Review of the Sacramental System of the Church of England* (1870) and *The Coming of the Son of Man to Judgment* (1873). In 1880, he moved to Hampshire to become second Vicar of St Clement's, Boscombe, Bournemouth, where, it is said, 'he held extreme Ritualistic views', so that 'the manner in which the services had been conducted at the church have been the cause of many an animated scene at vestry meetings' (*Gloucester Citizen*, 11 September 1891).

Purton died in office at the vicarage on 10 September 1891, of paralysis of the pneumo-gastric nerve. His wife, Mary, survived him. *A Memoir of William Purton, priest; together with two sermons preached in the Church of S Clement, Bournemouth, on the occasion of his death* appeared later the same year while, in the following one, the sculptor, George Frampton, produced a memorial portrait relief of Purton for St Clement's Church.

Idylls of the King
Between 1859 and 1885, the Poet Laureate, Alfred Tennyson, published 12 narrative poems retelling the story of King Arthur and his knights. Obsessed with the Arthurian legends from childhood, and familiar with Sir Thomas Malory's *Le Morte Darthur* (first published in 1485), he employed the subject as a 'parable of ideal imperial order and an image of that order's decadence' (Jonathan Freedman, 'Ideological Battlegrounds: Tennyson, Morris, and the Pastness of the Past', in Christopher Baswell and William Sharpe (eds), *The Passing of Arthur*, New York: Garland, 1988, page 235).

The first set of the idylls, published in 1859 as *The True and the False*, comprised poems about four very different women: 'Enid', 'Vivien', 'Elaine' and 'Guinevere'. This early edition almost immediately inspired two volumes of plates, Paolo Priolo's *Illustrations of the 'Idylls of the King'* (1862) and Amy Butts' *Sixteen Illustrations to the 'Idylls of the King'* (1863), and the outline style of the former certainly influenced the present unpublished set by William Purton.

Later, 'Enid' would be divided into 'The Marriage of Geraint' and 'Geraint and Enid', 'Guinevere' would be expanded, and 'Vivien' and 'Elaine' renamed as 'Merlin and Vivien' and 'Lancelot and Elaine'.

The 'Enid' poems concern the unfounded suspicion of the knight, Geraint, that his wife has been unfaithful, and the quest that they undertake together to prove his prowess and, implicitly, her innocence. Having killed six knights, Geraint is wounded by Earl Limours and his followers, and taken in by Earl Doorm the Bull as dead [03]. However, Enid correctly insists that he is still alive and, on his recovery, the couple join King Arthur in his camp, where they are properly reconciled.

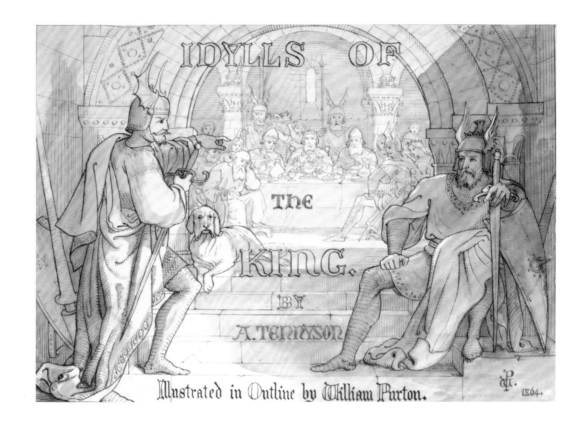

02 IDYLLS OF
THE KING
Signed with monogram
and dated 1864
Pen and ink with pencil
8 x 10 inches

In contrast to this tale of constancy, 'Merlin and Vivien' tells of the seduction of the wizard by a sorceress. Having failed to seduce King Arthur, Vivien turns her attention to Merlin, and wears down his resistance to her. He divulges how he works his magic, and she then uses it on him, imprisoning him in a hollow oak tree [04].

'Lancelot and Elaine' comprises an episode in the illicit love affair between Lancelot, 'the Chief of the Knights', and Guinevere, King Arthur's queen. At each of eight previous annual tourneys, Arthur has awarded Lancelot a diamond, and Lancelot plans to give them all secretly to Guinevere once he has secured the ninth and last. He goes to the last tournament in disguise, having borrowed armour, arms and colours from the remote Lord of Astolat [05], and having agreed to wear the favour of Elaine, the Lord's daughter [07]. Though he successfully battles 40 knights and wins

the diamond, he is wounded in the process, and is tended by Elaine, who has fallen in love with him [08]. When he is well, she expresses this love, but he rejects her and, soon after, she dies. According to her wishes, her body is then placed in a barge, with a note to Lancelot and Guinevere, and sent downstream to Camelot [09]. The appearance of her body and the contents of her letter touch the court deeply, and lead Guinevere privately to ask Lancelot for forgiveness.

The poem, 'Guinevere', which it seems that Purton did not illustrate, charts the queen's withdrawal from the court, and her subsequent death.

For further nineteeth-century illustrations on the subject of King Arthur, please see Chapter 02: Aubrey Beardsley, pages 41-48

03 WOULD SOME OF YOUR KIND PEOPLE TAKE HIM UP,
AND BEAR HIM HENCE OUT OF THIS CRUEL SUN?
(GERAINT AND ENID)
Signed with monogram
Pen and ink, 8 x 9 ¾ inches

04 BEFORE AN OAK, SO HOLLOW, HUGE AND OLD ...
AT MERLIN'S FEET THE WILY VIVIEN LAY
(MERLIN AND VIVIEN)
Signed with monogram
Pen and ink with pencil, 8 x 10 inches

05 THEN ANSWERED LANCELOT, THE CHIEF OF KNIGHTS:
KNOWN AM I, AND OF ARTHUR'S HALL ...
(LANCELOT AND ELAINE)
Signed with monogram
Pen and ink, 7 ¾ x 10 inches

06 WHOM THEY WITH MEATS AND VINTAGE OF THEIR BEST
AND TALK AND MINSTREL MELODY ENTERTAINED
(LANCELOT AND ELAINE)
Pen and ink with pencil
8 x 10 inches

07 SUDDENLY FLASHED ON HER A WILD DESIRE,
THAT HE SHOULD WEAR HER FAVOUR AT THE TILT
(LANCELOT AND ELAINE)
Signed with monogram
Pen and ink with pencil
8 x 9 ¾ inches

08 AND THE SICK MAN FORGOT HER SIMPLE BLUSH,
WOULD CALL HER FRIEND AND SISTER, SWEET ELAINE
(LANCELOT AND ELAINE)
Signed with monogram
Pen and ink, 8 x 10 ¼ inches

09 SO ARTHUR BAD THE MEEK SIR PERCIVALE
AND PURE SIR GALAHAD TO UPLIFT THE MAID
(LANCELOT AND ELAINE)
Signed with monogram
Pen and ink, 8 x 10 inches

JOHN LAWSON

John Lawson (born 1838)

Though he worked variously as a painter, sculptor and stained glass designer, John Lawson is best remembered as an illustrator of books and periodicals. His early, predominantly black and white, images mark him out as one of that striking generation of the 'Illustrators of the Sixties', and relate to those by his fellow Scotsman, Joseph Noel Paton, who is likely to have been a close friend. However, his later colour plates reveal his ability to adapt to a new market for popular children's books and annuals, and so work alongside his eldest daughter, Lizzie Mack.

John Lawson was born in Dunfermline, Fife, the youngest of the 10 children of Robert Lawson, a linen weaver, and his wife Ann (née Kirk). He was baptised on 10 June 1838. By 1850, the family was living at 9 Appin Terrace.

Nothing is known of Lawson's education, and he first appears as an artist when he begins to exhibit works at the Royal Scottish Academy in 1857. His two exhibits of 1858 comprised the horse and dogs of Sir Arthur Halkett of Pitfirrane Castle, Dunfermline, and a portrait of the sculptor, Amelia Paton, the sister of the artists, Joseph Noel and Waller Hugh Paton. The Patons also came from Dunfermline [see page 6], and were the children of a damask designer, so it is possible that they and the Lawsons grew up together.

On 13 July 1858, Lawson married Martha Carragher, the daughter of a Dunfermline labourer, in Edinburgh. It has been suggested that they married away from Dunfermline because Martha was already expecting Elizabeth, the first of their five children, who was born in the December. Initially, they returned to Dunfermline, and lived at Queen Anne Place, where their second child, Louisa, was born. However, by 1861, they had moved to Edinburgh, and were living at 76 Rosemount Buildings. At that stage, Lawson was describing himself as a 'glass stainer's designer', and family tradition has it that he contributed to the renewal of the stained glass windows in St Giles Cathedral.

However, soon after 1863, by which time he was living at 31 Dean Street, Lawson also established himself as an illustrator, initially working mainly with the Edinburgh publisher, William P Nimmo, and also contributing to periodicals, including *Once a Week* and *The Quiver*, both published in London. His early illustrative style has been compared to that of 'Paton, Frederick Sandys, Frederick Shields, and Edward Poynter – large figures, exactingly placed lines, the Dürer/Rethel woodcut school' (Gregory R Suriano, *The Pre-Raphaelite Illustrators*, New Castle: Oak Knoll Press/London: The British Library, 2000, page 291).

During the 1860s, Lawson became the father of three further children, Edwin (born 1862), Williamina (born 1867) and Noel Paton (born 1869), the name of the last surely confirming a close friendship between the Patons and the Lawsons. By the end of the decade, the family was living at 32 Upper Gray Street, and Lawson was describing himself as both 'artist on hand' and 'designer for stained glass'. However, at some point during the 1870s, they moved to London. Lawson worked with a number of publishers, including George Routledge and, in 1876, exhibited at Ernest Gambart's French Gallery, in Pall Mall, alongside Noel Paton, among others.

By 1881, both Lawson and his eldest child, Elizabeth, were working as artists from 23 Glebe Place, Chelsea. Gaining a reputation as an illustrator of children's books by the early 1880s, Lizzie Lawson married the writer and editor, Robert Ellice Mack, in September 1886, who would become Director of the London office of the publisher, Nister, in 1888. At various times, she and her husband worked both together and with her father.

By 1891, and at least until 1901, Lawson and his wife, Martha, lived at the Italian Villa, 62 Hurlingham Road, Fulham, and at that time he described himself as 'artist, painter, sculptor'. For much of that period, Lizzie – who gave birth to her daughter, Jenny, in 1890 – lived at the same address, and continued to do so until at least 1906. However, by the turn of the century, her husband, Robert, was based in Edinburgh and working for the Scottish publisher, Nelson's. Her mother, Martha, certainly died on 26 June 1905, but references to her father, John, fade from the records. His last published illustrations are likely to be those for Maria A Hoyer's *The Friend of Little Children*, which appeared in 1902. The colour plates are typical of his later style in their sweet sentiment.

Most published entries on John Lawson have confused him with another artist of the same name, a Scottish landscape painter who died at Carmunnock, Glasgow, on 9 September 1909.

Further reading:
Forrest Reid, *Illustrators of the Sixties*, London: Faber & Gwyer, 1928, pages 228-231

This entry is indebted to the website www.rankine-scott.me.uk, which is maintained by Niall Rankine Scott.

10 IN THE VALLEY OF THE
SHADOW
Signed with initials
Signed and inscribed with title
and '1691 VI' on reverse
Watercolour with bodycolour
on board
9 ½ x 7 ½ inches

Preliminary Checklist of Books Illustrated by John Lawson

1865

John Avery Collier
The Blade and the Ear. A Book for Young Men
Edinburgh: William P Nimmo

Joseph Avery Collier
The Young Men of the Bible: A Series of Papers Biographical and Suggestive
Edinburgh: William P Nimmo

Jean Ingelow
Stories Told to a Child
London: Alexander Strahan

1866

Robert Buchanan
Ballad Stories of the Affections. From the Scandinavian
London: George Routledge & Sons
[illustrated in collaboration with others]

Sarah Maria Fry
The Australian Babes in the Wood. A True Story. Told in Rhyme for the Young
London: Griffith & Farran
[with others]

Pen and Pencil Pictures from the Poets
Edinburgh: William P Nimmo
[with others]

1867

Ballads: Scottish and English
Edinburgh: William P Nimmo

Golden Thoughts from Golden Fountains: arranged in 52 divisions
London: Frederick Warne & Co
[with others]

Emilia Marryat Norris
The Early Start in Life
London: Griffith & Farran

Nursery Times; or, Stories About the Little Ones. By an Old Nurse
London: Griffith & Farran

D Richmond
The Children of Blessing
London: George Routledge & Sons

Roses and Holly: A Gift-Book for All the Year
Edinburgh: William P Nimmo [with others]

1868

Robert Burns
The Poems and Songs of Robert Burns (The 'Edina' Burns)
Edinburgh: William P Nimmo
[with others, including Sir Noel Paton and Waller Hugh Paton]

The Golden Gift. A Book for the Young
Edinburgh: William P Nimmo [with others]

Jane and Ann Taylor
Original Poems for Infant Minds
London: George Routledge & Sons
[with others]

1869

A L O E [A Lady of England, the pseudonym of Charlotte Maria Tucker]
Precepts in Practice, or Stories illustrating the Proverbs
London: T Nelson & Sons
[with others]

Frances Feeling Broderip
The Daisy and her Friends: simple tales and stories for children
London: Frederick Warne & Co
[with others]

1870

Barbara Hutton
Tales of the White Cockade
London: Griffith, Farran, Okeden & Welsh

1872

William Ballingall
The Shores of Fife
Edinburgh: Edmonston & Douglas
[with others, including Sir Noel Paton and Waller Hugh Paton]

The Garland of Poetry and Prose by celebrated authors
Edinburgh: William P Nimmo
[with others]

The Golden Gift, or Choice Gleanings from Great Authors (Nimmo's Elegant Gift Books)
Edinburgh: William P Nimmo
[with others]

Fanny Wheeler Hart
The Runaway: A Story for the Young
London: Macmillan & Co

1873

Alfred Elwes
Swift and Sure; or, the Career of Two Brothers
London: Griffith & Farran

Frances Ridley Havergal
Bruey: A Little Worker for Christ
London: James Nisbet & Co

Coventry Patmore (ed)
The Children's Garland from the Best Poets
London: Macmillan & Co

1875

Barbara Hutton
The Fiery Cross, or The Vow of Montrose!
London: Griffith, Farran, Okeden & Welsh

George Walter Thornbury
Historical and Legendary Ballads and Songs
London: Chatto & Windus
[with others; reprinted from *Once a Week*]

1877

E Lynn Linton
The World Well Lost
London: Chatto & Windus

The Little Folks Picture Album
London: Cassell, Petter & Galpin
[with others]

Little Talks with Little People
London: Cassell, Petter & Galpin
[with others]

1878

Little Rosebud's Picture Book
London: George Routledge & Sons
[with others]

1883

The Brothers Grimm
Clever Hans
London: Thos de la Rue & Co

1888

Constance Wilde
There Was Once. Grandma's Stories
London: Ernest Nister

1889

Childhood Valley. The Favourite Songs of Childhood with New Pictures in Colour by John Lawson, &c
London: Ernest Nister
[with others]

Matilda Horsburgh
Jottings from the Diary of the Sun (The Sunday Library for Young People series)
London: Hodder & Stoughton
[frontispiece attributed to Lawson]

1890

Mrs L Haskell
God is Love. Bible Stories and Pictures for the Young
London: Ernest Nister

1893

The Rev Charles John Ridgeway
Some Sweet Stories of Old: Boys of Bible Story No 3
London: Griffith Farran & Co
[with Henry Ryland]

1898

Helen Marion Burnside, R K Mounsey, Edric Vredenburg and others
Stories of Land and Sea (Father Tuck's 'Golden Gift' Series)
London: Raphael Tuck & Sons
[with others]

1902

Maria A Hoyer
The Friend of Little Children. A Short Life of Christ
London: T Nelson & Sons

FRANK DADD

Frank Dadd, RI ROI (1851-1929)

The Victorian tradition of genre subjects thrived into the twentieth century through the work of such artists as Frank Dadd. Both highly prolific and historically accurate, Dadd produced a wide range of narrative imagery, from the eighteenth century to the First World War, and became virtually synonymous with boys' adventure stories.

Frank Dadd was born at 54 Whitechapel High Street, London, on 28 March 1851, the third of six children of Robert Dadd, a chemist. Robert was the brother of the artist, Richard Dadd, and had to take responsibility for the entire Dadd family when Richard murdered their father, in 1843, and was confined to an asylum.

Educated privately, Frank Dadd spent much of his spare time in the Thames-side dockyard of his grandfather, the shipbuilder, Thomas Carter. The knowledge that he acquired there influenced his later paintings of coastal and river scenes.

Dadd studied art at the National Art Training School, South Kensington, and from 1871 at the Royal Academy Schools. Learning most about drawing from a visiting teacher, Lord Leighton, he won a silver medal for Drawing from Life and began to sell his drawings while still a student. He gained some of his earliest commissions from publishers with the help of the engraver, John Greenaway, a distant cousin and father of Kate Greenaway, the illustrator. His brother, Edward Martin Dadd, would marry Kate's sister, Fanny.

By 1872, Dadd was living at 4 Campshill Terrace, Ryecroft Road, Lewisham, and establishing himself as a genre painter and narrative illustrator. During the early 1870s, he exhibited at the Society of British Artists and contributed to periodicals, notably *The Cornhill Magazine*. Later in the decade, he began to work regularly for *The Graphic* (from 1876) and *The Illustrated London News* (from 1878), joining the staff of the former in 1884. He received regular commissions for book illustrations from the late 1870s, many from the Society for Promoting Christian Knowledge [see list overleaf].

While Dadd developed a speciality in monochrome illustrations to boys' adventure stories, he was also a skilful colourist, as is best seen in his contributions to *Holly Leaves* and *Pears' Annual*, and Christmas numbers of *The Graphic*, as well as his paintings for exhibition. Becoming a member of the Royal Institute of Painters in Watercolours in 1884, and a member of the Royal Institute of Painters in Oils four years later, he also showed work

at the Royal Academy of Arts, at leading provincial galleries and internationally.

From 1903, Dadd and his family lived at Morwenstow, Springfield Road, Wallington, Surrey. Though he left the staff of *The Graphic* in 1910, he continued to produce illustrations through the following decade. In 1919, he retired to West Lawn, Higher Brimley, Teignmouth, dying there on 7 March 1929. His wife, two sons and a daughter survived him.

15

11 HOP PICKING IN KENT
Signed with initials and dated 1909
Watercolour, 10 x 6 ¼ inches

A Preliminary List of Books Illustrated by Frank Dadd

1878

Lizzie Alldridge
Clare: A Narrative (Blue Bell Series),
London: Marcus Ward & Co

Geraldine Butt
A Spring of Heather (Blue Bell Series),
London: Marcus Ward & Co

Sarah Tytler
Summer Snow (Blue Bell Series)
London: Marcus Ward & Co

1879

C C Fraser-Tytler
Making or Marring (Blue Bell Series)
London: Marcus Ward & Co

Elizabeth Glaister
A Constant Woman (Blue Bell Series)
London: Marcus Ward & Co

1880

Miss Sale Barker (ed)
Little Wide Awake
London: George Routledge and Sons
[illustrated in collaboration with others]

1881

Stories in Pictures
New York: E P Dutton
[with others]

1882

Mrs G Linnaeus Banks
The Watchmaker's Daughter and Other Tales
Manchester: Heywood & Son
[with G C Banks]

The Changing Year; Being Poems and Pictures of Life and Nature
London: Cassell & Co
[with others]

1883

Mary Davison
Lucile, or, Faithful in a Few Things
London: SPCK

1884

J Bayford Harrison
A Good Copy, and other stories
London: SPCK

M L Molesworth
Lettice
London: SPCK

1885

Henry Frith
For King and Queen: Or, the Loyal 'Prentice. A Story of Old London
London: Cassell & Co

John Hunt and others
The Good Fight, or More than Conquerors: Stories of Christian Martyrs and Heroes
London: Hodder & Stoughton
[with F Barnard, E F Brewtnall, F A Fraser and others]

Constance E Miller
The Mill in the Valley; or, Truth Will Out
London: SPCK

1886

Mary Dow Brine
From Gold to Grey. Being Poems and Pictures of Life and Nature
New York: Cassell & Co
[with others]

Mary Linskill
A Garland of Seven Lilies
London: SPCK

'Author of *The Valley of Baca*' [Kathleen Mary Smith]
The Tents of Kedar
London: SPCK

1887

Phoebe Allen
Minon; or that Cat that the king looked at …
London: SPCK

The Rev Edward N Hoare
Foxholt, and the Light that burned there
London: SPCK

M L Molesworth
The Abbey by the Sea, and another story [*Felix, an Outcast*, from the French of Madame de Pressensé]
London: SPCK

John Henry Newman
Lead, Kindly Light
London: Thomas Nelson & Sons

'Author of *Mike and his Brother Ben*'
Two of Them
London: SPCK

'Author of *Our Valley*' [Julia Cartwright]
Cecily's Birds
London: SPCK

Mrs Mary Newman
Her Will and Her Way: and other stories
London: SPCK

Mrs Isla Sitwell
A Railway Garden (Jubilee Series)
London: SPCK

Mrs Isla Sitwell
Baby's Prayer-Book (Jubilee Series)
London: SPCK

Mrs Isla Sitwell
Northope Cave (Jubilee Series)
London: SPCK

Esmé Stuart [Amélie Claire Leroy]
The Goldmakers
London: SPCK

1888

Adelaide Anne Boodle
The Children's Guest
London: SPCK

Brotherhood, or, In the Way of Temptation (Rose Series)
London: SPCK

Austin Clare
In the Garden of Eden
London: SPCK

John W Diggle
Rainbows
London: SPCK

Erminda Rentoul Esler
Almost a Pauper: A Tale of Trial and Triumph
London: SPCK

George Manville Fenn
Dick o' the Fens. A Tale of the Great East Swamp
London: Blackie & Son

S W Landor
The Pupil Teachers of St Martin's
London: SPCK

F E Reade
Polly Rivers, or, What Must I Renounce?
London: SPCK

May Wentworth
Getting on, or, How Reuben Bond Became Rich
London: SPCK

W B Woodgate
Boating (Badminton Library of Sports and Pastimes)
London: Longmans, Green & Co

1888-90

Henry Irving and Frank Albert Marshall (eds)
The Works of William Shakespeare
London: Blackie and Son (8 vols)
[with others]

1889

George Manville Fenn
Quicksilver: or, the Boy with no Skid to his Wheel
London: Blackie & Son

16

1890
Mrs G Linnaeus Banks
Miss Pringle's Pearls
London: Hutchinson & Co

1890?
The Story Album for Little Folks
London: Glaisher
[with others]

1891
Sabine Baring-Gould
Urith: Tale of Dartmoor
London: Methuen & Co

S W Landor
Find a Way or Make It; or, George Watson's Motto
London: The Religious Tract Society

C E M
The Valley Mill, or, Truth Will Out
London: SPCK

Samuel J Pipkin
A Run Around the World, or, The Adventures of Three Young Americans, Boston: De Wolfe, Fiske and Company

Robert Weir; J Moray Brown
Riding; Polo (Badminton Library of Sports and Pastimes)
London: Longmans, Green & Co
[with J Stuart Allan and J D Giles]

1893
Sir Walter Scott
Old Mortality (Waverley Novels, Dryburgh Edition)
London: A & C Black

Sir Walter Scott
Peveril of the Peak (Waverley Novels, Border Edition)
London: John C Nimmo

Flora Maud Wootton
In the Days of '54: A Story of Love and Sacrifice
London: The Sunday School Union
[with others]

1896
Sabine Baring-Gould
The Broom-Squire
London: Methuen & Co

Pears' Annual
London: A & F Pears
[with others]

1897
Sabine Baring-Gould
Guavas the Tinner
London: Methuen & Co

1898
W Edward Chadwick
Brotherhood; or, In the Way of Temptation (Rose Series)
London: SPCK

Frank Mundell
Stories of Alpine Adventure
London: The Sunday School Union

Sir Reginald Percy Pfeiffer Rowe and Charles Murray Pitman,
Rowing (Badminton Library of Sports and Pastimes)
London: Longmans, Green & Co
[with the Hon Walter J James and photographers]

1898-1902
Pears' Annual
London: A & F Pears
[with others]

1901
Miss Mary E Palgrave
Deb Clavel – A Story of a Sister's Love
London: Religious Tract Society

Sir Max Pemberton
Love the Harvester: a story of the shires
New York: Dodd, Mead & Co

1902
Sir Max Pemberton
I Crown Thee King
London: Methuen & Co
[with Amédée Forestier]

George Robert Sims
Nat Harlowe, Mountebank
London: Cassell & Co

1904
Percy Fitzgerald
Christmas Days with Charles Dickens
London: A & F Pears
[also contains images by Hablot Knight Browne]

Pears' Annual
London: A & F Pears
[with others]

Sir Max Pemberton
Beatrice of Venice: a romance of the last days of the Venetian Republic and of Napoleon's campaign in Italy
London: Hodder & Stoughton

1906
James P Boyde (ed)
Russia and Japan including The Tragic Struggle by Land and Sea for the Empire in the Far East
London: The Historical Company
[with others and with photographers]

1906-16
Pears' Annual
London: A & F Pears
[with others]

1907
Hilda T Skae
Stories from English History (Stories from History)
London: T C & E C Jack

1910
Caesar, The King's Dog [Sir John Ernest Hodder-Williams]
Is That Lamp Going Out? To the Heroic Memory of Florence Nightingale
London: Hodder & Stoughton

Ethel Turner
Fair Ines
London: Hodder & Stoughton

1913
James Burnley (ed)
Pears' Shilling Cyclopaedia
London: A & F Pears

1916
Washington Irving
Old Christmas
New York & London: G P Putman's Sons

1917
Young England: an illustrated annual for boys throughout the English-speaking world
London: Pilgrim Press
[with others]

17

GORDON FRASER

George Gordon Fraser (1859-1895)

Able to match the talents of his better-known brothers in his atmospheric watercolours, Gordon Fraser also developed an independent career as a humorous illustrator – a career cut short by a fatal accident.

George Gordon Fraser was born in Cramond, Edinburgh, on 11 April 1859. The family moved to Bedford in 1861 and, eleven years later, he began to attend the local grammar school. While there, he studied art under Bradford Rudge. During his youth, he enrolled his younger brother, Anderson, and a group of mainly Scottish school friends into a band of like-minded youths called the Cudgel Community, and recorded their exploits in neatly written and illustrated books.

At the age of 18, in 1877, Gordon Fraser began to establish himself as an artist with a single watercolour at 'The Annual Exhibition of Modern Painters' at the Walker Gallery, Liverpool. Four years later, he published his first illustrations – those to Wilfred Meynell's article, 'Little-Known Sketching Grounds' – in The Art Journal. Between 1884 and 1893, he exhibited eight watercolours at the Royal Academy. In 1886, E E Leggatt became his agent.

The Ballad of Oriana

My heart is wasted with my woe, Oriana.
There is no rest for me below, Oriana.
When the long dun wolds are ribb'd with snow,
And loud the Norland whirlwinds blow, Oriana,
Alone I wander to and fro, Oriana.

Ere the light on dark was growing, Oriana,
At midnight the cock was crowing, Oriana:
Winds were blowing, waters flowing,
We heard the steeds to battle going, Oriana;
Aloud the hollow bugle blowing, Oriana.

In the yew-wood black as night, Oriana,
Ere I rode into the fight, Oriana,
While blissful tears blinded my sight
By star-shine and by moonlight, Oriana,
I to thee my troth did plight, Oriana.

She stood upon the castle wall, Oriana:
She watch'd my crest among them all, Oriana:
She saw me fight, she heard me call,
When forth there stept a foeman tall, Oriana,
Atween me and the castle wall, Oriana.

The bitter arrow went aside, Oriana:
The false, false arrow went aside, Oriana:
The damned arrow glanced aside,
And pierced thy heart, my love, my bride, Oriana!
Thy heart, my life, my love, my bride, Oriana!

Oh! narrow, narrow was the space, Oriana.
Loud, loud rung out the bugle's brays, Oriana.
Oh! deathful stabs were dealt apace,
The battle deepen'd in its place, Oriana;
But I was down upon my face, Oriana.

They should have stabb'd me where I lay, Oriana!
How could I rise and come away, Oriana?
How could I look upon the day?
They should have stabb'd me where I lay, Oriana
They should have trod me into clay, Oriana.

O breaking heart that will not break, Oriana!
O pale, pale face so sweet and meek, Oriana!
Thou smilest, but thou dost not speak,
And then the tears run down my cheek, Oriana:
What wantest thou? whom dost thou seek, Oriana?

I cry aloud: none hear my cries, Oriana.
Thou comest atween me and the skies, Oriana.
I feel the tears of blood arise
Up from my heart unto my eyes, Oriana.
Within my heart my arrow lies, Oriana.

O cursed hand! O cursed blow! Oriana!
O happy thou that liest low, Oriana!
All night the silence seems to flow
Beside me in my utter woe, Oriana.
A weary, weary way I go, Oriana.

When Norland winds pipe down the sea, Oriana,
I walk, I dare not think of thee, Oriana.
Thou liest beneath the greenwood tree,
I dare not die and come to thee, Oriana.
I hear the roaring of the sea, Oriana.

(Alfred Tennyson, from Poems Chiefly Lyrical, 1830)

12 ORIANA
'O PALE, PALE FACE, SO SWEET AND MEEK, ORIANA!
THOU SMILEST, BUT THEN DOST NOT SPEAK'
(TENNYSON)
Signed
Watercolour and bodycolour
13 ¼ x 20 inches
Exhibited: Royal Institute of Painters in Water Colours, 1895, no 596

18

On 9 September 1884, Fraser married Catherine Home Ramsay Ross of Larne, at Larne, Antrim, Ireland. Remaining in Ireland for an extended honeymoon, he would make the country a significant subject of his watercolours and illustrations. On returning to England, he and his wife settled in London, at 27 Ingersoll Road, Shepherds Bush. In 1886, she would give birth to the first of their four children. The growing family led to moves, first to Hemingford Abbots, Huntingdonshire, in 1887, and then, in 1889, to nearby Houghton.

Through an introduction from his brother, the illustrator, Frank, Gordon Fraser contributed a large number of full-page strip cartoons to *Fun*, from January 1889 until his death. In the June of that year, three of those drawings were exhibited by the Dalziel Brothers at an 'Exhibition of Works of English Humourists in Art' at the Royal Institute of Painters in Water Colours. His other work for magazines included contributions to *Ally Sloper's Half-Holiday* and *Larks!*, while his book illustrations comprise those to Jerome K Jerome's *The Diary of a Pilgrimage* (1891) and his own booklets, *O'Brien's Breeches* (1892) and *The Moonlighters* (undated).

While skating, on 15 February 1895, Fraser drowned beneath the ice near Hemingford Abbots. However, his body was not recovered until 6 April. He was buried with his father in the churchyard at Hemingford Grey. A collection of his cartoons, entitled *Humorous Pictures*, was published posthumously in 1896.

JOHN TENNIEL

Sir John Tenniel, RI (1820-1914)

While best remembered as the illustrator of Lewis Carroll's Alice books, John Tenniel contributed greatly to the look of *Punch* during the later nineteenth century. Beautifully drawn and highly allusive, his political cartoons remain startling in presenting fantastic imagery with classical polish.

For a biography of John Tenniel, please refer to *The Illustrators*, 2009, page 24. For an essay on the critical reception of Tenniel's work, see *The Illustrators*, 1996, pages 127-131.

Key works illustrated: Thomas Moore, *Lalla Rookh* (1861); Lewis Carroll, *Alice's Adventures in Wonderland* (1865), *Through the Looking-Glass* (1872); chief political cartoonist of *Punch* (1864-1900)

His work is represented in the collections of the British Museum and the V&A.

Further reading:
L Perry Curtis Jnr, 'Tenniel, Sir John (1820-1914)', H C G Matthew and Brian Harrison (eds), *Oxford Dictionary of National Biography*, Oxford University Press, 2004, vol 54, pages 131-134; Rodney Engen, *Sir John Tenniel: Alice's White Knight*, London: Scolar Press, 1991; Roger Simpson, *Sir John Tenniel: Aspects of His Work*, Cranbury: Associated University Presses, 1994

Chris Beetles Gallery is planning a major exhibition of the work of John Tenniel.

Pity the Poor Artist
In March 1895, Archibald Philip Primrose, 5th Earl of Rosebery (1847-1929), succeeded William Ewart Gladstone as Liberal Prime Minister. In this cartoon, John Tenniel suggests Lord Rosebery's lack of success during his first year in the office by representing him as a pavement artist who is attempting to meet the changing tastes of a demanding public. This comparison is particularly appropriate because the liberal laws on free speech and street hawking allowed pavement art to thrive more in the United Kingdom than anywhere else in the world. A decade before Tenniel produced this cartoon, in the mid 1880s, the streets of London supported over 300 self-employed 'screevers' (as explained by Philip Battle on his website, *All My Own Work! – A history of pavement art!*).

With his coronet upturned to receive contributions, Rosebery sits on the ground next to examples of his work, five of which each symbolise an element of his programme for the session. These appear to be on board or paper, and are clearly labelled. A further three seem to have been drawn in *trompe l'oeil* on the pavement itself, and may offer commentary on this programme, as a broken plate, two fish and bread and cheese all suggest issues of basic subsistence.

Local Veto
From the mid nineteenth century, elements of the British population began to call for the prohibition of alcohol. This led to the foundation, in 1853, of the United Kingdom Alliance for the Suppression of the Traffic in All Intoxicating Liquors. From 1857, the Alliance pushed for a *Local Veto* allowing 'a majority of two-thirds of the rate-payers in a locality to suppress the drink trade in their area'. During the early 1890s, 'the Liberal government introduced local-veto bills but failed to press them through with any vigour'. Support for prohibition in the United Kingdom declined altogether after the First World War, as Nonconformists 'dwindled in numbers' (Jack S Blocker Jr, David M Fahey, Ian R Tyrrell, *Alcohol and Temperance in Modern History. A Global Encyclopedia*, Santa Barbara CA: ABC-CLIO Inc, 2003, vol 1, page 627).

Irish Land Bill
From 1870, the British government introduced a number of Irish Land Acts in order to deal with the question of the peasant proprietorship of land in Ireland. During Rosebery's administration, John Morley, as Chief Secretary of Ireland, focussed on an *Irish Land Bill* that clarified and tightened Gladstone's 1881 legislation. That act 'had established the revolutionary principle that Irish tenants had a share in the ownership of the land they worked, with the statutory right to have a fair rent fixed judicially, and an entitlement to the full benefit of any increases in value resulting from their own improvements' (Patrick Jackson, *Morley of Blackburn*, Plymouth: Fairleigh Dickinson University Press, 2012, page 279). Morley's amendment failed to be completed, and the next Irish Land Act to be passed, in 1903, was that drafted by the Conservative Chief Secretary of Ireland, George Wyndham.

Welsh Disestablishment
Between 1870 and 1885, Gladstone had gradually come to accept the argument for separating the Anglican Church in Wales from the Church of England. Rosebery's Home Secretary, Herbert Henry Asquith, introduced a *Welsh Disestablishment Bill* in January 1895, and got a second reading for it in the April. The act would eventually be passed in 1914, during the time that Asquith was Prime Minister.

Naval Programme
During the late nineteenth century, Britain and Germany became rivals at sea. When Gladstone had returned to power in August 1892, he opposed the Sea-Lords' idea of increased naval expenditure. However, Lord Rosebery, as Foreign Secretary, and Lord Spencer, as First Lord of the Admiralty, favoured naval expansion, and it is this that led Gladstone to resign, in 1894, and Rosebery to replace him. In order to meet the needs of the *naval programme*, the Chancellor of the Exchequer, Sir William Vernon Harcourt, had to engineer a strongly redistributionary budget, which alarmed Rosebery.

House of Lords

In 1894, Lord Rosebery told a meeting of Bradford Liberals that the reform of the *House of Lords* was 'the greatest issue since your fathers resisted the tyranny of Charles I and of James II' (quoted in Paul Readman, 'The 1895 General Election and Political Change in Late Victorian Britain', *Historical Journal*, vol 42, no 2, 1999, page 469). However, rather than succeeding in making this a unifying issue, he actually fuelled dissent 'as many of his colleagues preferred ending to mending the Lords' (Malcolm Pearce & Geoffrey Stewart, *British Political History 1867-2001*, Abingdon: Routledge, 2002 (third edition), page 58).

Rosebery's government suffered from internal division and, as a result, was largely unsuccessful. On 21 June 1895, a vote was passed to reduce the

13 PITY THE POOR ARTIST
Signed with monogram and dated 1895
Pencil on board
6 ¼ x 8 inches
Provenance: Henry Sotheran & Co, 1911, £14.14s
Illustrated: *Punch*, 9 February 1895, page 67

salary of Henry Campbell Bannerman, the Secretary of State for War, as a censure over deficient supply of cordite to the army. As he was the most popular minister of Rosebery's administration, the government considered this to be a vote of no confidence, and resigned.

14 THE TELEPHONE CINDERELLA;
OR, WANTED A GODMOTHER
Signed with monogram and dated 1892
Pencil
9 ½ x 7 ¼ inches
Illustrated: *Punch*, 2 April 1892, page 162

**The Telephone Cinderella;
or, Wanted a Godmother**

In 1880, the Post Office won a landmark legal action that defined a telephone as a telegraph, and a telephone conversation as a telegram, in line with the existing 1869 Telegraph Act. As a result, the Post Office was able to restrict its rivals and so control the development of the telephone. The other telephone companies had to obtain 31-year licences from the Postmaster-General in order to operate in tight geographical areas, and to submit 10 percent of its gross income for the privilege. Furthermore, the Post Office had the option of purchasing a telephone company at the end of 10, 17 or 24 years. Nevertheless, other companies continued to form, most notably the National Telephone Company (NTC), in 1881, which, aided by some relaxation of restrictions in 1884, would gradually control a large majority of the United Kingdom's telephone market.

Early in 1892, the NTC and the rival New Telephone Company promoted bills in parliament to gain extensive new powers. On 22 March in the House of Commons, the Postmaster-General, Sir James Fergusson, countered them by proposing to purchase the trunk lines of the NTC, confining its operations to local areas under new licences. The transfer of the trunk lines would eventually be achieved in 1896-97, and the NTC taken over by the Post Office in 1912. However, the restrictive approach of the Post Office during Fergusson's regime led *The Times* to comment that:

> Far from taking up and developing the new mode of communication thus given into its hands, it could not forget its attitude of hostility to the innovation, or conceive any larger policy than one of repressing the telephone in order to make people stick to the telegraph. ... The result is that England lags far behind all other civilised countries in the use of the telephone.

John Tenniel produced his cartoon as a visualisation of this statement. In presenting the telephone as a technological Cinderella, he may have been alluding to the popular musical burlesque, *Cinder Ellen up too Late*, which had opened at the Gaiety Theatre, in London, on 24 December 1891 and ran until 9 July 1892.

CHARLES KEENE
Charles Samuel Keene (1823-1891)

Becoming associated, from the 1860s, with his *Punch* cartoons of urban street life, Charles Keene developed a great reputation as a draughtsman, and was revered by many of his contemporaries.

For a biography of Charles Keene, please refer to *The Illustrators*, 2009, page 27.

Key works illustrated: Douglas Jerrold, *Mrs Caudle's Curtain Lectures* (1866); contributed to *Once a Week*; chief social cartoonist of *Punch* (1864-90)

His work is represented in numerous public collections, including the British Museum, the National Portrait Gallery, Tate and the V&A; and the Ashmolean Museum (Oxford) and The Fitzwilliam Museum (Cambridge).

Further reading:
Simon Houfe, *Charles Keene. 'the Artist's Artist' 1823-1891*, London: Christie's/Punch, 1991; Simon Houfe, 'Keene, Charles Samuel (1823-1891)', H C G Matthew and Brian Harrison (eds), *Oxford Dictionary of National Biography*, Oxford University Press, 2004, vol 31, pages 29-32; Simon Houfe, *The Work of Charles Samuel Keene*, London: Scolar Press, 1995; Derek Hudson, *Charles Keene*, London: Pleiades Books, 1947; Lewis Johnson, 'Keene, Charles (Samuel) (*b* London, 10 Aug 1823; *d* London, 4 Jan 1891)', Jane Turner (ed), *The Dictionary of Art*, London: Macmillan, 1996, vol 17, page 877

15 CABBY (DISPUTES THE FARE, AND INSISTS ON HAVING FITZBELGRAVE'S NAME AND ADDRESS – THE LATTER HAS NOT HIS CARD-CASE): 'WH' THERE'S WRITIN ! WHY DIDN'T YER SAY 'S Y'VOR A ONEDICATED MAN ? IF YER 'D 'A'RST ME, I'D A' DONE IT FOR YER !!'
Stamped with monogram
Watercolour with pencil and bodycolour
5 x 4 inches
Illustrated: *Punch*,
14 September 1867,
page 103 (in reverse)

16 CONCLUSIVE!
UNSEATED M P (INDIGNANTLY): 'ACTUALLY CHARGED ME WITH BRIBERY!'
FRIENDS: 'BUT DIDN'T YOU DENY IT?'
THE UNSEATED: 'CERTAINLY – MOST EMPHATICALLY – BUT – THEY AH – PROVED IT!!'
Pen and ink, 5 x 4 inches
Illustrated: *Punch*, 7 August 1880, page 52 (in reverse)

CHARLES KEENE

'the greatest artist in black and white England ever produced'

(Harry Furniss, quoted in Bryant and Heneage 1994, page 85)

17 A PROTEST

STEWARD (FOR THE THIRD OR FOURTH TIME): 'BAS'N, SIR? BAS'N, MISS?'
AMERICAN PASSENGER: 'I SAY, STEE-U-ARD, IF YOU KEEP TEMPTING US WITH
THOSE LITTLE DISHES, WE SHAN'T BE ABLE TO RE-SIST — WHAT — !'
Signed with monogram
Drawn on reverse of a draft of a letter to Mrs Alexander Stevenson
Pen and ink
4 ½ x 7 inches
Illustrated: *Punch's Almanack for 1885*, 9 December 1884, [unpaginated]

GEORGE DU MAURIER

George Louis Palmella Busson Du Maurier
(1834-1896)

Equally talented as artist and writer, George
Du Maurier developed a cartoon format for
Punch that balanced text and image in order
to record and satirise the fashions and foibles
of society.

For a biography of George Du Maurier, please refer
to *The Illustrators*, 2009, page 30.

Key works written and illustrated: *Trilby* (1895);
chief society cartoonist of *Punch* (1864-96)

His work is represented in numerous public
collections, including the British Museum and
the V&A.

Further reading:
Leonée Ormond, 'Du Maurier, George Louis Palmella
Busson (1834-1896)', H C G Matthew and Brian
Harrison (eds), *Oxford Dictionary of National
Biography*, Oxford University Press, 2004, vol 17,
pages 177-180; Leonée Ormond, *George Du Maurier*,
London: Routledge & Kegan Paul, 1969; Leonée
Ormond, 'Du Maurier, George (Louis Palmella
Busson) (*b* Paris, 6 March 1834; *d* London, 8 Oct
1896)', Jane Turner (ed), *The Dictionary of Art*,
London: Macmillan, 1996, vol 9, page 384

25

18 A VOCATION
AUNT: 'SHALL I GIVE YOU A NEW DOLL, MAGGIE?'
MAGGIE: 'NO THANKS, AUNTIE, I SHOULD NEVER LOVE ANOTHER DOLL LIKE THIS; FOR SEE IT HAS
ONLY GOT ONE EYE, ONE LEG, AND ONE ARM, AND NOBODY WOULD CARE FOR IT IF I DIDN'T.
PROPER DOLLS CAN TAKE CARE OF THEMSELVES, YOU KNOW!'
Signed
Pen and ink
5 ¼ x 4 ½ inches
Provenance: Ernest Brown & Phillips, The Leicester Galleries, London, WC
Illustrated: *Punch*, 23 February 1878, page 83

26

19 PAIRING AND REPAIRING

THE REASONS INDUCING TWO YOUNG PEOPLE TO ENTER THE HOLY BONDS OF MATRIMONY HAVE HITHERTO, AS A RULE, BEEN LOVE, INTEREST, INTELLECTUAL SYMPATHY, COMPATIBILITY OF TEMPER, PARITY OF SOCIAL RANK, AND SO FORTH. NOW, MR PUNCH (WHO IS AN INVETERATE MATCH-MAKER) THINKS IT HIGH TIME THESE SELFISH AND OLD-FASHIONED NOTIONS AS TO WHAT CONSTITUTE MUTUAL FITNESS FOR THE MARRIED STATE SHOULD BE IMPROVED AWAY IN THE INTERESTS OF THE ANGLO-SAXON RACE. HE BEGS TO PRESENT HIS READERS WITH A SKETCH OF TWO PRIZE COUPLES, EXHIBITED BY HIM (IN IMAGINATION) AT A 'MARRIED COUPLE SHOW' (EVOLVED FROM HIS OWN INNER CONSCIOUSNESS), AND EARNESTLY COMMENDS THE SAME TO THE THOUGHTFUL STUDY OF THE YOUTH OF ENGLAND. AND OH! SHOULD ONE SINGLE MISGUIDED PAIR OF GIFTED BUT DYSPEPTIC ENTHUSIASTS BE INDUCED HEREBY TO FOREGO THEIR INTENTION OF TAKING EACH OTHER FOR BETTER FOR WORSE — SHOULD ONE SINGLE CHAMPION OF THE RIVER AND THE CRICKET-FIELD, ON CONTEMPLATING THE ABOVE, TRANSFER HIS AFFECTIONS FROM SOME SIMPLE-MINDED AND CONGENIAL RINKER TO SOME SUCH INSPIRED LITTLE BEING AS THAT WHO DIVIDES THE FIRST PRIZE IN THE PICTURE — MR PUNCH WILL NOT HAVE THOUGHT AND WROUGHT IN VAIN. VERBUM SAP

Signed
Pen and ink
7 x 9 ¾ inches
Illustrated: *Punch*, 25 March 1876, page 112

20 A SENSITIVE EAR

INTELLIGENT BRITON: 'BUT WE HAVE NO THEATRE, NO ACTORS WORTHY OF THE NAME, MADEMOISELLE! WHY, THE ENGLISH DELIVERY OF BLANK VERSE IS SIMPLY TORTURE TO AN EAR ACCUSTOMED TO HEAR IT GIVEN ITS FULL BEAUTY AND SIGNIFICANCE BY A BERNHARDT OR A COQUELIN!'
MADEMOISELLE: 'INDEED? I HAVE NEVER HEARD BERNHARDT OR COQUELIN RECITE ENGLISH BLANK VERSE!'
INTELLIGENT BRITON: 'OF COURSE NOT. I MEAN FRENCH BLANK VERSE — THE BLANK VERSE OF CORNEILLE, RACINE, MOLIERE!'
MADEMOISELLE: 'OH, MONSIEUR, THERE IS NO SUCH THING!' [BRITON STILL TRIES TO LOOK INTELLIGENT.]

Signed twice, inscribed with an alternative caption and dated 'Hampstead Dec 1 90'
Inscribed '¼ p', 'Punch' and 'reduce' below mount
Pen and ink
8 ½ x 5 ½ inches
Illustrated: *Punch*, 28 February 1891, page 107

The inscribed alternative caption is as follows:

FEMALE LOGIC

HE: 'YES, I'VE NOT BEEN LUCKY WITH MY FISHING THIS YEAR. IN THE WHOLE SEASON I ONLY KILLED TWO SALMON — I MAKE OUT THEY COST ME A HUNDRED POUNDS A PIECE!'
SHE (SYMPATHETICALLY): 'DEAR ME! HOW FORTUNATE THAT YOU DIDN'T CATCH ANY MORE!'

27

21 SOCIAL AGONIES
HERR BAUER: 'ACH! MY LIDDLE VRENT, MY POOTS ARE NOT MUTTY! VY ARE
YOU TRYING TO PRUSH DEM?'
TOMMY: 'MAYN'T I? MUMMIE SAYS YOU WANT POLISH!'
Pen and ink on board
6 ½ x 11 ½ inches
Illustrated: *Punch*, 24 March 1894, page 138

22 A CONSULTATION

PATIENT: 'DOCTOR, MY MEMORY HAS RECENTLY BECOME SHOCKINGLY BAD'
DOCTOR: 'INDEED, IN THESE CASES, SIR, IT IS MY INVARIABLE RULE TO ASK
FOR MY FEE IN ADVANCE'
Signed
Signed, inscribed 'Half-page. Punch Xmas Number' and dated 'Hampstead
Oct 94' below mount
Inscribed with title in another hand on reverse
Pen and ink
6 ½ x 10 ½ inches
Illustrated: *Punch's, Almanack for 1895*, 1 January 1895, page 5

The Weaker Vessel

The Weaker Vessel is one of the many novels of the once popular writer, David Christie Murray (1847-1907). It first appeared as a serial in *Good Words* in 1888, with three illustrations by George Du Maurier, and then in three unillustrated volumes, published by Macmillan and Co later the same year. Du Maurier's illustrations seem to have been reproduced in an American edition, published by Harper & Brothers in 1894. The novel received a range of reviews, from 'a book … uniformly of so high a level of literary excellence' (*The Cambridge Review*) to 'a thoroughly inferior novel, a bad work of art, most evidently written with no other object than to procure a certain number of shekels' (*The Universal Review*).

23 SEBASTIAN, I LEAVE YOU AND MR DENHAM TO EACH OTHER
Signed
Signed, inscribed with title, publication details and 'Hampstead', and dated 'Oct 87' below mount
Pen and ink
5 x 7 ¼ inches
Illustrated: *Good Words*, 1888, page 12, 'The Weaker Vessel' by D Christie Murray; D Christie Murray, *The Weaker Vessel*, New York: Harper & Brothers, 1894

'The author's mouth-piece is Jack Denham, who relates the story of his friend, Walter Pole, a young Englishman, who is the hero of the story. Pole, as the result of some mistaken ideas about heroism and chivalry, makes a most unfortunate marriage with [Adelaide] a woman who renders his life wretched and unhappy. He provides ample support for her, and they live apart, although she harasses him by occasional visits and by the presentation of enormous bills for her extravagant expenditures. Her final stroke is to cause a false report of her death to be circulated, with the hope that Pole will marry a beautiful young woman of lovely character whom she knows he has long been acquainted with and for whom he has a strong friendship.

Sebastian, I leave you and Mr Denham to each other
'There is Mr Delamere's godson, Sebastian Dolmer Jones, who professes
high aestheticism "with his stale old inspiration" and "turns his own
cleverness into a shameful lie."' (From a review of *The Weaker Vessel* in
The Illustrated London News, 1888, page 515)

The Maker's Pal
'A caricature figure is that of [Adelaide's] unscrupulous ally, one Goldsmith,
a Jewish solicitor and money-lender, who presently concocts
to extort money from Pole' (From a review of *The Weaker Vessel* in
The Illustrated London News, 1888, page 587)

24 THE MAKER'S PAL
'HE WAS MAGNIFICENTLY ATTIRED IN, I THINK, THE CHECK SUIT
OF THE LARGEST PATTERN AND VIVIDEST COLOURS I HAD
EVER BEHELD'
Signed
Pen and ink
4 ¾ x 7 ¼ inches
Illustrated: *Good Words*, 1888, page 293, 'The Weaker Vessel'
by D Christie Murray; D Christie Murray, *The Weaker Vessel*,
New York: Harper & Brothers, 1894

By a strange chance Sister Constance, who is called to the hospital to take care of her, is [Mary Constance Delamere] the very woman whom
Pole had come so near to marrying, and who, after Adelaide Pole's plot was discovered, had devoted herself to taking care of the sick and
helping the sorrowing and needy. Her sweet gentleness and patience soften the heart of the dissolute Adelaide, and when she dies she holds
the hand of Walter Pole in one hand, while the other clasps that of Sister Constance, and the word "Forgive" is upon her lips.'

(A summary of the plot of *The Weaker Vessel*, from a review of the novel published in *Public Opinion:*
A Comprehensive Summary of the Press Throughout all the World, 1889, pages 64-65)

WILLIAM RALSTON

William Ralston (1841-1911)

The Scottish artist, William Ralston, is a fascinating figure of the later nineteenth century, who straddled careers in photography, binding design, illustration and cartooning. He is now best remembered for his episodic cartoons and illustrations for *The Graphic* and *The Daily Graphic*.

William Ralston was born in Milton, Dunbartonshire, in the summer of 1841, the elder son of Peter Ralston, a pattern designer for a calico printer, and Catherine McLaren, a calico printer's daughter. By 1845, the family had moved to Glasgow, and was living at 475 Gallowgate, Peter Ralston continuing to work as a pattern designer. Subsequent addresses included 143 London Street (1848) and 30 Charlotte Street (1851).

Ralston attended the Normal School until the age of 12, when he left to serve as a cabin boy on one of the Clyde Steamers. He soon moved to work at the wholesale warehouse of Messrs William Gilmour & Sons. At the age of 17, he began to show signs of delicate health, and so was sent on a voyage to Australia, leaving Greenock in November 1858 and arriving in Victoria four months later. During his three years in the country, he worked as a gold digger and a vineyard worker. Nine of his sketches of Victoria would appear in *The Australasian Sketcher in Pen and Pencil* in 1879 as 'Digging Life 25 Years Ago'.

In 1856, Ralston's father and younger brother, John (or Jack) McLaren Ralston, had set up as professional photographers at 195½ Argyle Street, Glasgow, initially under the name J Ralston, but from 1861 as Peter Ralston. When a branch establishment opened, at 11 Jamaica Street, Ralston was invited to return home and take charge of it, and this he did, in about 1862, the company then becoming Ralston & Sons. He seems to have worked as a photographer and also a designer of bindings for books through the 1860s. During this time, he is likely to have lived in the family home, which was probably at 73 Sauchiehall Street. In 1871, he married the Glaswegian, Grace Sutherland Hilliard.

At some point, Ralston began classes at the Glasgow School of Art, but quickly abandoned them in favour of teaching himself drawing with the support of his brother, Jack, who was 'embarking on a career as an artist' and would produce some illustrations (Jones and Brown 2003, page 175). At the end of the 1860s, William was designing bindings for London publishers, including Frederick Warne, and beginning to produce his first illustrations. He befriended the wood engraver, Joseph Swain, who, in 1870, sent two of his sketches to Shirley Brooks, editor of *Punch*, one of which was then published in the weekly magazine. Many commissions followed, and the fruitful relationship led Ralston to name his third child Shirley Brooks Ralston (1874-1952). He continued to contribute to *Punch* until 1886.

In 1870, Ralston also began to contribute to *The Illustrated London News* (1870-73) and *The Graphic* (1870-1911). The founder of *The Graphic*, William Luson Thomas, encouraged him to move to London, and this he did in about 1875, spending 'the happiest fourteen years of his life' (according to *Who's Who in Glasgow in 1909*, Glasgow: Gowan & Gray, page 176), and 'in Hampstead and Islington had five further children' (Jones and Brown 2003, page 176). Arguably, his best work was produced for *The Graphic* and *The Daily Graphic*, for which he was a founding artistic contributor in 1890. This shows him to have been a master of episodic illustrations and strip cartoons.

Through the 1880s, Ralston established himself as a book illustrator with such volumes as John Strange Winter's *Bootles' Baby. A Story of the Scarlet Lancers* (1885) and *Houp-la* (1889); three collaborations with his friend, Charles W Cole: *Tippoo. A Tale of a Tiger* (1886), *Messrs Kamdene, Barnesburie and D'Alston's Tour in the North* (1888) and *The Demon Cat. A Naval Melo-Drama* (1889); and George Outram's *Legal and Other Lyrics* (1887), illustrated with Alexander Stuart Boyd.

In the wake of the deaths of his brother (1883) and his father (1888), Ralston returned to Glasgow in 1889, and attempted to manage the family photography business (becoming W Ralston Ltd at 259 Sauchiehall Street) while still working as an illustrator. If he contributed less frequently to periodicals, he still illustrated books, mainly with comic subjects, including further collaborations with Charles W Cole, and also produced some collections of sketches.

In 1906, Ralston sold the photography business to James W Robertson, who retained the Ralston name, and in the following year returned to London. He died there, at 73 Roderick Road, Hampstead, on 26 October 1911.

Further reading:
G V Jones and J E Brown, 'Victorian Binding Designer WR: William Ralston (1841-1911), not William Harry Rogers', *The Book Collector*, vol 52, 2003, pages 171-198

25 THE END OF THE
HOLIDAYS – GOING BACK
TO SCHOOL
Signed with initials
Pen and ink with watercolour
13 x 9 ½ inches
Illustrated: *The Graphic*,
19 September 1891, page 340

LINLEY SAMBOURNE

Edward Linley Sambourne (1844-1910)

Linley Sambourne developed a firm and intricate style of draughtsmanship that enabled him to complement and eventually succeed John Tenniel as the political cartoonist of *Punch*. An enthusiastic exponent of the new art of photography, and a member of the Camera Club, he took many of the photographs that comprised his research library and informed his detailed preparation.

Linley Sambourne was born at 15 Lloyd Square, Pentonville, London, on 4 January 1844, the son of Edward Mott Sambourne, a prosperous wholesale furrier, and his wife, Frances (née Linley). He was educated at the City of London School (1855-56) and Chester Training College School (1857-60), and then apprenticed as a draughtsman to a firm of marine engineers in Greenwich. Though he undertook only a little formal art study, at the National Art Training School, South Kensington, in 1860, he spent much of his spare time drawing caricatures. When Mark Lemon, editor of *Punch*, saw one of his sketches in 1867, he was engaged to work for the periodical, and four years later joined the staff. He began by filling gaps and covering absences and, by way of the influence of the work of Charles Bennett, developed his own distinctively intricate style. Promoted to producing decorative initial letters to *Punch*'s 'The Essence of Parliament', he gradually expanded these images, usurping the importance of Shirley Brooks' text and so providing a second political cartoon. In 1878, he was appointed 'cartoon junior', while, from the 1890s, he understudied Tenniel as political cartoonist, finally replacing him on his retirement in 1901. In parallel, he allowed himself a more purely surreal vein by producing a series of 'Fancy Portraits', such as Ruskin as Narcissus (18 December 1880).

Sambourne compensated for any lack of natural graphic fluency by developing a meticulous approach to his work founded on detailed research. He built up a library of 100,000 photographs, many of which he had taken himself. He posed his family and servants in elaborate set pieces with props and costumes, while, as a member of the Camera Club from 1893, he had access to a number of nude models. Contemporaries disapproved of this reliance on the camera. Harry Furniss complained that Sambourne was 'a slave to the camera and a mere copyist', to which Sambourne replied that 'The camera is my pencil and these photos are my "notes" which I am always making'. Certainly, his use of the camera saved little in the way of time or labour. Subjects for drawings were chosen on a Wednesday at the *Punch* table, with the work to be delivered that Friday. Sambourne spent most of Thursday either consulting his archives or producing new cyanotypes, photographs which involved sunshine in their development. Adverse weather conditions or problems with props would place strain on Sambourne to meet his deadline. Whatever the doubts,

regarding his methods, his results have been greatly admired. Tenniel once said of his work 'although a little hard and mechanical, it is of absolutely inexhaustible ingenuity and firmness of touch', and Low commented that he 'evolved a style which for sheer purity of line and solid correctness of draughtsmanship has not been excelled among British artists'.

In addition to his work for *Punch*, Sambourne contributed to a few other magazines and illustrated books, including Charles Kingsley's *The Water Babies* (1885) and *Three Tales of Hans Andersen* (published posthumously in 1910). He exhibited at the Royal Academy between 1885 and 1910, and his only solo show, at the Fine Art Society in 1893, was a sell-out success. However, by the time of his death – at home on 3 August 1910 – his precise images were being passed over in favour of the more apparently spontaneous drawings of Phil May. His wife, Mary Ann (née Herapath), and their two children, Mawdley (known as Roy), and Maud, all survived him.

His house, at 18 Stafford Terrace, Kensington, is now open to the public as the most complete record of Victorian domestic life.

Further reading:
Simon Jervis and Leonée Ormond, *Linley Sambourne House*, London: The Victorian Society, 1980; R C Lehmann (rev Shirley Nicholson), 'Sambourne (Edward) Linley (1844-1910)', H C G Matthew and Brian Harrison (eds), *Oxford Dictionary of National Biography*, Oxford University Press, 2004, vol 48, pages 792-793; Robin Simon, *Public Artist, Private Passions: The World of Edward Linley Sambourne*, London: British Art Journal/The Royal Borough of Kensington and Chelsea Libraries and Arts Service, 2001

Let Sleeping Dogs Lie

At the dinner that followed the revue of the 4th Army Corps at Erfurt, on 14 September 1891, the German Emperor, Wilhelm II, gave a particularly bellicose speech. Reproduced a few days later in the *Reichsanzeiger*, the official newspaper of the German Reich, it included the following statement:

> It is in this town [Erfurt] that the Corsican conqueror [Napoleon] deeply humiliated the German princes and our battered country. At this time the thought of pushing resistance to the extreme germinated in the soul of my grandfather [Wilhelm I]

The German ambassador to Paris reported that the entire French press was 'very excited' by these words and that even the otherwise moderate *Temps* found Wilhelm's 'language warlike, and the revival of memories, on which the implacable resentment of German chauvinism feeds, very questionable'.

Furthermore, on 19 September 1891, Wilhelm's mother, Victoria, wrote to her mother, Queen Victoria, that 'Wilhelm gave in Erfurt one of his

extremely unfortunate speeches in which he called Napoleon the "Corsican Parvenu"'. Indeed, there had been some discrepancy as to whether Wilhelm had actually called Napoleon 'conqueror' or 'parvenu', and this had added to the controversy. On the page opposite Sambourne's cartoon in *Punch* sat the following short article:

> The German Emperor going Nap – It now appears that the words descriptive of Napoleon Buonaparte used by the German Emperor, and to which the French too so strong an exception, were not '*Le parvenu Corse*' but '*Le conquérant Corse*,' which, of course, makes all the difference. At this banquet it would have been better had each course been omitted from the *menu*.

26 LET SLEEPING DOGS LIE
Signed and dated 'September 21 '91'
Pen and ink
7 x 10 inches
Illustrated: *Punch*, 3 October 1891, page 158

36

27 'ARRY ON ARRIUS
WITH SOME CONSIDERATION CONCERNING COMPULSORY CLASSICS
Signed and dated 'December 18 1891'
Pen and ink
8 ½ x 7 inches
Illustrated: *Punch*, 26 December 1891, page 302

'Arry on Arrius

Edwin James Milliken (1839-1897) made many written contributions to *Punch* between 1875 and his death, and the magazine's editor, F C Burnand, once described him as 'one of the most invaluable of Mr Punch's staff' (*Records and Reminiscences*, London: Methuen & Co, 1904, vol 2, page 214). His most popular contributions were 'The 'Arry Papers', the protagonist of which M H Spielmann called 'the great creation … for which Mr Milliken is most applauded' (*The History of Punch*, London: Cassell and Company, 1895, page 378).

Artists and writers in *Punch* had developed the figures of 'Arry and 'Arriet as the generic Cockney man and woman. However, Spielmann believed that Milliken's 'Arry was not 'the descendant … of the "gent" of Leech and the "snob" of Thackeray and Albert Smith' and meant much more than the 'similar character conceived by Charles Keene and Mr Anstey', being an 'impersonal symbol' representing the 'self-declared cad, without either hope or desire, or even thought, of redemption' (loc cit). While promoted from the 'rougher classes … to be characteristic of the low sort of shop-lad and still lower kind of mechanic', he developed almost 'into a type of humanity', so that there was even an ''Arryism of the "upper classes"'. What connected these manifestations was not only 'his materialistic philosophy' (op cit, page 379), but also his amusing 'forms of speech' and 'the quaint turns of his vulgar thought' (op cit, page 380).

The present image illustrates a poem by Milliken in which 'Arry reflects on his Classical counterpart, Arrius, the subject of a comic poem by the Roman writer, Catullus (circa 84-54 BC). As the *St James's Gazette* criticises 'Arry for dropping his 'haitches', so Catullus criticised Arrius for the affectation of aspirating the 'h' at the beginning of his words in order to sound more Greek. 'Arry concludes that 'larks are more important than 'Igher Heducation' (Patricia Marks (ed), *The 'Arry Ballads. An Annotated Collection of the Verse Letters by* Punch *Editor E J Milliken*, Jefferson NC: McFarland & Company, 2006, page 19).

28 TOUR DU MONDE
Signed 'Linley Sambourne. Inventr et Delr' and dated 'November 1889'
Pen and ink
13 ¼ x 10 inches
Illustrated: *Punch's, Alamanck for 1890*, 5 December 1889, title page

Scene in the L C Circus

Linley Sambourne here represents the failed attempt of the Conservative Prime Minister Lord Salisbury (1830-1903) to curb the power of the London County Council, and even abolish it. Dressed as a circus ringmaster, Salisbury holds a whip high above the kicking donkey that is the LCC. However, it is Salisbury's Secretary of State for the Colonies, Joseph Chamberlain, long critical of the LCC, who addresses the donkey. Dressed as a Union Jack jacketed clown, he admits that they will no longer 'sit' on it, in the wake of the LCC elections of 3 March 1898, which inflicted the heaviest blow yet sustained by Salisbury's government. The Progressives (aligned to the Liberal Party) won a large majority, which they retained until 1907.

Sambourne may have been inspired to use the circus metaphor by the residence of the American company, Barnum & Bailey's Greatest Show on Earth, at Olympia, which was close to his home at 18 Stafford Street, in Kensington. He had certainly visited the circus on one of its previous visits to London, in 1890, and had published a 'Fancy Portrait' of P T Barnum in *Punch* on 9 February 1884.

In his diary entry for 4 March 1898, Sambourne noted his preparation for this cartoon, and described the creature that represents the LCC as specifically a 'Blondin donkey'. This was not actually an animal at all, but two performers dressed in a costume, akin to a pantomime horse, who walked a rope in emulation of the famous French tightrope walker and acrobat, Charles Blondin. This popular animal burlesque act was devised by Fred Delaney and Joe Ridgeway who, since 1877, had worked together as 'the Griffiths Brothers'. Sambourne recorded seeing their 'Blondin donkey' at the Empire Theatre, Leicester Square on 3 October 1889. His use of a high wire donkey to represent the London County Council prefigures David Low's coalition ass and Trades Union Congress carthorse.

37

29 SCENE IN THE L C CIRCUS
JOEY: 'ME AND MR SALISBURY WERE GOING TO SIT ON YOU; BUT WE SHA'N'T NOW!'
Signed and dated 'March 5 1898'
Pen and ink
10 ¾ x 8 ½ inches
Illustrated: *Punch*, 12 March 1898, page 110

PHIL MAY

Philip William May, RI RP NEAC (1864-1903)

Sometimes referred to as the 'grandfather of British illustration', Phil May was one of the most influential black-and-white artists of his generation. Earthy, street-wise, and redolent of the music hall, his work is the antithesis of that of Aubrey Beardsley.

For a biography of Phil May, please refer to *The Illustrators*, 2009, page 38. For a caricature of the artist by E T Reed, see *The Illustrators*, 1999, page 46; for a photograph of the artist, see *The Illustrators*, 1992, page 70; for self-portraits, see *The Illustrators*, 1991, page 52, and 1999, page 60.

Key works illustrated: William Allison, 'The Parson and the Painter' (serialised in *St Stephen's Review*, 1890); *Phil May Annual* (1892-1904); contributed to *Punch* (from 1893), *Guttersnipes* (1896)

Further reading:
David Cuppleditch, *Phil May. The Artist and His Wit*, London: Fortune Press, 1981; Simon Houfe, 'May, Philip William [Phil] (1864-1903)', H C G Matthew and Brian Harrison (eds), *Oxford Dictionary of National Biography*, Oxford University Press, 2004, vol 37, pages 556-558; 'Simon Houfe, *Phil May. His Life and Work*, 1864-1903, Aldershot: Ashgate, 2002; James Thorpe, *Phil May*, London: Art and Technics, 1948

His work is represented in numerous public collections, including the British Museum, the National Portrait Gallery, Tate and the V&A; Leeds Art Gallery; the Fine Arts Museums of San Francisco; and the National Library of Australia (Canberra).

30 BARBER (WHO HAS ACCIDENTALLY STUCK HIS LATHER BRUSH IN OLD GENT'S EYE): 'AWFULLY SORRY, SIR, QUITE AN ACCIDENT.' OLD GENT: 'ACCIDENT! OF COURSE; THAT MAKES IT ALL THE WORSE. IF YOU'D INTENDED IT I'D HAVE FORGIVEN YOU FOR MAKING SUCH A DARNED GOOD SHOT.'
Signed and dated /93
Signed and inscribed with title on original mount
Pen and ink
11 ½ x 9 inches
Provenance: Fine Art Society
Illustrated: *Phil May's 1893 Illustrated Annual*, 1892, page 54

31 FRANKNESS
AMATEUR BEGGING LETTER WRITER: '–
AND DEAR SIR, IF YOU WOULD FAVOUR
ME WITH THE LOAN OF TEN POUNDS. I
SHOULD BE ETERNALLY INDEBTED TO YOU'
Signed and dated 1902
Inscribed with title below mount
Pen and ink
9 ½ x 7 inches
Illustrated: *The Tatler*, 3 January 1906,
page 19, 'The Humour of Life – as seen
by the Late Phil May'

PHIL MAY

32 A SHARP CONTRAST
Signed and inscribed with title
Inscribed with title and stamped with M W Ingram Collection mark
on reverse
Pencil drawing of a horse and rider on reverse
Pen and ink
6 ¼ x 5 ½ inches
Provenance: M W Ingram
Illustrated: *Fifty hitherto unpublished pen-and-ink sketches by Phil May*,
London: The Leadenhall Press, 1900, no 50

33 TRY SAM SMITH'S ANTI FAT
Signed
Stamped with M W Ingram Collection mark on reverse
Pen and ink
6 ¼ x 5 ½ inches
Provenance: M W Ingram
Illustrated: *Fifty hitherto unpublished pen-and-ink sketches by Phil May*,
London: The Leadenhall Press, 1900, no 3

AUBREY BEARDSLEY

Aubrey Vincent Beardsley (1872-1898)

Though Aubrey Beardsley was initially influenced by the Pre-Raphaelites, he soon outgrew them, and developed his own unique style, at once sophisticated and provocative. During his brief flowering in the *fin de siècle*, the elegant restraint of his art emulated Japanese prints and Rococo painting, while the elegant restraint of his life surpassed those of his friends and rivals, James McNeill Whistler and Oscar Wilde.

Aubrey Beardsley was born at 12 Buckingham Road, Brighton, Sussex, on 21 August 1872, the son of Vincent Beardsley and his wife, Ellen Agnus (née Pitt).

He grew up in an atmosphere of genteel poverty, in which his ambitious mother ensured that he became a precocious student of literature and music. At the age of seven, he contracted the then incurable disease of tuberculosis and was sent off to improve his health, first at nearby Hurstpierpoint, and then at Epsom. In 1884, he returned to Brighton and soon became a boarder at Brighton Grammar School, where it was recognised that he had a talent for drawing.

In 1888, at the age of 16, Beardsley moved with his family to London, where financial circumstances forced him to work as a clerk in an Islington surveyor's office, and later at the Guardian Fire and Life Assurance Company in Lombard Street. He made the most of his brief periods of good health, developing his artistic skills, and – particularly in 1891 – absorbing the visual delights of the capital, such as the Peacock Room that James McNeill Whistler had designed for Frederick Leyland's house. He visited Edward Burne-Jones and, spurred on by the artist's encouragement, took his advice, attending evening classes under Fred Brown at the Westminster School of Art. From early in his career, he was absorbing many disparate influences, from Mantegna to Japanese printmakers, and boasting of working in several styles.

In 1892, Beardsley was introduced by the bookseller, Frederick Evans, to the publisher, J M Dent, and asked by him to illustrate a new edition of Malory's *Le Morte Darthur*. This major commission enabled Beardsley to resign from his clerical position and establish himself as a major modern artist; this he achieved by refining a style that challenged and parodied the historicist approach of the Kelmscott Press, and was at the same time appropriate to reproduction by the new photo-mechanical line-block process. However, Beardsley soon became tired of the demands of this large-scale project, so that Dent had to rekindle his interest by issuing another commission, that for the three-volume series of *Bon-Mots*. The grotesque, even sinister, vignettes with which he decorated the series comprised perhaps his first truly mature work.

The importance of Beardsley was confirmed in April 1893 by the first number of the immediately influential periodical *The Studio*, in which he appeared as the subject of an illustrated article by Joseph Pennell. Among the illustrations was a drawing based on an episode from Oscar Wilde's *Salome*, and its presence prepared the way for Beardsley to meet its author, and then to illustrate the first translation of that symbolist play from French to English, in an edition by John Lane. The result, published in February 1894, attracted wide attention, even controversy, and permanently linked author and illustrator in the mind of the public. The provocative character of Beardsley's work was then further emphasised, in April 1894, with the issue of the first number of *The Yellow Book*, also published by John Lane, which Beardsley helped edit and illustrate. Words and images of sophisticated economy, bound in yellow, summed up the decadence of the decade.

41

34-55 are all illustrated in Sir Thomas Malory, *Le Morte Darthur*, London: J M Dent & Co, 1893-94

34 SNAKE AMONG DANDELIONS
Pen and ink
3 ¾ x 2 ¾ inches
Illustrated: vol 1, title page: printer's device [printed in red], and on back cover of each volume, gilt embossed

Exactly a year later, in 1895, Wilde was arrested on a charge of committing indecent acts, placed on trial and imprisoned. Beardsley was considered guilty by association, and more sanctimonious contributors forced his dismissal from *The Yellow Book*. Yet by the end of the year, he had defiantly developed *The Savoy* as a rival periodical, with help from the decadent poet, Arthur Symons, and the pornographic publisher, Leonard Smithers. The presence of Smithers also facilitated the publication of his great late illustrated volumes, especially *The Rape of the Lock* by Alexander Pope and *Lysistrata* by Aristophanes (both 1896). Becoming increasingly plagued by tuberculosis, he attempted to aid his physical health by spending time on the Continent, and his spiritual health by converting to Roman Catholicism. He died in Menton, on the French-Italian border on the 16 March 1898, at the age of twenty-five.

For essays on various aspects of the artist's achievements, see *The Illustrators*, 1999, pages 64-66; *The Illustrators*, 2000, page 8; and *The Illustrators*, 2008, page 15.

His work is represented in numerous public collections, including the British Museum, the National Portrait Gallery, Tate and the V&A; the Ashmolean Museum (Oxford) and The Fitzwilliam Museum (Cambridge); and the Museum of Fine Arts (Boston, MA) and Harvard University Art Museums (Cambridge, MA).

Further reading:
Stephen Calloway, *Aubrey Beardsley*, London: V&A Publications, 1998; Alan Crawford, 'Beardsley, Aubrey Vincent (1872-1898)', H C G Matthew and Brian Harrison (eds), *Oxford Dictionary of National Biography*, Oxford University Press, 2004, vol 4, pages 541-545; Haldane MacFall, *Aubrey Beardsley. The Man and His Work*, London: John Lane The Bodley Head, 1928; Brian Reade, *Aubrey Beardsley*, London: Studio Vista, 1967; Robert Ross, *Aubrey Beardsley*, London: John Lane, 1909; Matthew Sturgis, *Aubrey Beardsley: A Biography*, London: Harper Collins, 1998; Simon Wilson, 'Beardsley, Aubrey (Vincent) (*b* Brighton, 21 Aug 1872; *d* Menton, 16 March 1898)', Jane Turner (ed), *The Dictionary of Art*, London: Macmillan, 1996, vol 3, pages 444-446; Simon Wilson and Linda Zatlin, *Aubrey Beardsley: A Centenary Tribute*, Japan: Art Life, 1998; Linda Zatlin, *Aubrey Beardsley and Victorian Sexual Politics*, Oxford: Clarendon, 1990; Linda Zatlin, *Beardsley, Japonisme and the Peversion of the Victorian Ideal*, Cambridge University Press, 1997

36 PEACOCK
Pen and ink
1 ¾ x 2 inches
Illustrated: vol 1, pages 42, 113 & 221; vol 2, pages 339 & 383; vol 3, pages 668 & 876

35 TRELLISED GRAPE VINE
Pen and ink
3 ½ x 2 ½ inches
Illustrated: vol 1, page 21; vol 2, page 550

37 CURLING LEAVES
Pen and ink
2 ½ x 2 ¾ inches
Illustrated: vol 1, pages 48, 153 & 266; vol 2, page 628

Aubrey Beardsley and *Morte Darthur*

The demanding task of illustrating Sir Thomas Malory's epic *Morte Darthur* (1893-94) launched the career of Aubrey Beardsley. He was required to emulate the Medievalist style developed by Edward Burne-Jones and William Morris for Morris's Kelmscott Press, the pre-eminent publishing venture of second generation Pre-Raphaelitism. And, while the scale of the project tested his patience, and led him to parody his model in order to keep up his interest, he still created a striking set of images that retain the spirit of Kelmscott, most notably in his floral decorations.

By the time that he began to work on *Morte Darthur*, Beardsley had met both Burne-Jones and Morris. On 12 July 1891, he went with his sister, Mabel, to one of Burne-Jones' 'open studios', at his home in West Kensington, showing the artist a portfolio of his work, and receiving the encouraging response that 'I *seldom* or *never* advise anyone to take up art as a profession, but in *your* case I can do nothing else' (reported by Beardsley in a letter written to A W King on 13 July 1891).

A year later, on a Sunday afternoon, 'in the spring or early summer of 1892', Beardsley joined Aymer Vallance on a visit to William Morris's house in Hammersmith. Vallance was a member of Morris's circle and, knowing that he was in search of illustrators for the Kelmscott Press, suggested that Beardsley make a drawing of the title character from Wilhelm Meinhold's *Sidonia von Bork*, a translation of which Morris was planning to publish. However, Morris was unenthusiastic about this and the other drawings in Beardsley's portfolio, and merely remarked, 'I see you have a feeling for draperies, and I should advise you to cultivate it' (Aymer Vallance, in *The Magazine of Art*, 21 May 1898, page 363).

38 POPPIES
Pen and ink
2 ¾ x 2 ¾ inches
Illustrated: vol 1, page 61; vol 2, page 508

39 FLOWERING TENDRILS
Pen and ink
2 ½ x 2 ¼ inches
Illustrated: vol 1, page 64; vol 2, page 505; vol 3, pages 772, 828 & 924

40 WISTERIA
Pen and ink
2 ¾ x 2 ½ inches
Illustrated: vol 1, pages 91 & 263; vol 2, pages 41 & 557

41 VINE
Pen and ink
2 ¾ x 2 ½ inches
Illustrated: vol 1, pages 66 & 246; vol 2, pages 342, 387 & 539

43

44

During 1892, publishers began to hear that the Kelmscott Press was preparing to issue *The Work of Geoffrey Chaucer*, though it was formally advertised only in the December of that year, and did not appear until 1896. In response, J M Dent planned to publish a new, illustrated edition of *Morte Darthur*, a canny choice of text, for the famous compilation of tales concerning King Arthur and the Knights of the Round Table had already proved key to the Pre-Raphaelites. Furthermore, like the works of Chaucer, *Morte Darthur* had first appeared in print in the fifteenth century in an edition by William Caxton, the inspiration for so many English printers and publishers. However, though it was 'designed in imitation of Morris's mock-medieval Kelmscott Press style' and woodcut technique, Dent intended to print his edition 'at a fraction of the price by using photo-mechanical reproduction processes for the illustrative material' (Sturgis 1998, pages 107-108).

In order to proceed with the venture, Dent needed to find an appropriate illustrator. He was explaining this difficulty to his friend, the bookseller, Frederick Evans, on a visit to Jones & Evans, 77 Queen Street, Cheapside, when Beardsley walked in. Beardsley worked as a clerk in nearby Lombard Street and, during his lunch hour, had become a frequent visitor to the shop, gradually getting to know Evans, and giving him drawings in exchange for books. His arrival suggested to Evans 'that there was the young man for the "Morte"', and he 'introduced him to Mr Dent as the illustrator of his "Morte d'Arthur"'. Though Beardsley initially 'looked bewildered', Dent was sufficiently encouraged to ask him to make 'a specimen drawing as soon as possible … and if it was successful he should at once have the commission' (as reported by Evans in a letter published in *The Saturday Review*, 1913, page 394).

42 A DAMOSEL
WITH PEACOCKS
IN A GARDEN
Pen and ink
6 ½ x 3 ½ inches
Illustrated: vol 1,
page 69; vol 2,
page 332

Beardsley chose as his subject the climax of the book, 'The Achieving of the Sangreal', and produced a spectacular showpiece that revealed his close study of the work of Burne-Jones. Even though it combined tonal washes with the pen lines, making it unsuitable for reproduction by the line-block process, it completely convinced Dent, who offered Beardsley an irresistible deal.

This specimen drawing would eventually appear as the frontispiece to the second volume. The book was to be issued to subscribers in 12 monthly parts, from June 1893, in 1500 ordinary copies, with 300 copies on Dutch handmade paper. Initially presented in card covers, the parts would then be bound in volumes, the ordinary edition in two and the more limited edition in three.

Beardsley agreed to Dent's original contract, which had offered '£50 for the 20 odd full page drawings, £25 for the 40 small drawings & designs & 5/- each for the initial letters', approximately totalling 350 drawings (according to a letter from Beardsley to Dent of about 8 October 1892). This major commission enabled him to resign his clerical position and begin to establish himself as a major modern artist.

According to Haldane MacFall, 'Beardsley flung himself at the achievement of the *Morte d'Arthur* with almost mad enthusiasm' (MacFall 1928, pages 28-29), and produced most of the decorations that Dent wanted during the second half of 1892. When he began to tire of the demands of this large-scale project, Dent then attempted to rekindle his interest, first by drawing up a more generous formal contract for the Malory project, then by issuing another commission, that for the three-volume series of *Bon-Mots*. The grotesque, even sinister, vignettes with which he decorated the series revealed a Japanese inspired strain in his

43 DAISIES
Pen and ink
1 ¾ x 1 ¾ inches
Illustrated: vol 1, pages 146 & 278;
vol 2, page 586

44 POINTED LEAVES
Pen and ink
2 x 1 ¾ inches
Illustrated: vol 1, page 150;
vol 2, pages 295 & 598

**45 INITIAL S
WITHIN AN OLIVE TREE**
Pen and ink
3 ¾ x 2 ½ inches
Illustrated: vol 1, page 105, [printed in red]

46 WATER LILY BUDS
Pen and ink
2 x 1 ¾ inches
Illustrated: vol 1, page 200;
vol 2, page 381; vol 3, page 675

46

47 SINUOUS DAISIES
Pen and ink
3 x 2 ½ inches
Illustrated: vol 1, page 224; vol 2, page 356;
vol 3, page 757

48 APPLE TREE
Pen and ink
2 ¾ x 2 ¾ inches
Illustrated: vol 1, page 260; vol 2, page 384;
vol 3, page 722

49 INITIAL I
ENTWINED BY TENDRILS
Pen and ink
3 ¾ x 2 ½ inches
Illustrated: vol 2, page 291, (printed in red)

art, and suggested how quickly he could absorb and outgrow each new influence in developing his style.

Certainly, Beardsley was outgrowing Kelmscott, and perhaps with good reason. Close to Christmas 1892, Vallance made a failed attempt to persuade him to go back to Morris and win him over. All he would do was agree that Vallance could show Morris a printed proof of *The Lady of the Lake telling Arthur of the Sword Excalibur*. On seeing it, Morris became very angry that the young, inexperienced artist that he had dismissed six months earlier was now 'mastering the Kelmscott idea and in one fell drawing surpassing it and making the whole achievement of Morris's earnest workers look tricky and meretricious and unutterably dull'. He called it 'an act of usurpation' and 'was prevented from writing an angry remonstrance to Dent … only at Sir Edward Burne-Jones's earnest urging' (op cit, page 31).

By April 1893, Beardsley was trying out new expressions of his style, as was signalled by Joseph Pennell's illustrated article on the artist in the first number of *The Studio*. This stage in his career has been summed up as his wanting '*Salome* and wickedness' (Crawford 2004, page 543), a reference to the illustration to Oscar Wilde's *Salome* that he had made speculatively, but which would lead to his providing images for a complete edition of the play, which was published in the following year, and proved something of a *succès de scandale*.

By contrast, *Morte Darthur* received little in the way of critical response, mainly because of the serial nature of its publication. Nevertheless, its slow appearance between June 1893 and November 1894 did allow Dent to continue pressing Beardsley to complete the illustrations and, when that failed, to reuse the most ornamental of the designs, sometimes more than once. The result of this repetition is actually to give unity to the work, and to emphasise Beardsley's genius for decoration, especially floral decoration. His friend, Robert Ross, noted in a sensitive early monograph of the artist, that 'The initial- and tail-pieces are delightful in themselves, and among the most exquisite of his grotesques and embellishments' (Ross 1909, page 43).

50 LA BEALE ISOUD
Pen and ink
3 ¼ x 2 ¾ inches
Provenance: Mark Samuels Lasner
Illustrated: vol 2, page 404;
vol 3, page 911
Exhibited: 'Beautiful Decadence', The Museum of Fine Arts, Gifu, Japan, and touring, April-May 1998, no 11; 'The Long Nineteenth Century: Treasures and Pleasures', March - April 2014, no 135

51 FIERY FLOWER
Pen and ink
2 ½ x 2 ¼ inches
Illustrated: vol 2, pages 298 & 493

52 FLOWERS
Pen and ink
2 ½ x 2 ¼ inches
Illustrated: vol 2, page 400;
vol 3, page 787

53 INITIAL W
SINUOUS POPPY
Pen and ink
3 x 2 ½ inches
Illustrated: vol 3, page 741,
[printed in red]

47

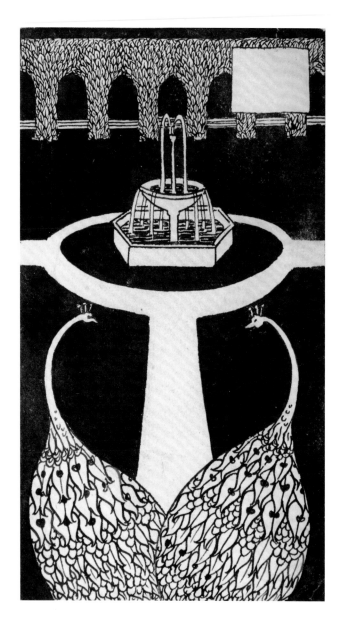

48

55 IN A WOOD
Pen and ink
4 x 4 ¼ inches
Provenance: Pickford Waller; Miss Sybil Waller
Illustrated: vol 2, page 846
Exhibited: 'The Long Nineteenth Century: Treasures and Pleasures',
March - April 2014, no 134

54 PEACOCKS IN A FORMAL GARDEN
Pen and ink
6 x 3 ¾ inches
Illustrated: vol 3, page 874

ANTICYRA · TELEVISMA

GEORGE ARLISS
IN
THE PRIVATE LIFE
OF
MR · BALDWIN
UNITED PLANETS RELEASE

03

HUGH THOMSON

'pen drawings by Hugh Thomson can be said with reasonable justification to mark the beginning of a new era in English book illustration'

(Edward Hodnett, *Five Centuries of English Book Illustration*, Aldershot: Scolar Press, 1988, page 187)

HUGH THOMSON

Hugh Thomson, RI (1860-1920)

The Irish-born artist, Hugh Thomson, helped introduce a new approach to illustration through his closely observed and carefully researched pen and ink drawings. He was particularly associated with editions of classics of and about the Georgian and Regency periods. However, his versatility enabled him to capture both contemporary life and native topography with a relaxed energy.

Hugh Thomson was born at 9 Church Street (now Kingsgate Street), Coleraine, County Londonderry, on 1 June 1860. He was the eldest of the three children of John Thomson, a tea merchant, and Catherine (née Andrews), a shopkeeper.

Two or three years after the death of Hugh's mother, in about 1871, his father married Maria Lennox, a widow with one son, of the Manor House, Kilrea, about 14 miles south of Coleraine. John Thomson settled in Kilrea, and opened a drapery, haberdashery and hosiery warehouse in Maghera Street, though left the running of it to his wife as he pursued other business interests.

Hugh attended Coleraine Model School and, while there, often stayed at Breezemount, with his maternal aunt, Jayne Hunter, becoming very close to his cousins. Then, on leaving school at the age of 14, he entered an apprenticeship with E Gribbon & Sons, linen manufacturers, on Strand Road. Having drawn from an early age, his artistic talent was soon recognised, probably by John Campbell, who worked in the linen trade. Campbell then recommended him to his friend, John Vinycomb, who was head of the art department of Marcus Ward & Co, the leading Belfast printer and publisher.

In 1876, at the age of 16, with his indentures having been cancelled, Hugh Thomson left for Belfast in the company of his brother, Richard, who was also a fine artist. He lived at 7 Park View Terrace, Ballynafeigh (since renumbered), close to Marcus Ward's Royal Ulster Works on the south side of the city. His work there included the production of Christmas cards and box covers. He received encouragement from John Vinycomb, and attended a few classes at Belfast School of Art, but was mostly self-taught. In 1879, he and Vinycomb were among the 16 members of Ward's staff to found the Belfast Ramblers Sketching Club (which later became the Belfast Art Society).

On 1 December 1883, Thomson moved to London to further his career, at the urging of his cousin, Ellen. He returned to Belfast to marry Jessie Naismith Miller, of Ballynafeigh, on 29 December 1884, but the couple settled in Putney, on the River Thames. By then, he had established himself through his drawings for Macmillan & Co's recently founded periodical, *The English Illustrated Magazine*, and would become particularly well known for those that illustrated eighteenth-century ballads and stories. These contributions led to *Coaching Days and Coaching Ways* (1888), the collaboration with the illustrator, Herbert Railton, and the writer, W Outram Tristram, which confirmed his reputation.

56 THE CHASE
Signed, inscribed with title and dated 95
Pen ink and watercolour
12 x 9 inches
Illustrated: William Somerville, *The Chase*, London: George Redway, 1896, frontispiece [published in black and white and subsequently coloured by the artist]

From the late 1880s, Thomson was continually in demand as an illustrator of fiction and poetry that had been written or set in Georgian or Regency times, such as that of Jane Austen and his own close friend, Austin Dobson. In visualising this world, Thomson himself was equally influenced by the writings of Thackeray and the illustrations of Edwin Austin Abbey and Randolph Caldecott. In turn, he influenced the Brothers Brock, who soon became his chief rivals in the field of historical illustration. Like them, he thoroughly researched his subjects and, in order to do so, made visits to the British Museum and the Victoria and Albert Museum. However, Thomson was more versatile than this suggests.

Living in or close to London for much of his career, Thomson produced vital and perceptive studies of contemporary city life for publication in *The Graphic* (1890-1905) and other periodicals. He also illustrated a number of topographical volumes, for Macmillan's series 'Highways and Byways', including that on his home territory, *Donegal and Antrim* (1899), with a text by Stephen Gwynn.

Thomson was well equipped to satisfy the increasing demand for colour illustration that occurred in the 1890s, for he had been regularly exhibiting watercolours at various dealers (the Fine Art Society, the Leicester Galleries, Walker's Galleries, the Continental Gallery) and at the Royal Institute of Painters in Water Colour. He was elected to the RI in 1897, but retired from the society a decade later. Though also nominated to the Royal Society of Painters in Water-Colours, he turned the offer down. Retaining connections to Belfast, he was elected a member of the Ulster Arts Club in 1903.

Macmillan attempted to stretch his skill as a colourist by launching a series of 'Hugh Thomson's Illustrated Fairy Books', which began and ended with *Jack the Giant Killer* (1898). However, his imagination lacked the edge of fantasy that made Dulac, Rackham and Heath Robinson the leaders in the field of the gift book; so he returned to produce the detailed, observant work that still characterises his name.

Having lived in West Kensington and then Sidcup, Kent, Hugh and Jessie Thomson moved to 8 Patten Road, Wandsworth Common, London, in 1913. Hugh would die there on 7 May 1920, his wife and only child, John Thomson, both surviving him. Three years later a memorial show was held at the Leicester Galleries.

His work is represented in the collections of Ulster Museum (Belfast).

Further reading:
Olivia Fitzpatrick, 'Thomson, Hugh (1860-1920)', H C G Matthew and Brian Harrison (eds), *Oxford Dictionary of National Biography*, Oxford University Press, 2004, vol 54, pages 515-516; M H Spielmann & Walter Jerrold, *Hugh Thomson. His Art*, London: A & C Black, 1931

51

57 A COUNTY COURT
Inscribed with title and publishing details on reverse
Pen and ink
9 ½ x 8 ¾ inches
Illustrated: Mrs E T Cook, *Highways and Byways in London*, London: Macmillan and Co, 1902, page 130

'Who has not heard of the Man who broke the Bank at Monte Carlo, and who has not been fired by the wish to emulate him? If "the man" really broke it, it has been put together again, and anybody who cares may smash it if he can. In order to go from England, he must first of all cross the silver streak – which isn't always silver, but very much the reverse – and a black and stormy crossing which disturbs Little Mary will have the effect of causing many intending gamblers to lose something at this stage long before they reach the tables.'

(Hugh Thomson, 'An Artist's Visit to Monte Carlo – I', *The Graphic*, 13 May 1905, page 556)

58 CROSSING THE CHANNEL
Inscribed 'Monte Carlo' below mount
Inscribed with title on reverse
Pencil sketch of figures on reverse
Pen and ink with coloured pencil
8 ¾ x 15 inches
Illustrated: *The Graphic*, 13 May 1905, page 556, 'An Artist's Visit to Monte Carlo – I' by Hugh Thomson

An Artist's Visit to Monte Carlo
Hugh Thomson's commissions for *The Graphic* occasionally gave him opportunities to observe life beyond London, and to record his responses in words as well as images. So in the spring of 1905, he visited Monte Carlo, and produced three reports, which appeared as spreads in the 'weekly illustrated paper' during the May.

59 A HALT AT AVIGNON: WELCOME REFRESHMENTS
IN THE EARLY MORNING
Inscribed 'Monte Carlo' below mount
Inscribed 'Avignon' on reverse
Pen and ink with coloured pencil
7 x 11 ½ inches
Illustrated: *The Graphic*, 13 May 1905, page 556, 'An Artist's Visit to
Monte Carlo – I' by Hugh Thomson

54

61 FOR THE WEARY: PILLOWS FOR HIRE
Inscribed 'Rest for the Weary' and 'Monte Carlo'
below mount
Inscribed 'Pillows' on reverse
Pen and ink
7 x 5 ¾ inches
Illustrated: *The Graphic*, 13 May 1905, page 556,
'An Artist's Visit to Monte Carlo – I'
by Hugh Thomson

60 ON THE PARIS, LYONS AND
MEDITERRANEAN RAILWAY:
NIGHT STUDIES
Inscribed 'On the Paris Lyons & Mediterranean
Railway' and 'Monte Carlo' below mount
Inscribed 'Sleeping Positions' on reverse
Pen and ink with coloured pencil
9 ½ x 7 inches
Illustrated: *The Graphic*, 13 May 1905, page 556,
'An Artist's Visit to Monte Carlo – I'
by Hugh Thomson

'On arrival at Monte Carlo no obstacles are placed in the way of those intending to attack the Bank … one passes through the central hall, and there, before ten o'clock in the morning, one will find two queues of waiting gamesters, who, directly the doors open, burst helter-skelter into the gaming rooms, the women gathering up their skirts in order to cope, if possible, with the less impeded men in a wild race for chairs and places at the tables.'

(Hugh Thomson, 'An Artist's Visit to Monte Carlo – I', *The Graphic*, 13 May 1905, page 557)

55

62 THE RUSH FOR CHAIRS ON THE OPENING OF THE CASINO DOORS
Inscribed with title and 'Monte Carlo' below mount
Inscribed 'Running up Room' on reverse
Pen and ink with coloured pencil
9 x 14 inches
Illustrated: *The Graphic*, 13 May 1905, page 557, 'An Artist's Visit to Monte Carlo – I' by Hugh Thomson

63 CROUPIERS COUNTING AND CHECKING THE MONEY UNDER THE EYES OF THE OFFICIALS
Signed and dated 1905
Inscribed 'Monte Carlo' below mount
Rough pencil sketch of the main composition below mount
Inscribed 'Counting the Money' on reverse
Pen ink and watercolour with pencil and coloured pencil
9 x 14 inches
Illustrated: *The Graphic*, 13 May 1905, page 557, 'An Artist's Visit to Monte Carlo – I' by Hugh Thomson
[published in black and white and subsequently coloured by the artist]

'Round every table, and passing to and fro between the tables, consulting their own cards and those of others for the sequences of number and colours which have turned up previously, are many players to whom the fate of their stake is no mere matter of amusement, but of considerable anxiety, to judge from the earnest study devoted to the run of the chances. Nearly all have their evident superstitions. One places his stake, but walks away from the table until the little ivory ball has come to rest, when he returns to learn his fate. Another gazes into the corner of the room, or anywhere but at the wheel of fate … All have their little tricks to propitiate fate.'

(Hugh Thomson, 'An Artist's Visit to Monte Carlo – I', *The Graphic*, 13 May 1905, page 557)

57

64 AT THE ROULETTE TABLE
Signed, inscribed 'Roulette' and dated 1905
Pen ink and watercolour with pencil
10 ½ x 16 inches
Illustrated: *The Graphic*, 20 May 1905, page 588, 'An Artist's Visit to Monte Carlo – II' by Hugh Thomson
[published in black and white and subsequently coloured by the artist]

65 FAIR GAMBLERS
Signed with initials
Inscribed 'Monte Carlo' on reverse
Pen ink and watercolour on paper on board
7 x 8 ½ inches
Illustrated: *The Graphic*, 20 May 1905, page 588,
'An Artist's Visit to Monte Carlo – II' by Hugh Thomson
[published in black and white and subsequently coloured
by the artist]

**66 GAMBLERS WITH SYSTEMS THAT DO NOT
ALWAYS WORK**
Signed, inscribed 'Systems' and dated 1905
Inscribed 'Monte Carlo' below mount
Pen and ink with coloured pencil
9 ¾ x 16 inches
Illustrated: *The Graphic*, 20 May 1905, page 588,
'An Artist's Visit to Monte Carlo – II' by Hugh Thomson

67 WINNERS
Signed and dated 1905
Inscribed with title and 'Monte Carlo' below mount
Pen ink and watercolour
9 ¾ x 7 ½ inches
Illustrated: *The Graphic*, 20 May 1905, page 589, 'An Artist's Visit to Monte Carlo – II' by Hugh Thomson [published in black and white and subsequently coloured by the artist]

68 A LOSER
Signed and inscribed with title
Inscribed 'Monte Carlo' below mount
Pen and ink with coloured pencil
10 ½ x 8 inches
Illustrated: *The Graphic*, 20 May 1905, page 589, 'An Artist's Visit to Monte Carlo – II' by Hugh Thomson

'When you are tired of the gaming-rooms there are other distractions …
The side of the mountain on which Monte Carlo is built is seamed by numberless courts for the playing of
bowls. Here the croupier, after breathing the hot air of the Casino, can find a little relaxation and healthy
exercise at a different game of ball from that practised inside the gaming-rooms.'

(Hugh Thomson, 'An Artist's Visit to Monte Carlo – III', *The Graphic*, 27 May 1905, page 624)

60

69 A GAME OF BOWLS
Inscribed 'The hillside is covered with courts for the playing of bowls', 'Bola Boules Bowls' and 'Monte Carlo' below mount
Pen and ink with coloured pencil
9 ½ x 15 inches
Illustrated: *The Graphic*, 27 May 1905, page 624, 'An Artist's Visit to Monte Carlo – III' by Hugh Thomson

70 A FRESH PIGEON AND THE SPANIEL WHICH RETRIEVES
THE SHOT BIRD
Inscribed with title below mount
Inscribed 'Retriever' on reverse
Pen and ink with coloured pencil
6 ¼ x 7 ¼ inches
Illustrated: *The Graphic*, 27 May 1905, page 624, 'An Artist's Visit to
Monte Carlo – III' by Hugh Thomson

71 SOMETIMES A PIGEON LIES LOW TILL PONTO'S
NOSE IS OVER IT, AND THEN GETS UP, TO
PONTO'S AMAZEMENT
Inscribed 'Sometimes a pigeon lies low & "says nuffin" till
Ponto's nose is over it' and 'Ponto's amazement' below mount
Pencil sketch of a standing man on reverse
Pen and ink
5 ¾ x 4 ¾ inches
Illustrated: *The Graphic*, 27 May 1905, page 624, 'An Artist's
Visit to Monte Carlo – III' by Hugh Thomson

72 PIGEON-SHOOTING
Inscribed with title and 'Monte Carlo' below mount
Pencil sketch of figures on reverse
Pen and ink
11 x 9 inches
Illustrated: *The Graphic*, 27 May 1905, page 624, 'An Artist's Visit to Monte Carlo – III' by Hugh Thomson

73 WATCHING THE SHOOTING
Inscribed 'The pigeon shooting from the terrace' and 'Monte Carlo' below mount
Inscribed 'Looking on' on reverse
Pen and ink
7 ¼ x 6 ½ inches
Illustrated: *The Graphic*, 27 May 1905, page 624, 'An Artist's Visit to Monte Carlo – III' by Hugh Thomson

74 AT THE KIOSK
Inscribed 'Monte Carlo'
Pen and ink with coloured pencil
7 x 10 ¼ inches
Illustrated: *The Graphic*, 27 May 1905, page 625, 'An Artist's Visit to Monte Carlo – III' by Hugh Thomson

04

IMAGING CHURCHILL

E T REED
(1860-1933)

NIBS
(1861-1928)

LEONARD RAVEN-HILL
(1867-1942)

H M BATEMAN
(1887-1970)

The text for Imaging Churchill *is written by Alexander Beetles, unless otherwise stated.*

detail of **81**

The Edwardian Churchill

Winston Churchill, the wartime Prime Minister, is surely the most recognisable British figure of the twentieth century. His bulldog expression, complete with cigar and v-sign is unmistakeable, captured as it was on a daily basis not only on camera, but also by cartoonists such as Sir David Low, Sidney Strube and Vicky (Victor Weisz). By the Second World War, he had provided ammunition for satirists for over 40 years. The Winston Churchill depicted by such Edwardian cartoonists as E T Reed and Leonard Raven-Hill is less instantly recognisable but no less striking. Baby-faced and ginger-haired, the Edwardian Churchill captured in these cartoons is an aggressively ambitious young politician, a charismatic presence that cartoonists found impossible to ignore.

Churchill's early career was shaped by the influence of his father, the former Chancellor of the Exchequer, Lord Randolph Churchill. Concerned that his son was not academically gifted enough to go to university, Lord Randolph Churchill arranged for the young Churchill to take the entrance exams for Sandhurst, which he passed at the third attempt. Despite issues with authority and a lack of self-discipline, he displayed a great aptitude for soldiering, passing out of Sandhurst 20th out of 130. Though his father's devotion to politics had left him feeling neglected as a child, his success at Sandhurst began to earn him his father's respect. Lord Randolph Churchill's sudden death at the age of 45 in 1895 convinced the young Churchill not only that he needed to live up to his father's expectations, but also that members of his family died young, so his time to make an impact was short.

Between 1895 and 1900, Winston Churchill's military career took him around the world; to Cuba, India, Sudan and South Africa. During this time, he began to earn a reputation not only as a talented soldier, but also as a first-class war correspondent, reporting on the various conflicts in which he fought for the *Daily Graphic,* the *Morning Post* and the *Daily Telegraph.* Though he enjoyed life in the military, Churchill's true ambition was to follow his father into the House of Commons. Whilst on leave from the army in 1899, he had stood as the Conservative candidate for Oldham but had been defeated. In November of the same year, while in Natal, Churchill was captured by Boer forces, before staging a dramatic escape. This incident found him a new level of fame and respect, which enabled him to be returned at Oldham in the general election of 1900.

His maiden speech in the Commons came on 18 February 1901, when he was just 26. He quickly became known as a self-confident, outspoken figure. He angered many Conservatives not only through his desire to see the Boers offered generous peace terms, but also for his frequent attacks on the Secretary of State for War, St John Brodrick. He was a strong supporter of free trade and regularly mocked the indecision of Prime Minister Arthur Balfour. Churchill's decision to cross the floor to David Lloyd-George's Liberal Party in May 1904 was ambitious, but paid off when the Liberals won a landslide victory in January 1906 and the new Prime Minister, Henry Campbell-Bannerman, appointed him to ministerial office for the first time as Under Secretary of State for the Colonies. With the Colonial Secretary in the House of Lords, this gave Churchill full responsibility for handling colonial affairs in the Commons. Though his speeches were not always well received – he developed a reputation for an occasionally overbearing, gloating oratorical style – his new role brought him more into the public eye.

In March 1908, at the age of 33, Winston Churchill was made the youngest member of the cabinet since 1866, when Prime Minister Herbert Henry Asquith named him President of the Board of Trade. Alongside Chancellor of the Exchequer David Lloyd George, he proved himself a vocal and dedicated supporter of social reform, before being named Home Secretary following the general election of 1910. In 1911, Churchill's impressive response to the Agadir Crisis prompted Asquith to name him First Lord of the Admiralty, a role that placed him at the centre of the country's involvement in the First World War. However, his involvement in the disastrous Gallipoli campaign would force his resignation and nearly irrevocably damage a career and reputation on a remarkable rise.

E T REED
Edward Tennyson Reed (1860-1933)

Preferring pencil to pen and ink, E T Reed developed into a superb draughtsman, using his confident line to express a rich imagination. Known equally for his political caricatures and his *Punch* series, 'Prehistoric Peeps', his range of subject and allusion was astonishingly wide.

For a biography of E T Reed, please refer to *The Illustrators*, 2011, page 80.

Further reading:
Shane Leslie (ed), *Edward Tennyson Reed*, London: Heinemann, 1957

65

An Exception to the Rule!
Published just a few weeks before Churchill crossed the floor to join the Liberal Party, this cartoon refers to a discussion that took place in the House of Commons on 5 May 1904 on alleged mistreatment of native labourers in South Africa. Churchill, then the Conservative MP for Oldham, brought it to the House's attention that although instances of flogging had been reduced under the previous Colonial Secretary Joseph Chamberlain, a commission report out of South Africa had complained about growing mistreatment of native labourers in the previous 12 months, through beatings and underpayment. This brought Churchill into conflict with the current Colonial Secretary, Alfred Lyttelton, portrayed here as a schoolmaster, whom Churchill implied had not done enough to prevent these abuses.

75 AN EXCEPTION TO THE RULE!
MR WINSTON CHURCHILL SAID THAT THE LATE COLONIAL SECRETARY HAD GREATLY REDUCED THE AMOUNT OF FLOGGING ALL OVER THE BRITISH EMPIRE (CHEERS). IT WAS A QUESTION ON WHICH THE RT HON GENTLEMAN HELD VERY STRONG VIEWS (WE STRONGLY SUSPECT THAT HIS DISLIKE OF FLOGGING IS NOT OF UNIVERSAL APPLICATION!)
Signed with monogram and inscribed with title
Pencil
7 ¼ x 4 ¾ inches
Illustrated: *Punch*, 11 May 1904, page 337

It Never Got Over My Escape and **The Duties of Confidential Adviser to Lord Roberts are not Light**

These two images of a twenty-seven-year-old Churchill were illustrated as part of a set of four vignettes, which accompanied an imagined interview with the young MP for Oldham, titled 'Mr Punch's Sketchy Interviews'. In the fictitious interview, Churchill and the interviewer admire a stuffed vulture that is revealed to be the very one which made its presence known to Churchill during his dramatic escape from a Boer POW camp in 1899. Churchill's revelation that he is confidential advisor to Lord Roberts, Commander-in-Chief of the British Forces, is a tongue-in-cheek reference to his growing reputation as a young politician with strong views on all political and military matters; he also laments in this interview that US President Theodore Roosevelt is 'impetuous and has to be constantly held in check'.

76 IT NEVER GOT OVER MY ESCAPE
Signed with monogram and inscribed with title
Pencil
7 ½ x 4 ½ inches
Illustrated: *Punch*, 10 September 1902, page 175

77 THE DUTIES OF CONFIDENTIAL ADVISER TO LORD ROBERTS ARE NOT LIGHT
Signed with monogram and inscribed with title
Pencil
7 ¼ x 4 ½ inches
Illustrated: *Punch*, 10 September 1902, page 175

78 SIDE-LIGHTS ON WINSTON'S STATE VOYAGE
OUR ARTIST HAS NEVER HAD THE PLEASURE OF MEETING AN
OKAPI IN REAL LIFE, SO HE FEELS THERE MAY BE SOMETHING
WRONG SOMEWHERE
Signed with monogram
Pencil, 10 x 9 ¼ inches
Illustrated: *Punch's Almanack*, 1 January 1908, [unpaginated]

79 WINSTON AT THE NETS (QUESTION TIME)
THE MORE BOWLING HE GETS THE BETTER HE LIKES IT
Signed with monogram and inscribed with title
Pencil, 7 ¾ x 4 ¾ inches
Illustrated: *Punch*, 16 May 1906, page 356

Side-Lights on Winston's State Voyage
In the autumn of 1907, as part of his duties as Under-Secretary
for the Colonies, Churchill embarked upon a tour of East Africa.
Initially, the trip began as little more than a hunting expedition, but
it soon turned into semi-official inquiry into colonial affairs. In the
Punch Almanack for 1908, Edward Tennyson Reed produced a trio
of pictures highlighting Churchill's visit to Africa, including this image
of Churchill playing polo atop the artist's estimation of an Okapi.

Winston at the Nets
As Under-Secretary of State for the Colonies, Churchill was responsible for
answering questions on colonial matters in the Commons, due to the Secretary of
State for the Colonies, Viscount Harcourt, being in the House of Lords. This
cartoon may refer to a day in the Commons on 14 May, when he faced an unusual
number of questions. Churchill responded to colonial queries from seven different
MPs, on issues ranging from the slave trade in British Northern Columbia to the
threat of Sleeping Sickness in Northern Rhodesia.

NIBS

Frederick Drummond Niblett, RSA (1861-1928), known as 'Nibs'

Though too little known today, Frederick Drummond Niblett produced some of the most striking caricatures of the Edwardian period in a style reminiscent of the posters and illustrations of William Nicholson and James Pryde, who worked together as the 'Beggarstaff Brothers'.

For a biography of Nibs, please refer to *The Illustrators*, 2008, page 26.

The Rt Hon Winston Churchill

Niblett, or 'Nibs', is best known for his caricature of *W L S Churchill, MP*, which appeared in *Vanity Fair* in 1911. However, four years earlier, the present image of Churchill was published in *The Crown: The Court and Country Families Newspaper*. Possibly only the second published caricature of Churchill by any artist (the first, by 'Spy', appearing in *Vanity Fair* in 1900), it is certainly more striking than Nibs' later drawing and more representative of his emphatic 'poster' style. It is virtually unknown because of the scarcity of surviving copies of *The Crown*, the very short-lived periodical in which it appeared. Other caricatures in the same series included King Edward VII, Lord Kitchener and the playwright, Sir Arthur Wing Pinero.

Churchill's shock of red hair, exaggerated brow and Puckish stance combine in a masterly caricature of the politician just at the beginning of his meteoric rise. At the time, he was Liberal Member of Parliament for Manchester North West and Under Secretary of State for the Colonies.

The drawing records a speech Winston Churchill gave on 18 May 1907, before 3,000 members of the Scottish Liberal Association at the King's Theatre, Edinburgh. Here, he addressed what had been discussed at the Imperial Conference, which had been concluded on 14 May and which Churchill had attended as Under Secretary of State for the Colonies. He criticised Conservative attempts to impose Imperial preference and declared that the Liberal, Radical and Labour majority would continue to defend free trade. He also accused the press of attempting to stir ill-feeling between the colonial premiers and the government. His final attack, as referred to here, was on the House of Lords, by calling upon the electorate to join in defending free trade and rescue Britain from the Lords.

The note on The Rt Hon Winston Churchill *is written by Alexander Beetles and David Wootton.*

80 THE RT HON WINSTON CHURCHILL
WHEN THE NEXT ELECTION CAME THEY WOULD APPEAL TO THE ELECTORS AND DEFEND FREE TRADE AND TO RESCUE THE LAND OF BRITAIN FROM THE LORDS
Signed and dated '07
Inscribed with title below mount
Signed and inscribed with artist's address on reverse
Bodycolour and ink
15 ¾ x 10 inches
Illustrated: *The Crown: The Court and County Families Newspaper*, 1907
Literature: R T Matthews & P Mellini, *Vanity Fair*, London: Quiller Press, 2001, pages 67 & 68, and colour plate 64

LEONARD RAVEN-HILL

Leonard Raven-Hill, RWA (1867-1942)

One of the most versatile of Edwardian artists, Leonard Raven-Hill became best known as an illustrator and cartoonist, and particularly for his contributions to *Punch* over 40 years.

Leonard Raven-Hill was born at 18 New Bond Street, Bath, Somerset, on 10 March 1867, the son of William Hill, an umbrella and parasol manufacturer. He was educated at Bristol Grammar School and Devon County School, West Buckland, and first studied at Bristol School of Art.

Following his move to Lambeth School of Art, in London, Raven-Hill contributed his first cartoons to *Judy* with the signature 'Leonard Hill' (1885). At that time, he shared lodgings with Charles Shannon, and fell under the influence of Charles Ricketts. Possibly on Ricketts' recommendation, he moved to Paris to study under William-Adolphe Bouguereau and Aimé Morot at the Académie Julian (1885-87); while there, he exhibited at the Paris Salon. In London, he exhibited history paintings and illustrations at the Royal Society of British Artists (1887-90) and the Royal Academy (1889-98), among other societies, and held solo shows at the Fine Art Society and with other dealers. In 1889, he married Annie Rogers, the daughter of the woodcarver, Mark Rogers. They lived at 45 Rossetti Mansions, Cheyne Walk, Chelsea, until 1892, and then at 20 North Side, Clapham Common. They seem to have had three children: Sylvia (born circa 1893), Arthur (born circa 1899) and Betty (born circa 1903).

Best known as a cartoonist and illustrator, Raven-Hill developed his approach by working with Phil May, and would become a member of the Savage Club. He was employed as art editor of *Pick-Me-Up* (from about 1890) and co-founded *The Butterfly* (1893) and the short-lived *The Unicorn* (1895). Contributing to *Punch* from 1895, he acted as second cartoonist to Bernard Partridge from 1910 to 1935. In drawing the topical themes of the week, he was compared to Charles Keene, an artist whom he had studied closely. He was also greatly admired for the revealing humour both of his military cartoons and his book illustrations, such as those for Rudyard Kipling's *Stalky and Co* (on its original appearance in *The Windsor Magazine* in 1898) and H G Wells' *Kipps* (1905). His own publications included *The Promenaders* (1894), *Our Battalion* (1902) and *An Indian Sketch-Book* (1903), the last based on his experience of the Delhi Durbar of 1903.

By 1896, Raven-Hill had acquired Battle House, Bromham, near Chippenham, in Wiltshire. Making it his main base, he added a studio in 1909. His experiences of the village – as Chairman of Bromham Parish Council and a member of the 2nd volunteer battalion of the Wiltshire Regiment – provided him with subject matter for his cartoons. However, his move to Bromham was not entirely a successful one: in 1899, his wife, Annie, began an affair with the eighteen-year-old Clive Bell, whose parents lived in the nearby village of Seend; it lasted, if intermittently, for 15 years, by which time he was married to the Bloomsbury painter, Vanessa Bell, and had published his book, *Art* (1914).

In the year following the death of Annie, in 1922, Raven-Hill married Marion Jean Lyon, *Punch*'s advertising manager. He may have left Bromham at this time to live in London and Surrey and on the Isle of Wight (he and Annie already having had a house on the latter at The Duver, St Helen's). He continued to work for *Punch* until 1935, when failing eyesight and general ill health necessitated his retirement. He died at Ryde on the Isle of Wight on 31 March 1942, two years after his second wife. His last address was Mayfield, 24 Queen's Road, Ryde.

His work is represented in numerous public collections, including the British Museum; and Birmingham City Museum and Art Gallery, and the Art Gallery of New South Wales (Sydney).

69

Further reading:
E V Knox (*rev* Simon Turner), 'Hill, Leonard Raven- (1867-1942), H C G Matthew and Brian Harrison (eds), *Oxford Dictionary of National Biography*, Oxford University Press, 2004, vol 27, pages 153-154

The biography of Leonard Raven-Hill *is written by David Wootton.*

detail of **82**

70

81 THE LIBERAL PLEASURE PARTY AT SEA
Signed
Pen and ink
10 ¼ x 9 inches
Illustrated: *Punch*, 2 July 1913, pages 20-21

The Liberal Pleasure Party at Sea
This cartoon presents the Liberal government in the setting of a pleasure boat, a motif that at first seems appropriately celebratory for a summer issue of *Punch*. However, it alludes to the long-established allegory of the Ship of Fools, and so critiques a political lack of direction, as is signalled by the loaded title phrase 'at sea' and the image of the Prime Minister, Herbert Asquith, steering a wheel emblazoned with his procrastinating coinage, 'Wait and See'. The ship itself is called 'The People's Will', a term appropriated by the Liberals and, especially, Lloyd George, the Chancellor of the Exchequer, who had published a book of essays with that title in 1910.

From left to right, the cartoon represents the following figures:

1. [seated at the prow, with coronet and cigar] **Richard Haldane**, 1st Viscount Haldane (1856-1928), was Lord Chancellor between 1912 and 1915.

2. [standing singing 'The Joy Song', with top hat and umbrella] **Charles Masterman** (1873-1927) was Financial Secretary to the Treasury, between 1912 and 1914, and was responsible for overseeing National Health Insurance. The author of the influential study, *The Condition of England* (1909), he was highly regarded as a rising politician, and even a potential Prime Minister, in the years before the First World War.

3. [ape hanging from the mast] **Charles Darwin** (1809-1882), swinging from the mast as an ape, possibly represents the abridged version of *On the Origin of Species* that was published in 1913.

4. [at the rear, in white suit and hat, and with upturned moustache] **Robert Crewe-Milnes**, 1st Marquess of Crewe (1858-1945), was Leader of the House of Lords between 1908 and 1916, and Secretary of State for India during most of that period.

5. [at the rear, in grey suit, with a hawk-like profile] **Edward Grey**, 3rd Baronet of Fallodon (1862-1933), served as Foreign Secretary from 1905 to 1916.

6. [at the front, recognisable by his gimlet eye and bushy moustache, holding *How To Make Fourpence Into Ninepence*] **David Lloyd George** (1863-1945) was Chancellor of the Exchequer from 1908 to 1915. In 1913, he finally put into effect the 1911 National Insurance Act, the first part of which provided for medical benefits by legislating that workers earning under £160 a year paid four pence a week to the scheme, the employer paid three pence, and general taxation paid two pence – hence Lloyd George's coinage 'ninepence for fourpence'.

7. [at the front, in a straw boater, with a flower in his button hole] **Rufus Isaacs** (1860-1935) was Attorney General for England between 1910 and 1913. Early in 1913, he was implicated in the scandal of insider trading in the shares of the Marconi Company (of which his brother, Godfrey, was managing director) – as indeed was Lloyd George. Along with Herbert Samuel [no 21], they were revealed as profiting directly from the policies of the government, but found not guilty of corruption. By linking Lloyd George and Isaacs so closely, Raven-Hill may have been suggesting that they had found a new way of making 'fourpence into ninepence'.

8. [represented by a sign with a pointing hand as attached to a rope ladder] **John Burns** (1858-1943) was President of the Local Government Board for the Liberal Government between 1908 and 1914, despite his reputation as an independent Radical.

9. [standing in a white suit, with his back to the viewer, hands on hips, and topped by an unmistakable profile] **Winston Churchill** (1874-1965) served as First Lord of the Admiralty between 1911 and 1915, which is why Raven-Hill has represented him as if he owned the yacht.

71

10. [at the rear, his long, narrow head seen between Churchill and the sail] **Lewis Harcourt** (1863-1922) served as Secretary of State for the Colonies between 1910 and 1915.

11. John Morley (1838-1923) served as Lord President of the Council between 1910 and 1914. He had previously held office as Chief Secretary for Ireland and Secretary of State for India.

12. Unidentified

13. [dressed in Irish costume, and playing a harp initialled TP] **Thomas Power O'Connor** (1848-1929), Father of the House of Commons, was an Irish Nationalist.

14. [near side, leaning over the side] **John Seely** (1868-1947) served as Secretary of State for War between 1912 and 1914. On the outbreak of the First World War, he left his post to fight on the front line, serving for the full duration of the war.

15. [far side, saying 'oh!'] **James Falconer** (1856-1931) was Liberal MP for Forfarshire. In 1912, he was appointed to the Select Committee set up by the House of Commons to look into the Marconi Scandal.

16. [shot by me in India] **Ramsay MacDonald** (1866-1937), Leader of the Labour Party, had made an electoral agreement with the Liberal whips.

17. [Ure's white wash] **Alexander Ure** (1853-1928) served as Solicitor General for Scotland from 1905 to 1909 and as Lord Advocate between 1909 and 1913.

18. [Board of Education primer] **Jack Pease** (1860-1943) was President of the Board of Education between 1911 and 1915. He would later become Chairman of the BBC between 1922 and 1926.

19. [Constable fishing for mermaids] **Reginald McKenna** (1863-1943) was Home Secretary between 1911 and 1915.

20. The **Mad Hatter** was used on a number of occasions by cartoonists and satirists to represent the Liberal Party, for example in Laurence Houseman's one-act play *Alice in Ganderland*, first performed at the Lyceum on 27 October 1911.

21. [man with phone] **Herbert Samuel** (1870-1963) was Postmaster General between 1910 and 1914 [see no 7].

22. [at the wheel] **H H Asquith** (1852-1928), Prime Minister, First Lord of the Treasury and Leader of the House of Commons from 1908 to 1915. In 1910, he coined the phrase, 'wait and see', regarding the creation of peers. However, this became something of a general approach, and was perceived as weakness. This is further referenced by the bound and gagged Lord being used as a figurehead.

23. [man in cloud blowing] This is possibly **Walter Hume Long** (1854-1924), former leader of the Irish Unionist Alliance.

24. [in the role of captain] **John Redmond** (1856-1918) was Leader of the Irish Parliamentary Party from 1900 until his death in March 1918.

25. [suggestive of a cabin boy] **Augustine Birrell** (1850-1933) was Chief Secretary for Ireland between 1907 and 1916.

26. [hanging off the stern] **Timothy Healy** (1855-1931) was a controversial and outspoken Irish nationalist politician. He became the 1st Governor-General of the Irish Free State in 1922.

27. [in a lifeboat] **1st Baron Murray of Elibank** (1870-1920) served as Parliamentary Secretary to the Treasury between 1910 and 1912, before his involvement in insider trading in the Marconi Scandal forced his resignation [see no 7 for more information].

The note on The Liberal Pleasure Party at Sea *is written by Alexander Beetles and David Wootton.*

LEONARD RAVEN-HILL

82 WHEN CONSTABULARY DUTY'S TO BE DONE

MR LLOYD GEORGE (TO THE NEW HOME SECRETARY): 'I SUPPOSE YOU'RE GOING TO SETTLE DOWN NOW?'

MR WINSTON CHURCHILL: 'YES; BUT I SHAN'T FORGET YOU. IF YOU FIND YOURSELF IN TROUBLE I'LL SEE IF I CAN'T GET YOU A REPRIEVE, FOR THE SAKE OF OLD TIMES!'

Signed and inscribed with title

Pen and ink

12 ¾ x 10 inches

Illustrated: *Punch*, 23 February 1910, page 129

When Constabulary Duty's To Be Done

Following the general election in January 1910, Liberal Prime Minister Herbert Henry Asquith appointed Churchill to the Home Office as the new Home Secretary, where his responsibilities included the supervision of the Metropolitan Police. He had previously held the position of President of the Board of Trade, a role in which he worked closely with Chancellor of the Exchequer, David Lloyd-George. With Lloyd-George's encouragement, Churchill promoted a number of major reforms of social policy, such as state-run labour exchanges, and compulsory unemployment insurance. Together they campaigned at great public meetings, urging their radical strategy of social reforms on the rest of the cabinet. This period marked the start of a famously close working relationship between the two, one in which Churchill openly acknowledged his subordination to the older man. Violet Bonham Carter, the daughter of Asquith and close friend of Churchill, described David Lloyd-George as holding 'the only personal leadership I have ever known Winston to accept unquestioningly in the whole of his career' (Violet Bonham-Carter, *Winston Churchill as I Knew Him*, London: Eyre & Spottiswoode, 1965, page 161).

The title of this cartoon is taken from the Policemen's song, 'When a felon's not engaged in his employment', in Gilbert & Sullivan's *Pirates of Penzance*, which was first performed in New York in 1879.

H M BATEMAN
Henry Mayo Bateman (1887-1970)

H M Bateman established his inimitable style before the First World War when, as he put it, he 'went mad on paper', by drawing people's mood and character. It reached its zenith with 'The Man Who …', his famous series of cartoons dramatising social gaffes.

For a biography of Henry Mayo Bateman, please refer to *The Illustrators*, 2009, page 72; for an essay on the revolutionary and reactionary aspects of the artist's work, see *The Illustrators*, 2000, pages 21-22.

His work is represented in numerous public collections, including the British Museum.

Further reading:
Anthony Anderson, *The Man Who Was H M Bateman*, Exeter: Webb & Bower, 1982; John Jensen, 'Bateman, Henry Mayo (1887-1970)', H C G Matthew and Brian Harrison (eds), *Oxford Dictionary of National Biography*, Oxford University Press, 2004, vol 4, pages 299-301

For further works by H M Bateman, please see pages 130-133

73

Churchill: Once More into the Breach –
As First Lord of the Admiralty, Churchill was keen to play a central role in the First World War. However, his involvement in the disastrous failure at Gallipoli forced his resignation from the government in November 1915. He was so eager to continue to contribute to the war effort that he took command of the 6th battalion of the Royal Scots Fusiliers, serving briefly on the Western Front in 1916. The political crisis in 1916, which saw David Lloyd-George become Prime Minister as head of a wartime coalition, gave Churchill an opportunity to return to government. In July 1917, he was appointed Minister of Munitions, where he would be responsible for ensuring a continuous and increasing flow of production. The title of the cartoon is taken from the opening line of King Henry's famous speech in Act 3 of Shakespeare's *Henry the Fifth*.

83 CHURCHILL: ONCE MORE INTO THE BREACH –
Signed with initials and inscribed 'Once More into the Breach –'
Pen and ink with pencil on tinted paper
7 x 5 ½ inches

05
EDWARDIAN ILLUSTRATORS

ARTHUR RACKHAM
(1867-1939)

MARY VERMUYDEN
WHEELHOUSE
(1868-1947)

CHARLES ROBINSON
(1870-1937)

DUNCAN CARSE
(1876-1938)

EDMUND DULAC
(1882-1953)

ARTHUR RACKHAM
Arthur Rackham (1867-1939)

First and foremost among illustrators of the Gift Book, Arthur Rackham had a particular affinity for the northern literary tradition, from Andersen to Wagner, and developed a perfect visual response in his intensely observed characterisation and atmospheric depiction of setting. The images tend to be remembered as grotesque and spine tingling but, wide-ranging and always apt, their mood is as likely to be humorous or tender.

For a biography of Arthur Rackham, please refer to *The Illustrators*, 2007, pages 97-98; for essays on various aspects of the artist's achievements, see *The Illustrators*, 1997, pages 124-125; *The Illustrators*, 1999, pages 98-99; *The Illustrators*, 2000, pages 14-15; and *The Illustrators*, 2002, pages 26-27.

Drawing my pistol, I wheeled suddenly in my saddle, and fired straight at him.

84 DRAWING MY PISTOL, I WHEELED SUDDENLY IN MY SADDLE, AND FIRED STRAIGHT AT HIM
Signed, inscribed with title and dated 97
Pen and ink with bodycolour
11 x 7 ½ inches
Illustrated: Charles James Lever, *Charles O'Malley, The Irish Dragoon*, London: Service & Paton, 1897, page 341

Key works illustrated: S J A Fitzgerald, *The Zankiwank and the Bletherwitch* (1896); [R H D Barham], *The Ingoldsby Legends* (1898); Mrs Edgar Lewis (tr), *Fairy Tales of the Brothers Grimm* (1900); Washington Irving, *Rip Van Winkle* (1905); J M Barrie, *Peter Pan in Kensington Gardens* (1906); William Shakespeare, *A Midsummer-Night's Dream* (1908); Richard Wagner (tr Margaret Armour), *The Rhinegold and The Valkyrie* (1910); Richard Wagner (tr Margaret Armour), *Siegfried and The Twilight of the Gods* (1911); Charles S Evans, *Cinderella* (1919); Edgar Allan Poe, *Tales of Mystery and Imagination* (1935)

His work is represented in numerous public collections, including the British Museum and the V&A; and the Butler Library (Columbia University in the City of New York), The Cleveland Museum of Art (OH), The New York Public Library and the Harry Ransom Humanities Research Center (University of Texas at Austin).

Further reading:
James Hamilton, *Arthur Rackham: A Life with Illustration*, London: Pavilion Books, 1990; James Hamilton, 'Rackham, Arthur (*b* Lewisham, London, 19 Sept 1867; *d* Limpsfield, Surrey, 6 Sept 1939), Jane Turner (ed), *The Dictionary of Art*, London: Macmillan, 1996, vol 25, pages 835-856; James Hamilton, 'Rackham, Arthur (1867-1939)', in H C G Matthew and Brian Harrison (eds), *Oxford Dictionary of National Biography*, Oxford University Press, 2004, vol 45, pages 718-721; Derek Hudson, *Arthur Rackham: His Life and Work*, London: Heinemann, 1960

85 PETER PAN
Signed
Pen ink and watercolour
6 x 13 ½ inches
Illustrated: J M Barrie, *Peter Pan in Kensington Gardens*, London: Hodder & Stoughton, 1906, title page

86 EXIT MOONSHINE
Signed, inscribed with title and dated – 08
Pen ink and watercolour
6 ¼ x 6 ¼ inches
Illustrated: William Shakespeare, A *Midsummer-Night's Dream*, London: William Heinemann, 1908, page 127
[Published in black and white and subsequently coloured by the artist]

On the Great Wall

Puck of Pook's Hill is a volume of short stories by Rudyard Kipling, which was first published in 1906. Dan and Una (based on Kipling's own children) act out scenes from *A Midsummer Night's Dream* on Midsummer's Eve in an old fairy ring near Burwash, in Sussex. By so doing, they accidentally invoke the sprite, Puck, who provides them with a series of tales of old England, narrated either by him or by various historical characters, including Parsenius, a Roman centurion. In 'On the Great Wall', Parsenius recounts his efforts on Hadrian's Wall to protect the northern frontier of the Roman Empire. The present image represents the kinds of people that he says he is likely to meet in the far north. Parsenius's experience represents 'in miniature, Britain's endeavour to defend the margins of its present day empire, whether in India or in South Africa' (John McBratney, 'India and Empire', Howard John Booth (ed), *The Cambridge Companion to Rudyard Kipling*, Cambridge University Press, 2011, page 33).

87 THAT'S WHERE YOU MEET HUNTERS AND TRAPPERS FOR THE CIRCUSES, PRODDING ALONG CHAINED BEARS AND MUZZLED WOLVES
Signed and dated 06
Pen ink and watercolour
14 x 10 ½ inches
Illustrated: Rudyard Kipling, *Puck of Pook's Hill*, New York: Doubleday, Page & Co, 1906, facing page 152, 'On the Great Wall'

88 BEFORE THE BALL
Signed
Pen ink and watercolour
6 ¼ x 8 ¼ inches

Metzengerstein

'Metzengerstein' was the first published short story of Edgar Allan Poe (1809-1849), appearing as it did in the Philadelphia magazine, *Saturday Courier*, on 14 January 1832. Set in Hungary, in an unspecified period, the story concerns young Baron Frederick, the last of the Metzengersteins, who cruelly perpetuates a long-standing feud with the Berlifitzing family. Four days after Frederick receives his inheritance, the Berlifitzings' stables catch fire, and he is suspected of arson. At home, he meditates on a tapestry containing a huge horse that once belonged to the Berlifitzings. Outside, he encounters an actual horse that is the counterpart to the one in the tapestry. On its forehead are branded the initials, 'WVB', probably standing for Wilhelm Von Berlifitzing, who, it transpires, died in the fire. The Berlifitzings deny any knowledge of the animal, and Frederick takes ownership of it, just as his page comes to tell him that a portion of the tapestry is missing. Riding this horse becomes Frederick's obsession, and he does so to the exclusion of every other activity. One night, he mounts the horse and rides it into the forest. Some hours later, the Metzengerstein castle catches fire. As the gathering crowd watches, horse and rider leap into the flames and, soon after, a rising cloud of smoke settles into the shape of 'the distinct colossal figure of – *a horse'*.

89 THE YOUNG METZENGERSTEIN SEEMED RIVETED TO THE SADDLE
Pen and ink with pencil
10 ¾ x 7 ½ inches
Provenance: The Estate of Barbara Edwards, the artist's daughter
Preliminary drawing for Edgar Allan Poe, *Tales of Mystery and Imagination*, London: George G Harrap & Co, 1935, 'Metzengerstein'

79

MARY VERMUYDEN WHEELHOUSE

Mary Vermuyden Wheelhouse (1868-1947)

The artist, Mary Vermuyden Wheelhouse, developed three successful overlapping careers through the first half of the twentieth century, the first as a painter in oil and watercolour, the second as a book illustrator, and the third as a toymaker, especially of wooden dolls.

Mary Vermuyden Wheelhouse was born in Leeds, in Yorkshire. She was the youngest of three daughters of Claudius Galen Wheelhouse FRCS JP (1826-1909), a surgeon at the Leeds Public Dispensary who would become President of the Council of the British Medical Association, and Agnes Caroline Cowell (1824-1911), a daughter of the Reverend Joseph Cowell. Her creativity is likely to have been encouraged, as her father had been active as a photographer during the 1850s, while one of her sisters, Ethel Hamerton Wheelhouse (born 1865) grew up to become a professional violinist. The family lived in Hillary Place, Leeds, and at Cliff Point, Filey.

Wheelhouse studied under Albert Strange at Scarborough School of Art, during the mid 1890s. While there, she lived at 29c St Nicholas Street, and began to exhibit at the Royal Academy of Arts, in London, and also in York. However, she would later state that 'the only art school in which I ever worked was the Academie Delecture in Paris, where I spent some three years a long time ago' (Miller and Whitney (eds), *Contemporary Illustrators of Children's Books*, Boston: Bookshop for Boys and Girls, Women's Educational and Industrial Union, 1930, page 76).

By 1899, Wheelhouse had moved to London, and was sharing 3 Pomona Studios, 111 New Kings Road, Fulham, with three other artists, including Alice Kinkead. From there, she sent work to galleries in London and the provinces, and also to the Paris Salon. She made her name as an illustrator in 1907, when she won a competition organised by *The Bookman*, with *The Adventures of Merrywink*, written by her friend, Christina Whyte. From then she received commissions from a number of publishers, and especially George Bell, with whom she began a long collaboration. She became particularly associated with her interpretations of works by Louisa M Alcott, Juliana H Ewing and Elizabeth Gaskell, and continued to illustrate books until the early 1930s.

Active in the women's suffrage movement, Wheelhouse helped found the Artists' Suffrage League in January 1907, and exhibited with the Women's International Art Club from at least 1910. Other exhibitions of the time included one at the Baillie Gallery in 1912, which she shared with three other illustrators: L L Brooke, F L Griggs and C P Hawkes.

In 1915, Wheelhouse began making a range of toys – including wooden dolls – with her fellow artist, Louise Jacobs, who is probably best remembered for her 1912 poster, *The Appeal of Womanhood*. They showed these first with the Arts and Crafts Exhibition Society, in 1916, and soon after opened a shop, Pomona Toys, at 64 Cheyne Walk, in Chelsea (which they leased from the artist, Marion Dawson, who lived above). Though they dissolved the partnership in 1922, Wheelhouse then joined with A B Ellis, by 1926, and they continued to run Pomona Toys at Cheyne Walk until 1927. They then moved the shop to 14 Holland Street, and also opened a workshop at 28 Gunter Grove. The company supplied major stores, including Fortnum & Mason, Harrods and Liberty & Co, as well as the LCC with nursery bricks, before folding soon after the outbreak of the Second World War. Wheelhouse died in 1947.

80

'now recognised universally as "the" artist for a special type of book … We mean the type of book which touches tenderly and humorously and warmly upon the warm and tender ways of life – the type of book, whether it be for children or grown-ups, which tells of "first and last things" – Miss Wheelhouse interprets as few illustrators do; she gives her pictures the universal touch by which they might stand alone, yet never achieves this through any overshadowing of the author by the artist.'

(*The Nation*, 1914, page 366)

Cousin Phillis

Published in 1908, George Bell's edition of *Cousin Phillis* was the first of four novels by Elizabeth Gaskell illustrated by M V Wheelhouse, the others being *Cranford* (1909), *Sylvia's Lovers* (1910) and *Wives and Daughters* (1912). First appearing in 1864, *Cousin Phillis* is considered to be 'Gaskell's crowning achievement in the short novel' (Lynn M Alexander, 'Elizabeth Gaskell', Wilson, Schlueter and Schlueter (eds), *Women Writers of Great Britain and Europe*, New York: Garland, 1997, page 164). Narrated by Phillis's second cousin, Paul Manning, it concerns her development and sexual awakening. The present image depicts Paul's first meeting with Phillis, when he arrives at her home, at the Hope Farm, at the beginning of the novel.

90 A TALL GIRL ABOUT MY OWN AGE CAME AND OPENED IT, AND STOOD THERE SILENT, WAITING TO KNOW MY ERRAND
Signed and dated 08
Inscribed with title and story title below mount
Pen ink and watercolour on board
10 ½ x 6 ½ inches
Illustrated: Mrs Gaskell, *Cousin Phillis* (Queen's Treasures), London: George Bell & Sons, 1908, frontispiece

82

91 NOUS PARTIONS EN BANDE, LE MATIN, A TRAVERS LES PRES
Signed
Inscribed with title and 'Frontispiece' below mount
Pen ink and watercolour on board
9 ½ x 6 inches
Illustrated: George Sand, *Les Maîtres Sonneurs* (Les Classiques Français Illustrés: Oeuvres de George Sand), London: George Bell & Sons, 1908

Les Maîtres Sonneurs
First published in 1853, George Sand's novel concerns the lives of bagpipers in the central French regions of Berry and Bourbonnais during the eighteenth century, and provides an appreciation of folk culture. The present image illustrates a passage early in the novel in which the narrator, Etienne Depardieu, introduces his cousin, Brulette, and their friend, Joseph, to the reader. Joseph is driven by a passion for music that sets him apart from his fellow villagers, and especially his local master, Carnat, and takes him to the mountains where he finds a new mentor in the person of le Grand-Bûcheux. Returning to the village to outperform Carnat's son, he then heads south with le Grand-Bûcheux. However, his dead body is later discovered in a ditch, and his instruments broken on the road, as a result of his having taunted some other musicians.

92 IT WAS WHILE THEY WERE WALKING THROUGH EVESHAM, BESIDE OR BEHIND THE SLOWCOACH ... THAT JANET FELT A HAND ON HER ARM, AND LOOKING ROUND PERCEIVED A VERY SMALL AND VERY NEAT AND VERY ANXIOUS LITTLE SERVANT
Signed
Inscribed with title and 'Chap 14' below mount
Watercolour with pen and ink on board
11 x 6 ½ inches
Illustrated: E V Lucas, *The Slowcoach. A Story of Roadside Adventure*, London: Wells Gardner & Co, 1910

The Slowcoach

This children's novel by E V Lucas tells of a holiday taken by the younger members of the Avory family. While reflecting on the sad news that their 'regular landlady at Sea View, in the Isle of Wight' has become seriously ill [93], they receive a gypsy caravan as a gift from a mysterious benefactor. As a result, they are able to set off on a trip through Oxfordshire, Warwickshire, Worcestershire and Gloucestershire, accompanied by some friends and aided by their gardener, Kink, who acts as driver. By their first evening, they have settled into life on the open road, and are able to enjoy a hearty supper [94].

One of their many adventures concerns an invitation – issued by a maid [92] – to take tea with the children's author, Miss Redstone, who writes under the name 'Godfrey Fairfax'. She reads them 'Barbara's Fugitive', a romance of Cavaliers and Roundheads, which appears as a story within the story.

83

93 ONE DAY IN LATE JUNE THE AVORIES AND THE ROTHERAMS AND HORACE CAMPBELL WERE SITTING AT TEA UNDER THE CEDAR TALKING ABOUT A GREAT TRAGEDY THAT HAD BEFALLEN
Signed
Inscribed with title below mount
Pen ink and watercolour on board
11 x 6 ¾ inches
Illustrated: E V Lucas, *The Slowcoach. A Story of Roadside Adventure*, London: Wells Gardner & Co, 1910

84

94 BY HALF PAST SEVEN THEY WERE
SEATED ON THEIR RUGS ROUND THE
FIRE EATING THE MOST SUPREME STEW
OF THE SEASON, AS MARY ROTHERAM
CALLED IT
Signed
Inscribed with title and 'Chap 9' below mount
Pen ink and watercolour on board
11 x 6 ¾ inches
Illustrated: E V Lucas, *The Slowcoach.*
A Story of Roadside Adventure, London:
Wells Gardner & Co, 1910

The Mill on the Floss

In 1910, George Bell and Sons published an edition of George Eliot's *Silas Marner*, with illustrations by M V Wheelhouse. The same publisher may have commissioned her to illustrate an edition of Eliot's *The Mill on the Floss* but, if so, it appears not to have been issued. Originally published in 1860, *The Mill on the Floss* concerns the Tulliver family who live at Dorlcote Mill in Lincolnshire, and particularly the siblings, Maggie and Tom. The present image depicts the scene in which Tom's friend, Bob Jakin, brings the intellectually avid Maggie 'a superannuated "Keepsake" and six or seven numbers of a "Portrait Gallery"' in an attempt to make up for her lack of books.

95 SUDDENLY SHE WAS ROUSED BY THE SOUND OF THE OPENING GATE AND OF FOOTSTEPS ON THE GRAVEL
Signed and dated 1913
Inscribed with title and 'Book 4 Chap 3' below mount
Pen ink and watercolour on board
10 x 6 ½ inches
Drawn for an unpublished edition of *The Mill on the Floss* by George Eliot (Mary Ann Evans)

96 ON THE DAY OF GRANNY'S FUNERAL OLD JOHN TOOK
CARE OF JOHNNY
Signed
Inscribed with title and 'p 186' below mount
Watercolour with pen and ink on board
8 ½ x 6 ¾ inches
Illustrated: Mary E Phillips, *Tommy Tregennis*, London: Constable & Co,
1914, page 186

97 WE LOOKED IT OUT IN JOHNSON'S DICTIONARY
Signed
Inscribed with title and story title below mount
Pen and ink with watercolour on board
9 ½ x 5 ¾ inches
Illustrated: Juliana Horatia Ewing, *Mary's Meadow & Other Tales of Fields &
Flowers* (Queen's Treasures), London: G Bell & Sons, 1915, 'Sunflowers
and a Rushlight'

Tommy Tregennis

The mischievous, warm-hearted young son of a fisherman and his wife, Tommy Tregennis lives in a Cornish village. His mother takes in lodgers during the summer months, and many of the incidents concern Miss Margaret, the 'Blue Lady', and Miss Dorothea, the 'Brown Lady', who take a great interest in Tommy and his upbringing. The present image comes from late in the novel when, on the day of his Granny's funeral, Tommy stays with the fisherman, Old John [96].

Having originally published Mary E Phillips' *Tommy Tregennis* in 1912, Constable & Co reissued it in 1914 with illustrations by M V Wheelhouse. In reviewing this later edition, *The Nation* stated that 'the charming story has been illustrated by Miss M V Wheelhouse, now recognised universally as "the" artist for a special type of book – that to which "Tommy Tregennis" belongs. We mean the type of book which touches tenderly and humorously and warmly upon the warm and tender ways of life – the type of book, whether it be for children or grown-ups, which tells of "first and last things" – Miss Wheelhouse interprets as few illustrators do; she gives her pictures the universal touch by which they might stand alone, yet never achieves this through any overshadowing of the author by the artist.'

Sunflowers and a Rushlight

Juliana Horatia Ewing remained a highly popular and respected author of children's books long after her death in 1895. In the early 1900s, her publisher, George Bell reissued a number of her stories in the 'Queen's Treasures' series, including eight illustrated by M V Wheelhouse. The last of these, appearing in 1915, was *Mary's Meadow & Other Tales of Fields & Flowers*, including 'Sunflowers and a Rushlight', which the present image illustrates [97]. Grace, the narrator, and her elder sister, Margery, are orphans, and live with their Grandmamma. She has a vivid imagination and, while Margery is visiting an old friend of their father, becomes particularly attached to the sunflowers in the garden, which 'are quite as good as dolls to play with'. Indeed, she becomes so attached to them that she goes out into the garden to look at them at night and, as a result, catches a cold. Her Grandmamma is so angry that she threatens to have the sunflowers cut down, and they are saved only through the intervention of Dr Brown, the children's joint guardian.

The Story of Florence Nightingale

Amy Steedman was a prolific writer of children's books, both fiction and non-fiction, published mainly by T C & E C Jack during the early twentieth century. Though the present image suggests that M V Wheelhouse may have proved their ideal collaborator, she worked with both writer and publisher only on this one occasion, because she changed direction in 1915, by moving from illustrating to toy making. However, her illustrations to Steedman's text were reused for Doris Heale Evans' *The Story of Florence Nightingale*, which was published in 1933 by Thomas Nelson and Sons, the firm that absorbed Messrs Jack.

98 TALKING WITH THE DOCTORS, AND HOLDING MEETINGS WITH THE LADIES
Signed
Inscribed with title and 'Chap 3' below mount
Watercolour with pen and ink on board
9 ¼ x 6 inches
Illustrated: Amy Steedman, *The Story of Florence Nightingale*, London: T C & E C Jack, 1915

CHARLES ROBINSON

Charles Robinson, RI (1870-1937)

Charles Robinson produced distinctive illustrations and watercolours, evolving his style from the influences of Pre-Raphaelitism and Art Nouveau, Japanese prints and the work of Old Masters.

For a biography of Charles Robinson, please refer to *The Illustrators*, 2007, page 53

Further reading:
Geoffrey Beare, *The Brothers Robinson*, London: Chris Beetles, 1992;
Leo de Freitas, *Charles Robinson*, London:
Academy Editions, 1976

The Port of Pride

In 1914, Charles Robinson began a series of drawings to which he gave the collected title, 'A Dream of St Nicholas in Heaven'. As described in an article in *The Studio*, published in 1915, these drawings depict:

> a satire, in the form of a legend, on the modern aspect of maternity woven into the personality of the patron saint of children. St Nicholas dreamed a dream of a great ship freighted with numbers of baby souls setting out from the Port of Heaven and journeying to different ports on reaching the terrestrial sphere, the ports symbolising different aspects of life. The first port reached is *The Port of Pride*. This, says the artist, is an allegory or satire on the child born into wealthy surroundings. The naked soul from the ship is seen in luxurious surroundings; people are bringing presents; maids have washed him in beautiful basins and clothed him in the finest napery. Plans of his estate lie about him; the lawyer waits to confirm his titles. The grandfather scans the family tree, and everywhere there are the concomitants of luxury and wealth. The only person unconcerned is the mother in her bed in the background; she does not allow the affair to interfere with her daily round of ease. In a room beyond, the father is toasting his ancestors and outside church bells are ringing. In the other drawings forming the series the ports of Poverty, Shame, Pleasure, Joy, and Sorrow are allegorised. (page 153)

A special number of *The Studio*, entitled *Modern Book Illustrators and their Work*, and published in autumn 1914, showed another drawing in the series, that for the ship itself, loaded with the 'baby souls'. While Robinson had produced these drawings as the 'unfettered expression' of his 'own imaginings' (loc cit), he intended that an author should provide an accompanying text, so that the series could be published in book form.

However, this seems not to have come to fruition. Nevertheless, Robinson also produced a watercolour triptych on the same theme, which has *The Port of Pride* on the right. His eldest child, Edith Mary Robinson, bequeathed the triptych to the V&A in 1982.

The satirical dimension of 'A Dream of St Nicholas in Heaven' in general, and of *The Port of Pride* in particular, was surely inspired, at least in part, by the eighteenth-century moral comedies of William Hogarth, such as *The Rake's Progress* and *Marriage à-la-mode*. The Georgian mode was then filtered through the style that Aubrey Beardsley developed in 1896 in order to illustrate Alexander Pope's mock-heroic poem, *The Rape of the Lock*, of 1712.

In an article on Charles Robinson, published by *The Studio* in 1916, Malcolm Salaman agreed that the artist had responded to the work of Beardsley, but added that 'Mr Robinson will admit a deeper, stronger influence in the style and sentiment of Mr Laurence Housman's expressive designs; while the wonderful precision of Dürer's line and the noble beauty of that master's designs have no less sensibly influenced and inspired our artist' (page 182). The present work confirms that he is rightly placed among such exalted company.

99 THE PORT OF PRIDE
Signed
Pen and ink with pencil
22 ¼ x 14 ½ inches
Literature: *The Studio*, vol LXIII, 1915, pages 148-153

DUNCAN CARSE
Andreas [Andrew] Duncan Carse (1876-1938)

Of Norwegian and Scottish parentage, Duncan Carse was a wide-ranging artist and designer. As an illustrator, he is best known for his delightful and delicate fairy subjects.

For a biography of Duncan Carse, please refer to *The Illustrators*, 2010, page 76.

His work is represented in the collections of the Museum of Reading.

101-120 are all illustrated in Hans Andersen, *Hans Andersen's Fairy Tales*, London: A & C Black, 1912, unless otherwise stated

For further illustrations to Hans Andersen, see Chapter 13, pages 210-219 and Chapter 19, pages 282-290

101 GOBLINS
Pen and ink on paper on board
¾ x 2 ¼ inches
Illustrated: title page

100 THE COMMON VAPOURER
Signed
Signed and inscribed with title below mount
Pen ink and watercolour with pencil
10 ¾ x 8 ½ inches

102 THE STORYTELLER
Pen and ink on paper on board
2 ¾ x 3 ¼ inches
Illustrated: title page

The Garden of Paradise

Though a young prince with a love of reading has developed a great library, not one of his books has been able to answer his most burning question: where the Garden of Paradise is to be found. Eventually, the East Wind carries him to Eden, and he is shown the tree of knowledge and then tempted by a beautiful woman. When he kisses her, the garden disappears. Death approaches him and warns him to expiate his sins, for one day he will return and place him in a black coffin. Only if he has repented will he enter the Garden of Paradise that is Heaven.

103 THE GARDEN OF PARADISE
Signed with initials
Pen and ink on board
6 ¼ x 9 inches
Illustrated: page v, 'Contents'

The Tinderbox

A soldier acquires a magic tinderbox that has the power to summon three enormous dogs to do his bidding. When he orders one of the dogs to transport a sleeping princess to his room, he is sentenced to death, but saves his life by summoning the dogs.

The Emperor's New Clothes

Two weavers promise an emperor a new suit of clothes that is invisible to anyone incompetent or stupid. When the emperor shows off his new clothes to his people, all are silent until a child says, 'he has nothing on'.

104 THERE SAT THE DOG WITH EYES LIKE BIG TEACUPS, STARING AT HIM
Signed with initials
Pen and ink on board, 6 x 4 ½ inches
Illustrated: page vii, 'List of Illustrations'

105 HEAVEN PRESERVE ME! THE OLD MINISTER THOUGHT ... 'WHY I CANNOT SEE ANYTHING'
Signed with initials
Pen and ink on board
6 ½ x 5 ¼ inches
Illustrated: page 40, 'The Emperor's New Clothes'

106 THE LITTLE MERMAID
Signed with initials
Inscribed with story title below mount
Pen and ink on board, 5 ¾ x 4 ¼ inches
Illustrated: page 67, 'The Little Mermaid'

The Little Mermaid
A young mermaid is willing to relinquish her identity and way of life in
order to gain a human soul and the love of a human prince. She visits the
Sea Witch who, in exchange for her voice and tongue, gives her a potion
that transforms her tail into legs, though she always finds walking painful.
She is found by the prince, and becomes his favourite companion, but he
loves and marries a princess from a neighbouring country. While despairing
and thinking of death, her sisters rise out of the water and bring her a
knife with which to kill the prince. If she lets his blood drip on her feet,
she will become a mermaid once again. Instead, she throws the knife and
herself into the water and, because she strove with all her heart to obtain
an immortal soul, turns into a daughter of the air with the hope that she
may rise up into the Kingdom of God.

107 HOW DID YOU COME BY ALL THAT QUANTITY OF MONEY!
Signed with initials
Inscribed with story title below mount
Pen and ink on board, 5 x 5 inches
Illustrated: page 81, 'Little Klaus and Big Klaus'

Little Klaus and Big Klaus
Little Klaus is bullied by Big Klaus, his richer, more powerful neighbour, but,
in turn, repeatedly makes a fool of him and, in the process, gains in wealth.
His last trick is to make Big Klaus believe that he has gained a herd of
cattle from the bottom of a river. Big Klaus so wants a herd of his own
that he begs Little Klaus to put him in a weighted sack and throw him into
the water, which he does, leaving Little Klaus as the only Klaus in the village.

108 INITIAL W
THE SNOW QUEEN
Inscribed with story title below mount
Pen and ink on board
3 ½ x 3 inches
Illustrated: page 82, 'The Snow Queen'

The Snow Queen
A wicked sorcerer creates a distorting mirror that magnifies the negative
aspect of people and things. He tries to take it to heaven in order to make
a fool of God, but it slips from his hand and falls to earth, shattering into
billions of small pieces. Some splinters enter the heart of a boy called Kai,
who, as a result, argues with his devoted friend, Gerda, and destroys the
window-box garden that they have tended together. The only things that
he now enjoys are the snowflakes that he views through a magnifying glass.
During the winter, the Snow Queen carries him away and kisses him, so
that he forgets his family and friends. Gerda seeks for him and, after many
adventures, finds out that the Snow Queen has taken him to Lapland. Setting
out on a reindeer, she stops at the home of a Finnish woman, who
recognises that it is Gerda's innocence and purity that will save Kai. She is
able to enter the Snow Queen's palace by saying the Lord's Prayer, and
melts Kai's heart by weeping warm tears on him. She then releases him by
helping him to spell out the word 'eternity' in splinters of ice. They return
home older and wiser.

109 THE UGLY
LITTLE DUCK
Signed with initials
Inscribed with story title
below mount
Pen and ink on board
5 ½ x 5 inches
Drawn for but not
illustrated

110 INITIAL I
THE UGLY
LITTLE DUCK
Inscribed with story title
below mount
Pen and ink on board
2 ¼ x 2 inches
Drawn for but not
illustrated

The Ugly Little Duck
A homely little bird suffers abuse from those around him until, to his
delight, and their surprise, he matures into a beautiful swan.

94

111 INITIAL H
THE SHEPHERDESS & THE SWEEP
Inscribed with story title below mount
Pen and ink on board
3 x 3 inches
Illustrated: page 191, 'The Shepherdess and the Sweep'

The Shepherdess and the Sweep
The love shared between two china figurines is threatened by the jealousy of a carved mahogany satyr. The satyr gains the support of a nodding porcelain Chinaman, who considers himself to be the shepherdess's grandfather. However, when the Chinaman has an accident, and is so mended that he can no longer nod, the lovers are safe to marry.

The Red Shoes
Following the death of her mother, Karen is adopted by a wealthy lady, and is spoiled. Her adoptive mother agrees to buy her a pair of red shoes, and she wears them constantly, even to church. They begin to move by themselves, and eventually she is unable to take them off, so that she is forced to dance, night and day. An angel condemns her to dance even after her death in order to act as a warning to vain children. Driven to an extreme, she asks an executioner to amputate her feet, but this does not stop the shoed feet from dancing before her and barring her way. She takes a job as a maid at the clergyman's house, and remains there, beginning to pray to God for help. The angel then returns and gives her the mercy that she asked for, so that her heart breaks and her soul flies to Heaven, where her red shoes are not mentioned.

112 INCESSANTLY SHE HAD TO DANCE
Inscribed with story title below mount
Pen and ink on board
4 ¾ x 3 ½ inches
Illustrated: page 202, 'The Red Shoes'

113 INITIAL F
THE WILD SWANS
Inscribed with story title
below mount
Pen and ink on board
2 ½ x 3 inches
Illustrated: page 203,
'The Wild Swans'

114 THE WILD SWANS
Signed with initials
Inscribed with story title
below mount
Pen and ink on board
2 ¾ x 5 ½ inches
Illustrated: page 223,
'The Wild Swans'

115 SEE, HOW HE GALLOPS PAST
Inscribed with story title below mount
Pen and ink on board
4 ¾ x 4 ½ inches
Illustrated: page 239, 'The Sandman'

The Wild Swans
A king has 11 sons and one daughter, called Eliza. Unfortunately, he marries a wicked queen, who sends Eliza to live with peasants, and turns her brothers into swans. Eliza returns to the palace at the age of 15, but her stepmother smears her with dirt, so that her father cannot recognise her, and sends her away again. Soon after cleaning herself in a forest pool, Eliza discovers her brothers, who return to human form each night. They weave a basket and, as swans, use it to carry Eliza to another, safer land. A dream reveals to her how she can break the spell that has been cast on her brothers: taking a vow of silence, she must pick stinging nettles and knit shirts from their fibres for them to wear. While she is beginning to do this, the king of the country discovers her, takes her to the palace, and proposes to her. In secret, she continues the task of gathering nettles to weave the shirts, but is caught in the act by the archbishop, accused of being a witch and condemned to burn at the stake. She finishes the last of the shirts just as she is about to be burned, and is able to toss them to her brothers as they fly above the crowd. They turn back into humans and corroborate the innocence of their sister, who is able to speak again. In celebration, she marries the king.

The Sandman
Given the name 'Ole Lukøje' by Hans Christian Andersen, the Sandman sends children to sleep and, if they have been good, brings them happy dreams. In the tale, he visits a boy each night for a week and tells him stories. On the final night, the Sandman introduces him to his brother, Death, who 'wears the most beautiful hussar's uniform' and 'gallops past' on a 'fiery horse'.

116 THE SWINE HERD
Signed with initials
Inscribed with title below mount
Pen and ink on board
6 x 4 ½ inches
Drawn for but not illustrated

The Swine Herd
A prince disguises himself as a swineherd to woo an arrogant princess, and then finds her unworthy of his love.

117 THE SHADOW
Inscribed with title below mount
Pen and ink on board
6 x 4 inches
Drawn for but not illustrated

The Shadow
Having lost his shadow once in Africa, a writer encounters it again in an almost human form, and invites it to live with him. Over the following years, the shadow grows richer and fatter and the writer grows poorer and paler. Eventually the shadow marries a princess, and has the writer arrested and executed.

118 INITIAL P
TRAVELLING COMPANIONS
Inscribed with title below mount
Pen and ink on board
2 ¾ x 2 ½ inches
Drawn for but not illustrated

Travelling Companions

Having tended his father until his death, John is now alone in
the world. Deciding to travel, he soon comes across two
grave robbers who are about to break into a coffin, and pays
them not to do so. Then, further along the road, a stranger
with magical powers becomes his travelling companion.
Together they arrive at a city, in which a beautiful, cruel
princess offers to marry the first man who can guess the three
things of which she is thinking – but promises to kill anyone
who fails. When John sees her, she reminds him of the dream
that he had on the night that his father died: his father
presenting him with exactly this woman and saying 'see what a
bride you have won'. As a result, he determines to win her.
This he achieves through the powers of his fellow traveller,
who finds out which objects the princess has chosen, and then
tells John that they have appeared to him in dreams. He also
helps John purge the princess of the influence of an evil
magician. Living happily ever after, John and the princess invite
the traveller to remain with them. However, he says that he
has now paid his debt and must go, for he is the dead man
who was in the coffin that John had protected.

119 LITTLE IDA'S FLOWERS
Inscribed with title below mount
Pen and ink on board
5 ½ x 7 ½ inches
Drawn for but not illustrated

The Drop of Water

An old magician observes a drop of
water through a magnifying glass and
sees a thousand creatures jumping
against each other. In an attempt to
calm them down, he adds a drop of
witch's blood, but this only makes
them look wild and naked. Another
magician asks what he is looking at,
and is told that, if he guesses, he can
have it. However, he thinks that he
is looking at the people of
Copenhagen or another large city,
not a drop of ditchwater.

120 THE DROP OF WATER
Inscribed with title below mount
Pen and ink on board
2 x 2 inches
Drawn for but not illustrated

Little Ida's Flowers 97

When Little Ida wonders why the flowers
in the garden looked so tired, a student
friend of hers tells her that that is because
they have been to a ball. He so fills her
head with stories that she begins to
wonder if they might be true, so at night
goes into the garden to check. There she
witnesses the flowers dancing. When she
returns to the garden in the morning, she
is more accepting of the withered state of
the flowers and buries them.

EDMUND DULAC

Edmund Dulac (1882-1953)

The multi-talented artist, Edmund Dulac, contributed more than a dash of French panache to the illustration of English gift books. Developing an exquisite palette and eclectic style, that referenced Japanese prints and Persian miniatures, he complemented the work of his chief rival, Arthur Rackham.

For a biography of Edmund Dulac and an essay on *Princess Badoura* (1913), please refer to *The Illustrators*, 2003, pages 61-65.

Key works illustrated: *Stories from the Arabian Nights* (1907); Edward Fitzgerald (tr), *The Rubaiyat of Omar Khayyam* (1909); *Stories from Hans Andersen* (1911)

His work is represented in numerous public collections, including the British Museum, The Cartoon Museum, the Imperial War Museum, the Museum of London and the V&A; The Fitzwilliam Museum (Cambridge); and the Harry Ransom Humanities Research Center (University of Texas at Austin) and The New York Public Library.

Further reading:
Edmund Dulac: Illustrator and Designer, Sheffield City Art Galleries, 1983; James Hamilton, 'Dulac, Edmund [Edmond] (1882-1953)', H C G Matthew and Brian Harrison (eds), *Oxford Dictionary of National Biography*, Oxford University Press, 2004, vol 17, pages 168-170; Ann Conolly Hughey, *Edmund Dulac. His Book Illustrations. A Bibliography*, Potomac: Buttonwood Press, 1995; Colin White, *Edmund Dulac*, London: Studio Vista, 1976

98

Bluebeard

In a city near Baghdad, there lived a man so wealthy that he would have been greatly envied had he not had a blue beard, which made him frightfully ugly to women. In particular, Anne and Fatima, the two daughters of a neighbouring gentlewoman, failed to respond to his advances, and their lack of enthusiasm for him only increased when they discovered that he had been married seven times before and that his wives had disappeared. Nevertheless, he persevered in wooing them with various entertainments, including being 'rowed to the sound of music' (as illustrated in the present image). Gradually, he overcame the prejudices of Fatima and her mother, the former suggesting that his beard appeared less blue, and the latter stating that blue 'is a beautiful colour, and considered lucky'. As a result, and with the agreement of her family, Fatima married him.

A month later, Bluebeard had to go away on a long business trip, and gave Fatima a set of keys, telling her that she may open any door except that to the little closet on the ground floor. While she amused herself in the company of her friends, she could not forget what her husband had forbidden, so that, once alone, she went and opened the closet door. As her eyes became accustomed to the darkness, she saw, in horror, the bodies of seven dead women hanging above a pool of blood. Then, while locking the door again, she dropped the key and stained it with the blood, which she could not clean off. While still attempting to do so, she heard her husband's horn, so quickly hid the key inside her bodice. Entering his house, he told her that he had received letters on the road telling him that

his journey was unnecessary, and so had come back. Next morning, he asked her to return the keys, but had to repeat his demand several times before she yielded the key to the closet door. The blood on it confirmed to him that her curiosity had led her to disobey him, and that she would now share the fate of his former wives. However, he allowed her 10 minutes to say her prayers and, as she went off, fortuitously met her sister, Anne, who had just arrived on a visit. In the nick of time, Anne alerted their two stepbrothers, who killed Bluebeard, and left Fatima the sole heir to his estate.

121 THEY WERE ROWED TO THE SOUND OF MUSIC ON THE WATERS OF THEIR HOST'S PRIVATE CANAL
(BLUEBEARD)
Signed and dated 10
Pen ink and watercolour with bodycolour
12 ¼ x 10 inches
Illustrated: Sir Arthur Quiller-Couch, *The Sleeping Beauty and Other Tales from the Old French*, New York: Hodder & Stoughton, 1910, no 4
Exhibited: 'An Exhibition of Water-Colour Drawings Illustrating "The Sleeping Beauty" and Other Fairy Tales', The Leicester Galleries, London, December 1910, no 11, as 'Bluebeard Entertains Fatima and her relatives. They are rowed, to the sound of music, on their host's canal'

06

WILLIAM HEATH ROBINSON

A BIT MORE OFF
THE INCOME TAX

W
HEATH
ROBINSON

100

WILLIAM HEATH ROBINSON
William Heath Robinson (1872-1944)

Heath Robinson is a household name, and a byword for a design or construction that is 'ingeniously or ridiculously over-complicated' (as defined by *The New Oxford Dictionary of English*, 1998, page 848). Yet, he was also a highly distinctive and versatile illustrator, whose work could touch at one extreme the romantic watercolours of a Dulac or Rackham, at another the sinister grotesqueries of a Peake, and at yet another the eccentricities of an Emett.

For a biography of William Heath Robinson, please refer to *The Illustrators*, 2007, page 147. Essays on various aspects of Heath Robinson's achievements have appeared in previous editions of *The Illustrators*: on his illustrations to Rabelais in 1996, pages 112-113; on the relationship of his illustrations to those of Arthur Rackham in 1997, pages 124-125; on his illustrations to *The Arabian Nights Entertainments*, 1999, pages 73-74; and on one of his illustrations to *Twelfth Night* in 2000, pages 17-18.

Key works written and illustrated: *The Adventures of Uncle Lubin* (1902); *Bill the Minder* (1912)

Key works illustrated: H N Williams (intro), *The Poems of Edgar Allan Poe* (1900); *The Works of Mr Francis Rabelais* (1904); contributed to *The Bystander* (from 1905) and *The Sketch* (from 1906); *Hans Andersen's Fairy Tales* (1913); *Shakespeare's Comedy of A Midsummer Night's Dream* (1914); Walter de la Mare, *Peacock Pie* (1918)

His work is represented in the collections of the British Museum, The Cartoon Museum, the V&A and The West House and Heath Robinson Museum Trust.

Further reading:
Geoffrey Beare, *The Art of William Heath Robinson*, London: Dulwich Picture Gallery, 2003; Geoffrey Beare, *The Brothers Robinson*, London: Chris Beetles Ltd, 1992; Geoffrey Beare, *Heath Robinson Advertising*, London: Bellew, 1992; Geoffrey Beare, *The Illustrations of W Heath Robinson*, London: Werner Shaw, 1983; Geoffrey Beare, *William Heath Robinson 1872-1944*, London: Chris Beetles Ltd, 2011; Langston Day, *The Life and Art of W Heath Robinson*, London: Herbert Joseph, 1947; James Hamilton, *William Heath Robinson*, London: Pavilion Books, 1992; Simon Heneage, 'Robinson, William Heath (1872-1944)', H C G Matthew and Brian Harrison (eds), *Oxford Dictionary of National Biography*, Oxford University Press, 2004, vol 47, pages 428-431; John Lewis, *Heath Robinson. Artist and Comic Genius*, London: Constable, 1973

123 THE TRIALS OF SANTA CLAUS
SANTA CLAUS MAKES A LITTLE MISTAKE
Signed and inscribed with title
Pen and ink with bodycolour
14 x 9 ½ inches
Provenance: James Watson, Lecturer in
Agriculture who was at Edinburgh University
in 1912
Illustrated: *Pearson's Magazine*, 1912, page 628,
'The Little Trials of Santa Claus'

122 A BIT MORE OFF
THE INCOME TAX (opposite)
Signed
Pen ink and watercolour with pencil on board
12 x 9 inches

101

124 TRADING WITH THE ENEMY ON MARGATE SANDS
Signed and inscribed with title
Pen and ink with pencil
16 x 11 ¼ inches

125 HOW TO CROSS THE RHINE WITHOUT GETTING WET
Signed and inscribed with title
Pen ink and watercolour with bodycolour on board
16 x 12 ½ inches
Illustrated: *The Sketch*, 13 December 1939

126 ONCE UPON A TIME
Inscribed 'Rough Sketch'
Pen ink and watercolour
7 ¼ x 10 ¼ inches
Design for Liliane M C Clopet,
Once Upon a Time, London:
Frederick Muller, 1944,
dust jacket

Once Upon a Time

Once Upon a Time was the last of William Heath Robinson's illustrated books to be published in his lifetime, and was also his only collaboration with either the author, Dr Liliane Clopet, or the publisher, Frederick Muller. He and Muller had agreed the terms for his contribution by 25 September 1943, the date on which he wrote the following to Dr Clopet (from his last address at 25 Southwood Avenue, Highgate, N6):

> I think [your fairy stories] will lend themselves well to my style of fantastic illustration. No doubt you will like me to have a perfectly free hand in my interpreting and illustrating them, but I will welcome any suggestions you would wish to make.

He then worked on the illustrations through the closing months of 1943, though was 'slowed down by an attack of influenza', as he explained in a letter to Muller, dated 3 January 1944. Soon after, he sent the first 'batch' to Muller, who then sent the drawings, or perhaps proofs, on to Dr Clopet. She responded:

A letter from William Heath Robinson to Liliane Clopet, the author of *Once Upon a Time*, **dated 25 September 1943**

Liliane Marie Catherine Clopet (1901-1987) was a doctor and writer of novels and children's plays and stories, some of which were published under pseudonyms. From 1930s, she lived at Lark's Rise, Druidstone Road, St Mellons, Cardiff, with her friend, the author and educator, Kathleen Freeman (1897-1959).

104

Thank you very much for sending me on the utterly wonderful illustrations by Mr Heath Robinson. I didn't know that such a delightful artist existed – or had existed – in the world and I can scarcely believe in my good fortune to have him to do my stories. I like the fun and sweetness and of course, the sheer beauty of the drawings … what I like so much, as the author, is that the mood of the illustrations is the mood of the stories. (quoted by Geoffrey Beare in *The Illustrations of W Heath Robinson*, London: Werner Shaw, 1983, pages 103-104).

A letter from Robinson to Clopet, dated 9 August 1944, evidences that artist and writer also continued to correspond directly during the process. In that letter, he commiserated with her over the fact that 'Muller turned down your last book of stories', and attempted to console her by adding that 'I shall be interested to read them and if I find them suitable, to illustrate them should you find another publisher'. However, having explained that he had been ill, and adding that he had 'to go into hospital for an operation', he died of heart failure on 13 September 1944, before the operation took place.

Heath Robinson is unlikely to have seen a finished copy of *Once Upon a Time*. It seems not to have appeared until late in 1944, and is listed in *British Book News* for 1945. This is a shame, because, despite the modest format and thin paper that reflected wartime conditions, its contents brought the artist's career as an illustrator to a satisfying close. As Geoffrey Beare has explained in the most thorough appreciation of the book to date, the four original fairy stories had given Robinson

> a chance to return to many of his favourite subjects. The first story has a young man blown across the sea, as was Vammerdopper in *Uncle Lubin*, and also features a cat … The other three stories all feature animals and the reader is treated to a delightful Heath Robinson menagerie including a very robust family of pigs, horses, geese, bears and even ladybirds. There is none of the dramatic tension of his earlier fantasy work, but the drawings are made with a warmth and lively good humour that cannot fail to please. The dustwrapper design, which was printed in black, orange and green, is one of the best of the drawings, full of life and movement and serving as an excellent advertisement for the good things inside. (op cit, page 103)

127-138 and **140-146** are all illustrated in Liliane Clopet, *Once Upon a Time*, London: Frederick Muller, 1944

127 AND THAT'S THE LAST I SAW OF HER
Inscribed with title and story title below mount
Pen and ink
7 ½ x 6 inches
Illustrated: frontispiece, 'The Woodcutter and his Three Sons'

The Apothecary's Assistant

128 AND EAT HIS SANDWICHES
Inscribed with title and 'The Apothecary's Assistant (Pt 1)' below mount
Pen and ink
8 x 6 ½ inches
Illustrated: page 8

129 THE LITTLE KNIGHT CHALLENGES HIM TO FIGHT
IN THE TOURNAMENT
Inscribed with title and 'The Apothecary's Assistant (Pt 2)' below mount
Pen and ink
7 ½ x 6 inches
Illustrated: page 17

130 TOOK PENNYWORT AND THE KITCHEN CAT
INTO PARTNERSHIP
Inscribed with title
Pen and ink, 5 ½ x 6 inches
Illustrated: page 24

The Scarlet Boots

THE MAYOR
GIVES CHASE.

131 THE MAYOR GIVES CHASE
Inscribed with title
Pen and ink
5 ½ x 6 ½ inches
Illustrated: page 39

132 SHE GAVE HIM A HOT BATH
Inscribed with title
Pen and ink
8 ½ x 6 ½ inches
Illustrated: page 43

133 TIED A BLUE BOW ON TIMOTHY'S LEFT ARM
Inscribed with title and story title
Pen and ink
8 ½ x 6 ½ inches
Illustrated: page 27

The House with the Glass Key

134 LADYBIRDS
Inscribed 'Heading' below mount
Pen and ink, 1 ¾ x 5 ½ inches
Illustrated: page 46

—TO SEND YOU INTO
THE WORLD TO FEND
FOR YOURSELF

135 TO SEND YOU INTO THE WORLD
TO FEND FOR YOURSELF
Inscribed with title
Pen and ink
5 ½ x 6 ½ inches
Illustrated: page 46

136 UNTIL THE OTHER CHILDREN CAME HOME
Inscribed with title
Pen and ink
9 x 6 inches
Illustrated: page 47

The Woodcutter and his Three Sons

137 HE WORKED
BY DAY AS A
WOODCUTTER
Inscribed with title and
story title below mount
Pen and ink
4 ¾ x 5 inches
Illustrated: page 58

138 AND GATHERED
UP THE IMMENSE
PUMPKIN IN
HIS ARMS
Inscribed with title
below mount
Pen and ink, 5 x 4 inches
Illustrated: page 72

108

139 HIS SONGS
THOUGH PRETTY
WERE SHORT
Inscribed with title and
story title
Pen and ink
8 ¼ x 6 inches
Drawn for but not
illustrated in Liliane
Clopet, *Once Upon a
Time*, London: Frederick
Muller, 1944, 'The
Woodcutter and his
Three Sons'

140 WILLIAM
BEGAN TO SING
Inscribed with title
Pen and ink
9 x 6 inches
Illustrated: page 69

141 THE SCHOOL
CHILDREN RANG A PEAL
OF BELLS AT SIX IN THE
MORNING
Inscribed with title
Pen and ink
9 ¾ x 5 inches
Illustrated: page 81

142 SHE WOULD TURN
AND SAY SOMETHING
UNPLEASANT TO IT
Inscribed with title
Pen and ink
9 ½ x 6 ½ inches
Illustrated: page 91

143 AND LET OUT JOLT
Inscribed with title
Pen and ink
4 x 6 ½ inches
Illustrated: page 73

— AND LET OUT JOLT, —

144 HE SNIPPED
AT ERNEST'S
HAIR
Inscribed with title
and story title
below mount
Pen and ink
4 ½ x 5 inches
Illustrated: page 79

145 THEN THE MOTHERS CAME TO LOOK FOR THE
CHILDREN
Inscribed with title
Pen and ink
9 x 6 inches
Illustrated: page 97

146 AND FLEW AWAY WITH HIM
Inscribed with title and story title below mount
Pen and ink
8 ½ x 6 ½ inches
Illustrated: page 102

FLORENCE HARRISON

07

FLORENCE
HARRISON

Florence Susan Harrison (1877-1955)

The late Pre-Raphaelite illustrations of Florence Harrison have always stood out from those of her contemporaries, the colour plates having the luminosity and strong outlines of stained glass, and the line drawings having a decorative efflorescence.

For a biography of Florence Harrison, please refer to *The Illustrators*, 2014, page 146.

Further reading:
Mary Jacobs, 'Florence Susan Harrison', *Studies in Illustration*, Imaginative Book Illustration Society, no 46, Winter 2010, pages 22-59 (with a bibliography of published illustrations)

147-156 are all illustrated in *Poems by Christina Rossetti,* London: Blackie & Son, 1910

147 HE CAME ACROSS THE GREEN SEA
Pen and ink
3 ¼ x 5 inches
Illustrated: page 187, tailpiece to 'Songs in a Cornfield'

148 THESE LOVING LAMBS SO MEEK TO PLEASE
Pen and ink
2 ¼ x 3 ¾ inches
Illustrated: page 223, tailpiece to 'The Lambs of Grasmere 1860'

149 AND BORE THE CROSS
Pen and ink with bodycolour
5 ½ x 4 inches
Illustrated: page 264, tailpiece to 'A Portrait'

111

151 START WITH LIGHTENED HEART UPON THE ROAD
Pen and ink
3 x 5 ¼ inches
Illustrated: page 304, tailpiece to 'Who Shall Deliver Me'

150 THEY SHALL MEET AGAIN
Pen and ink with bodycolour
5 ½ x 3 ½ inches
Illustrated: page 287, tailpiece to 'One Day'

152 OPEN THY DOOR TO ME
Pen and ink
2 ¼ x 4 inches
Illustrated: page 309, tailpiece to 'Despised and Rejected'

154 ANGELS, ARCHANGELS CRY
ONE TO OTHER CEASELESSLY
Pen and ink with bodycolour
1 ¾ x 4 ¾ inches
Illustrated: page 337, tailpiece to 'Christian and Jew: A Dialogue'

155 I INFUSE LOVE, HATRED,
LONGING, WILL
Pen and ink with bodycolour
2 ¼ x 2 ¼ inches
Illustrated: page 350, tailpiece to
'A Bruised Reed Shall He Not Break'

153 YET WILL I WAIT FOR HIM
Pen and ink
4 ¼ x 2 ½ inches
Illustrated: page 320, tailpiece to 'From House to Home'

156 SHALL THERE BE REST FROM TOIL, BE TRUCE FROM SORROW
Pen and ink with bodycolour
5 x 8 inches
Illustrated: page 364, tailpiece to 'Dost Thou Not Care?'

Dost Thou Not Care?

I love and love not: Lord, it breaks my heart
To love and not to love.
Thou veiled within Thy glory, gone apart
Into Thy shrine, which is above,
Dost Thou not love me, Lord, or care
For this mine ill? –
I will love thee here or there,
I will accept thy broken heart, lie still.

Lord, it was well with me in time gone by
That cometh not again,
When I was fresh and cheerful, who but I?
I fresh, I cheerful: worn with pain
Now, out of sight and out of heart;
O, Lord, how long? –
I watch thee as thou art,
I will accept thy fainting heart, be strong.

'Lie still,' 'be strong,' today; but, Lord, tomorrow,
What of tomorrow, Lord?
Shall there be rest from toil, be truce from sorrow,
Be living green upon the sward
Now but a barren grave to me,
Be joy for sorrow? –
Did I not die for thee?
Do I not live for thee? leave Me tomorrow.

(Christina Rossetti)

157-164 are all illustrated in *Early Poems of William Morris*, London:
Blackie & Son, 1914

157 HOLDING PICTURES
Pen and ink with bodycolour
2 ½ x 5 inches
Illustrated: page xiv

158 LAUNCELOT FALLS
Pen and ink with bodycolour
3 x 2 ¼ inches
Illustrated: page 31,
'King Arthur's Tomb'

159 WE HEARD A SWEET
VOICE SING (far right)
Pen and ink with bodycolour
5 ½ x 2 ½ inches
Pencil drawing of a woman on reverse
Illustrated: page 40, 'Sir Galahad.
A Christmas Mystery'

115

160 AND EVER THE GREAT BELL
OVERHEAD,
AND THE TUMBLING SEAS MOURN'D
FOR THE DEAD
Pen and ink with bodycolour
5 ½ x 2 ¾ inches
Illustrated: page 100, 'The Blue Closet'

161 I KISS THE LADY MARY'S HEAD,
HER LIPS, AND HER HAIR GOLDEN RED,
BECAUSE TO-DAY WE HAVE BEEN WED
Pen and ink
7 ¼ x 4 ½ inches
Illustrated: page 118, 'A Good Knight in Prison'

162 HO, YOU REAPERS, AWAY FROM THE CORN,
TO MARCH WITH THE BANNER OF FATHER JOHN!
Pen and ink with bodycolour
2 ¾ x 6 ¼ inches
Illustrated: page 138, 'Father John's War Song'

163 SHE SHOOK HER HEAD AND GAZED AWHILE
AT HER COLD HANDS WITH A RUEFUL SMILE
Pen and ink with bodycolour
2 x 4 ½ inches
Illustrated: page 175, 'The Haystack in the Floods'

164 A SHIP WITH SAILS BEFORE THE WIND
Pen and ink
2 ¼ x 4 ¾ inches
Illustrated: page 186, 'Near Avalon'

FRANK REYNOLDS

Frank Reynolds, RI (1876-1953)

Drawing mainly from memory, Frank Reynolds was much admired for his direct characterisation of middle-class and low-life types and situations.

For a biography of Frank Reynolds, please refer to *The Illustrators*, 2011, page 130

Further reading:
Percy V Bradshaw, *The Art of the Illustrator: Frank Reynolds*, London: Press Art School, [1918]; A E Johnson, *Frank Reynolds*, London: A & C Black, 1907

165 THE BATSMAN
Signed with initials
Pen ink, watercolour and bodycolour on tinted board
11 ½ x 9 ½ inches

166 THE BOWLER
Signed
Pen ink, watercolour and bodycolour on tinted board
12 x 9 inches

167 THE BOUNCER
Signed
Pen ink, watercolour and bodycolour on board
9 ½ x 7 inches

168 OUR VILLAGE FAST BOWLER: ALWAYS AN OPPORTUNIST
– INCREASES HIS RUN
Signed
Inscribed with title below mount
Rough pencil sketch of bowler on reverse
Pen and ink with bodycolour on board
8 x 12 inches
Illustrated: *Punch*, Summer Number, 16 June 1924, [unpaginated]

169 PURELY DEFENSIVE BATSMAN: I SAY, I DON'T MIND YOU
CROWDING IN, BUT NEED YOU BREATHE SO HARD
Signed
Inscribed with title below mount
Also signed with initials by Frank Reynolds in the role of art editor of *Punch*
Pen and ink with bodycolour on board
8 x 12 inches
Illustrated: *Punch*, Summer Number, 2 July 1923, [unpaginated]

170 SOMETHING TO LOOK FORWARD TO
PROFESSOR: THAT WILL DO FOR THE 1ST LESSON SAH – NEXT TAHM I
WANTA MAKE YOU WHAT I CALL 'PUNCH CONSCIOUS!'
Signed
Inscribed with title below mount
Pen and ink on board
12 ½ x 9 ½ inches
Illustrated: *Punch*, 3 July 1935, page 2

171 ARDENT GOLFER (ON HIS ETERNAL SUBJECT): AND AT
THE 17TH I DROVE OUT OF BOUNDS
ROMANTIC LADY: I'M AFRAID I DON'T KNOW WHAT THAT
MEANS BUT IT SOUNDS DELICIOUS
Signed
Inscribed with title below mount
Also signed with initials by Frank Reynolds in the role of art editor of *Punch*
Pen and ink with bodycolour on board
11 x 9 inches
Illustrated: *Punch*, 6 February 1924, page 127

172 INSULT TO INJURY
Signed
Inscribed with title and 'full colour'
below mount
Pen ink and watercolour on board
12 ½ x 9 ½ inches
Illustrated: *Punch*, Summer Number,
6 May 1940, [unpaginated]

BERT THOMAS

Herbert Samuel Thomas, MBE PS (1883-1966)

Though Bert Thomas has become best known for his war cartoons – gaining a national reputation with one entitled *'Arf a mo' Kaiser* – he was wide ranging in his subjects and technically versatile.

For a biography of Bert Thomas, please refer to *The Illustrators*, 2011, page 94

His work is represented in the collections of the British Museum, the National Portrait Gallery and the V&A; and the British Cartoon Archive, University of Kent (Canterbury).

173 THE NEW MINISTER: 'BOY. D'YE NO' KEN IT'S THE
SAWBATH?'
BOY: '– OH. AY. FINE. – BUT THIS IS WORK O' NECESSITY.'
MINISTER: 'AN' HOO IS THAT?'
BOY: 'THE MEENISTERS' COMIN' TAE DINNER. AN' WE'VE
GOT NAETHIN' TAE GIE 'IM.'
Signed, inscribed with title and 'To Dear George Stampa', and dated 1920
Pen and ink, 13 ½ x 9 ½ inches
Provenance: George Loraine Stampa
Illustrated: *Punch*, 28 January 1920, page 65

BRUCE BAIRNSFATHER

Charles Bruce Bairnsfather (1887-1959)

Bruce Bairnsfather is best remembered for 'Old Bill', the pipe-smoking Tommy that he created during the First World War. Old Bill proved so significant to the morale of British troops that Bairnsfather was promoted to Officer Cartoonist. The character remained popular in peacetime, on both sides of the Atlantic, through a range of media and merchandise, and gained new currency during the Second World War, when Bairnsfather became Official War Artist to the US Army in Europe.

Bruce Bairnsfather was born at Strawberry Bank Cottage, Murree, Punjab, India, on 9 July 1887. He was the eldest son of Thomas Henry Bairnsfather, a Scottish officer in the Bengal Infantry, and his wife, Amelia Jane Eliza Every. Arriving in England at the age of eight, he stayed with his maternal uncle, the rector of Thornbury, near Bromyard, Herefordshire, before attending Rudyard Kipling's old school, the United Services College, at Westward Ho!, Devon, between 1898 and 1904. He went on to an army crammer, Trinity College, Stratford-upon-Avon, and served with the Third Militia Battalion of the Royal Warwicks, while also attending evening classes in art at the local technical college. Though he gained a commission as a second lieutenant with the Cheshires, he soon became disillusioned with army life, and resigned to become an artist.

In 1907, Bairnsfather studied under Dudley Hardy and Charles van Havermaet at John Hassall's New Art School, in London. However, he was unable to establish himself as a poster artist, so returned to Warwickshire to live with his parents, and worked as an electrical engineer at Spensers Ltd, in Stratford. In his spare time, he took part in amateur theatricals. Through this activity, he met the novelist, Marie Corelli, who in turn introduced him to the tea merchant, Sir Thomas Lipton. Sir Thomas commissioned some of his earliest advertising drawings.

At the outbreak of the First World War, Bairnsfather rejoined the Royal Warwickshire Regiment and served as a machine-gun officer in France, eventually achieving the rank of captain. He sent comic drawings from the Front, which appeared in *The Bystander* as 'Fragments from France' from January 1915. During the second battle of Ypres, later that year, he suffered shell shock and hearing damage, and was hospitalised. While recovering, he invented his most famous character, the pipe-smoking Tommy, 'Old Bill' Busby, who was introduced to the readership of *The Bystander* on 15 September 1915 in the cartoon, *When the 'ell is it going to be strawberry.* Two months later, he drew his most celebrated cartoon, *Well, if you knows of a better 'ole, go to it.* His work proved so popular with the troops that he was appointed Officer Cartoonist and transferred to the Intelligence Department of the War Office.

Despite the end of the First World War in 1918, 'Old Bill' had so taken on a life of his own that he continued to appear not only in periodicals and books, but also on stage and screen, and through a range of merchandise. In addition, he was the subject of a number of lectures, given by Bairnsfather on both sides of the Atlantic for many years. Bairnsfather's popularity in the United States was such that he was appointed Official War Artist to the US Army in Europe in the Second World War (1942-44).

Bairnsfather died in the Royal Infirmary, Worcester, on 29 September 1959. His wife, Cecilia, and his daughter, Barbara, both survived him.

Further reading:
Mark Bryant, 'Bairnsfather, (Charles) Bruce (1887-1959)', H C G Matthew and Brian Harrison (eds), *Oxford Dictionary of National Biography*, Oxford University Press, 2004, vol 3, pages 352-354; Tonie and Valmai Holt, *In Search of a Better Hole: The Life, the Works and the Collectables of Bruce Bairnsfather*, Portsmouth: Milestone Publications, 1985

Swigging the Last Drop
The present painting by Bruce Bairnsfather may relate to the advertisements that he produced for the West Midlands brewery, Mitchells and Butlers, later in his career.

174 SWIGGING THE LAST DROP
Oil on canvas
29 ¼ x 20 ½ inches

125

FOUGASSE

Cyril Kenneth Bird, CBE (1887-1965), known as 'Fougasse'

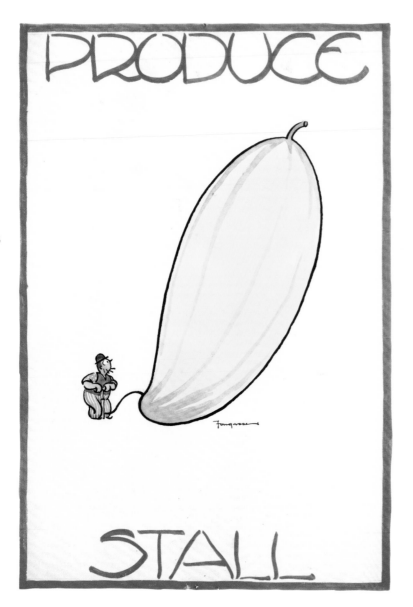

As cartoonist, art editor and editor, Cyril Bird transformed the style of *Punch*. His own contributions pared down human activity with such economy as to suggest the essence of modern life. This approach also had a significant influence on advertising, as in the emphasis on the elegant streamlining of Austin Reed's 'New Tailoring'.

For a biography of Fougasse, please refer to *The Illustrators*, 2009, page 77.

His work is represented in the collections of the London Transport Museum and the V&A.

Further reading:
Bevis Hillier (ed), *Fougasse*, London: Elm Tree Books, 1977; Peter Mellini, 'Bird, (Cyril) Kenneth [*pseud*. Fougasse] (1887-1965)', H C G Matthew and Brian Harrison (eds), *Oxford Dictionary of National Biography*, Oxford University Press, 2004, vol 5, pages 818-820

175 PRODUCE STALL
Signed and inscribed with title
Pen ink and watercolour
14 ¼ x 9 ¾ inches

It's only fair that occupants of boxes should be allowed to look like celebrities during the intervals ——

176 IT'S ONLY FAIR THAT
OCCUPANTS OF BOXES
SHOULD BE ALLOWED TO LOOK
LIKE CELEBRITIES DURING
INTERVALS – CONSIDERING HOW
THEY HAVE TO SPEND THE REST
OF THE EVENING
Signed and inscribed with title
Signed and inscribed 'Allowed to look like
celebrities in the intervals' and 'No 632' on
A E Johnson artists' agent label on reverse
Pen and ink
13 x 10 inches
Illustrated: *Punch*, 5 July 1933, page 13

Considering how they have to spend the rest of the evening.

177 HEADSTRONG
Inscribed with title below mount
Pen and ink on board
5 x 4 ½ inches
Drawn as an advertisement for Austin Reed, March 1936

178 BLACK ON WHITE TIE
Signed
Inscribed with title below mount
Pen and ink on board
4 ½ x 4 inches
Drawn as an advertisement for Austin Reed, April 1933

179 HAT SO?
Inscribed with title below mount
Pen and ink on board
3 ½ x 5 ½ inches
Drawn as an advertisement for the 'London Evenings Regent St Campaign',
for Austin Reed, January 1935

181 FOR HOT GOLF
Inscribed with title below mount
Pen and ink on board
4 ½ x 4 ½ inches
Drawn as an advertisement for the 'London Evenings Regent St
Campaign', for Austin Reed, January 1935

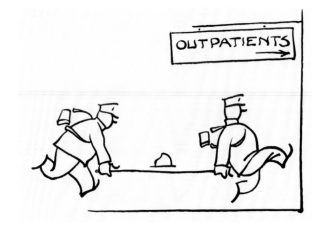

180 ZIP AHOY
Inscribed with title below mount
Pen and ink on board
9 x 6 ½ inches
Drawn as an advertisement for 'Regent Street Campaign', for Austin Reed,
May 1936

182 OUTPATIENTS
Pen and ink on board
5 x 7 inches
Drawn as an advertisement for 'Regent Street Campaign', for Austin Reed,
November 1935

H M BATEMAN
Henry Mayo Bateman (1887-1970)

H M Bateman established his inimitable style before the First World War when, as he put it, he 'went mad on paper', by drawing people's mood and character. It reached its zenith with 'The Man Who …', his famous series of cartoons dramatising social gaffes.

For a biography of Henry Mayo Bateman, please refer to *The Illustrators*, 2009, page 72; for an essay on the revolutionary and reactionary aspects of the artist's work, see *The Illustrators*, 2000, pages 21-22.

His work is represented in numerous public collections, including the British Museum.

Further reading:
Anthony Anderson, *The Man Who Was H M Bateman*, Exeter: Webb & Bower, 1982; John Jensen, 'Bateman, Henry Mayo (1887-1970)', H C G Matthew and Brian Harrison (eds), *Oxford Dictionary of National Biography*, Oxford University Press, 2004, vol 4, pages 299-301

For a further work by H M Bateman, please see page 73

Desmond Coke: A Patron of H M Bateman
The writer, teacher and connoisseur, Desmond Coke (1879-1931), began to publish novels in 1903, initially under the pseudonym, Belinda Blinders. Invalided out of the army in 1917, he became a housemaster at Clayesmore School, and numbered the illustrator, Edward Ardizzone, among his first pupils. His experiences as a teacher informed the subjects of his school stories, some of which were illustrated by H M Brock. He was also a major collector of British drawings, especially the work of Thomas Rowlandson, and patronised such contemporary artists as Sidney Herbert Sime and Austin Osman Spare. He published *Confessions of an Incurable Collector* in 1928.

In 1923, Desmond Coke suggested to H M Bateman the subject of his cartoon, *The Prefect – The Triumph of Brains over Brawn* [**184**], though Bateman modelled the figure of the prefect on his friend, the writer and artist, William Caine (making a pun with cane). It was reproduced in *Punch* on 19 September 1923, and subsequently coloured by Bateman for Coke (as is mentioned by Bateman in a letter to Coke dated 24 September 1923).

In the following year, Bateman illustrated Coke's book, *Our Modern Youth: An Exuberance*, including the cover design, showing a boy nonchalantly smoking to the astonishment of his teacher [**183**]. Again the drawing was the subject of a letter by Bateman (27 November 1924) and entered the collection of Coke.

183 OUR MODERN YOUTH
Signed, inscribed 'Cover Design for "Our Modern Youth"' and dated 1924
Pen ink and watercolour
12 x 8 inches
Provenance: Desmond Coke; W Russell Button Gallery, Chicago
Illustrated: Desmond Coke, *Our Modern Youth. An Exuberance*, London: Chapman & Hall, 1924, dust jacket

184 THE PREFECT – A TRIUMPH OF BRAINS OVER BRAWN
Signed and dated 1923
Pen ink and watercolour on tinted paper
14 x 10 inches
Provenance: Desmond Coke; W Russell Button Gallery, Chicago
Illustrated: *Punch*, 19 September 1923, page 272
[Published in black and white and subsequently coloured by the artist]

132

185 ETON
FILIAL LORDLINESS AND
PARENTAL SERVITUDE
Signed and dated 1919
Signed, inscribed 'Eton' and
numbered '925' on A E Johnson
artists' agent label on reverse
Pen ink and watercolour on board
13 ¼ x 10 ¼ inches
Provenance: Desmond Coke;
W Russell Button Gallery, Chicago

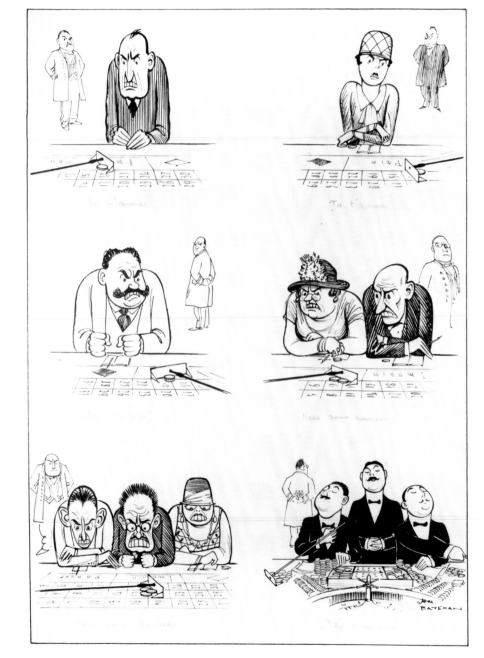

186 A MONTE CARLO
DECLENSION
JE M'AMUSE; TU T'AMUSE; IL S'AMUSE;
NOUS NOUS AMUSONS; VOUS VOUS
AMUSEZ; ILS S'AMUSENT
Signed and inscribed with captions
Inscribed with title below mount
Signed, inscribed with title and dated
1927 on A E Johnson artists' agent stamp
on reverse
Pen and ink with pencil
14 ½ x 10 ¼ inches
Illustrated: *The Tatler*, 1927

JOSEPH LEE
Joseph Booth Lee (1901-1975)

Joseph Lee established his reputation as a newspaper cartoonist with the *Pall Mall Gazette* at the age of nineteen. Working for various periodicals during the 1920s and early 30s, he joined the London *Evening News* in 1934, when he produced his initial 'London Laughs'. 'London Laughs' comprised the first series of non-political topical cartoons in a British newspaper, and would make Lee the longest-running daily cartoonist in history.

For a biography of Joseph Lee, please refer to *The Illustrators*, 2007, page 252.

His work is represented in the collections of the British Museum and the Cartoon Museum; and the British Cartoon Archive, University of Kent (Canterbury).

134

187 LONDON LAUGHS: BARBER SHOPS
'THE GUV'NOR JUST HAD TO SACK THE FELLOW. HE HADN'T A TIP FOR THE DERBY!'
Signed
Dated 21-5-37 below mount
Pen and ink on board
14 x 10 ½ inches
Illustrated: *Evening News*, 21 May 1937

188 LONDON LAUGHS: HARLEY STREET
'APPLES! ... APPLES! ... APPLES!'
Signed
Dated 6-6-34 below mount
Pen and ink with coloured pencil on board
15 x 12 inches
Illustrated: *Evening News*, 6 June 1934

189 LONDON LAUGHS: VOLUNTEERS
'... AND I STARTED BAYONET FIGHTING AT THE DRILL HALL LAST NIGHT'
Signed
Inscribed with title and dated 31-5-39 below mount
Pen and ink on board
14 x 10 inches
Illustrated: *Evening News*, 31 May 1939

190 LONDON LAUGHS: CUSTOMS
'COULDN'T WE TALK THIS OVER QUIETLY SOMEWHERE
OVER A COUPLE OF GLASSES'
Signed
Inscribed with title and dated 14-7-39 below mount
Pen and ink on board
15 x 10 ½ inches
Illustrated: *Evening News*, 14 July 1939

191 SMILING THROUGH: ARMY RUGGER
'I HOPE YOU DON'T CONSIDER THAT I, AS A PRIVATE, AM SHOWING ANY
DISRESPECT FOR YOUR COMMISSIONED RANK, SIR, IN THUS PREVENTING
YOU SCORING AN ALMOST CERTAIN TRY?'
Signed
Inscribed with title and dated 24-2-40 below mount
Pen and ink on board
13 x 10 ½ inches
Illustrated: *Evening News*, 24 February 1940

192 THE PAPERS ARE QUITE RIGHT, COX. WHAT I NEED IS
MEAT ... MEAT ... MEAT!
Signed
Inscribed with title and dated 'Sat 17-1-48' below mount
Pen and ink with coloured pencil and charcoal on board
14 x 10 inches
Illustrated: *Evening News*, 17 January 1948

193 ... AND LOOK YOUR BEST FOR THE CAMERAMEN. IT'LL BE NICE FOR THE PUBLIC TO SEE SOME SIMPLE, STUPID BRAWN FOR A CHANGE AFTER ALL THE BRAINS THEY'VE BEEN HAVING LATELY
Signed
Inscribed with title below mount
Pen and ink with coloured pencil on board
14 ½ x 10 ½ inches
Illustrated: *Evening News*, 28 February 1950

194 AUTUMN SHOULD BE REALLY NICE WHEN THEY HAVE TECHNICOLOUR TV
Signed
Inscribed with title and dated 12-11-52 below mount
Pen and ink on board
16 x 11 inches
Illustrated: *Evening News*, 12 November 1952

TONY WYSARD

Roy Alexander Edward Antonio Wysard (1907-1984), known as Anthony, Antony and Tony Wysard

The cartoonist and illustrator, Tony Wysard, is best remembered for the society caricatures that he contributed to many leading periodicals before and after the Second World War. The most impressive of these – as with the present example – are in full colour and contain large groups of personalities.

Tony Wysard was born in Pangbourne, Berkshire, on 18 September 1907, one of two children of Walter Wysard, a merchant and director of a number of companies, and his wife, Delia, who as Delia Mason had been an actress and singer. Educated at Harrow, he began to learn accountancy in the City, before deciding that he would rather work as an artist. While employed as the secretary to Phormium Cavity Blocks Limited, in the late 1920s, he began to contribute caricatures to many leading magazines and newspapers, including *The Bystander*, the *Daily* and *Sunday Express*, *Harper's Bazaar*, *The Sphere* and *The Tatler*. Many of the best of these appeared in 'Caricatures and Cartoons of People of Importance', a solo show at Walker's Galleries, Bond Street, in November 1936. By then, he was also working as advertising manager for Alexander Korda's London Films Productions at its new studios at Denham, Buckinghamshire. In 1939, he married Ruth McDougall, of the famous flour milling family.

Having been commissioned in the Queen's Westminsters, an infantry regiment of the Territorial Army in 1938, Wysard served with the Royal Green Jackets during the Second World War, and then returned to Denham.

He also became associate editor for *Harper's Bazaar*, and continued to produce caricatures for various periodicals, including the series, 'The Uncommon Man', for *The Strand Magazine* (1948-50). During the 1950s, he began to illustrate a number of books, beginning with Ted Kavanagh's *Colonel Chinstrap* (1952), Gilbert Harding's *Treasury of Insult* (1953) and two books by Spike Hughes: *The Art of Coarse Cricket* (1954) and *The Art of Coarse Travel* (1957).

Wysard was a habitué of Wheeler & Co, in Old Compton Street, Soho, and an active member of its lively Thursday Club. He proposed that this restaurant should have its own quarterly magazine, and this was launched in 1954 with himself as editor. By the end of the decade, it was available in all branches of Wheeler's. Through his association with Wheeler's, he also produced and edited a promotional booklet for the 40th anniversary of Woodhouse Hume, a London wholesale butcher (1958). Later, in 1974, he would illustrate *Wheeler's Fish Cookery Book*, written by Macdonald Hastings and Carole Walsh.

By 1965, Wysard had set up his own advertising consultancy, Excelads Imprint Ltd, which specialised in design and print production for a diverse clientele.

Wysard lived at Stanford Wood, Tutts Clump, near Bradfield, west Berkshire, where his friend, Sir Osbert Lancaster, made a number of drawings on the walls of the flower room. He died in November 1984.

His work is represented in the collections of the National Portrait Gallery.

'The Shape of Things to Come': First Night: London, AD 2036

H G Wells loosely adapted his own novel, *The Shape of Things to Come* (1933), for the film, *Things to Come*, which was directed by William Cameron Menzies, and released in 1936. Providing a speculative 'future history' for the period from 1940 to 2036, the film has been considered 'the first true masterpiece of science fiction cinema' (on the website, *Gary Westfahl's Bio-Encyclopedia of Science Fiction*) and 'a landmark in cinematic design' (Christopher Frayling, *Things to Come*, London: BFI Publishing, 1995, page 56).

Tony Wysard was involved with *Things to Come*, as he had recently become the advertising manager for its producer, Alexander Korda, and worked at his new studio, at Denham, Buckinghamshire, where the film was made. At once insider and outsider, Wysard was well placed to caricature the evolving social world of the period between the wars. His pictorial satire on the world premiere of *Things to Come* was published two days before the actual first night, which took place at the Leicester Square

Theatre on 21 February 1936. He probably knew who had been invited to attend and, at least in part, used his image of the guests to promote the film. It shows his awareness of the film's design by Alexander Korda's brother, Vincent, and more generally of contemporary cinema.

A year later, Denham produced another of his multi-figure caricatures, showing *Diners at Denham Studios Restaurant*, which is now in the collections of the National Portrait Gallery.

195 'THE SHAPE OF THINGS TO COME': FIRST NIGHT: LONDON, AD 2036
Signed and dated 36
Pen ink and watercolour with pencil
13 ½ x 21 inches
Illustrated: *The Tatler*, 19 February 1936

Key

1 Mr H G Wells
2 Mr Alexander Korda
3 Lady Oxford and Asquith
4 Duke of Sutherland
5 Viscountess Weymouth
6 Sir Thomas Beecham
7 Lady Cunard
8 Baron Franckenstein
9 Viscount Weymouth
10 Lady Melchett
11 Lord Melchett
12 Duke of Marlborough
13 Duchess of Marlborough
14 Lord Cowdray
15 Hon Wilfred Egerton
16 Marchioness of Dufferin and Ava
17 Sir Richard Sykes

18 Viscount Castlerosse
19 Lord Beaverbrook
20 Lord Lonsdale
21 Lord Kemsley
22 Rosita Forbes
23 Osbert Sitwell
24 Edith Sitwell
25 Lady Eleanor Smith
26 Mr James Agate
27 Mr Hannen Swaffer
28 Lord Donegall
29 Mr Eddie Tatham
30 Mr Cecil Beaton
31 Mr Noel Coward
32 Miss Penelope Dudley-Ward
33 Mr Douglas Fairbanks
34 Lady Ashley
35 Hon Richard Norton
36 Mr Charles Laughton
37 Mr George Arliss

38 Miss Merle Oberon
39 Earl of Cromer
40 Mr Edward Marsh
41 Mr Stanley Baldwin
42 Mrs Stanley Baldwin
43 Mr A Duff Cooper
44 Lady Duff Cooper
45 Hon Maurice Baring
46 Lord Lurgan
47 Baroness Erlanger
48 Mr Gordon Selfridge
49 Sir Connop Guthrie
50 Sir Robert Horne
51 Mr Montagu Norman
52 Mr John Sutro
53 Lady Mary Lygon
54 Mr Randolph Churchill
55 Sir A Lindsay-Hogg
56 Hon A Asquith
57 Lord Beatty

JAMES MONTGOMERY FLAGG

James Montgomery Flagg (1877-1960)

An illustrator, cartoonist and portrait painter strongly influenced by John Singer Sargent, James Montgomery Flagg contributed to a golden age of American illustration, alongside contemporaries such as Howard Chandler Christy, J C Leyendecker and Norman Rockwell. He was the creator of one of the most famous and reproduced poster illustrations of all time, the iconic Uncle Sam 'I Want YOU' recruitment poster.

James Montgomery Flagg was born in Pelham Manor, New York, on 18 June 1877. At the age of 12, he sold his first drawing to the magazine, *St Nicholas*, and by the age of 15, he was a staff cartoonist for *Judge* and *Life*, then two of America's most popular and successful periodicals. In 1894, he enrolled at the Art Students League in New York City, where he studied until 1898. Whilst a student in New York, he began to feature prominently on the city's social scene, as a member of the Lotos Club, The Players Club, the Dutch Treat Club and the Society of Illustrators.

In 1898, Flagg travelled to England to continue his studies at the Herkomer School in Bushey, Hertfordshire. He also studied briefly in Paris before returning to America in 1900. That year, he illustrated his first book, *Yankee Girls Abroad*, which established his reputation for producing illustrations of all-American beauties in the manner of Howard Chandler Christy and Harrison Fisher. He accepted commissions for countless cartoons, posters, advertisements, illustrations and magazine covers across his career. One of his most popular creations, the cartoon strip 'Nervy Nat', appeared in *Judge* between 1903 and 1907.

In 1917, Flagg created a recruitment poster for the United States Army that would become his most famous work. His image of Uncle Sam, modelled on himself, with the caption 'I Want YOU for US Army', would become one of the most famous, iconic and reproduced poster images of all time. He produced 46 posters for the American Government between 1917 and 1919 and, following the First World War, was reported to have been the highest paid magazine illustrator in America.

A close friend of the publishing tycoon, William Randolph Hearst, Flagg presented himself as a bohemian, moving in high society circles. He produced portraits of many of his friends and admirers, including Mark Twain, John Barrymore and Jack Dempsey. He died in New York City on 27 May 1960.

Further reading:
Robert L Gale, 'Flagg, James Montgomery (18 June 1877-27 May 1960)', John A Garraty and Mark C Carnes (eds), *American National Biography*, Oxford University Press, 1999, pages 73-74

The text for The American Century *is written by Alexander Beetles, unless otherwise stated.*

Helen Wills Moody

Helen Wills Moody (1905-1998) was an American tennis player who won 19 Grand Slam singles titles between 1923 and 1938. Her record of eight Wimbledon titles stood until 1990, when it was broken by Martina Navratilova. Her athletic ability coupled with her beauty made her one of America's first female celebrity athletes.

141

196 HELEN WILLS MOODY
Signed and inscribed 'Moody'
Charcoal
11 ¾ x 9 ¼ inches
Drawn on reverse of an advertising booklet for the American version of the magazine, *House Beautiful*

JOHNNY GRUELLE

John Barton Gruelle (1880-1938)

A prolific cartoonist and children's illustrator, Johnny Gruelle is best known for creating two of the most iconic and popular characters of American childhood – Raggedy Ann and Andy.

John Gruelle was born in Arcola, Illinois, on 24 December 1880. At the age of two, he moved with his family to Indianapolis, Indiana. This was in order for his father Richard Gruelle, a talented impressionist painter, to associate and exhibit with the Hoosier Group, a collective of Indiana painters.

Encouraged to draw from a young age by his father, Gruelle discovered a flair and passion for cartooning, and in 1901, at the age of 20, joined the Indianapolis-based tabloid, the *People*. After a short spell at the *Indianapolis Sun*, he joined the rival *Indianapolis Star* as assistant illustrator in June 1903. In 1905, he accepted a freelancing job with the World Color Printing Company of St Louis to produce four-colour Sunday comics. He continued this association after relocating to Cleveland in 1906 to work for the *Cleveland Press* and the Newspaper Enterprise Association. Between 1906 and 1911, his cartoons appeared in numerous newspapers across the country, including the *Pittsburgh Press*, the *Spokane Press* and the *Tacoma Times*. He enjoyed greater exposure in 1911, when he beat over 1,500 other entrants in a cartooning competition sponsored by the *New York Herald*. He would go on to produce the cartoon he created, *Mr Twee Deedle*, for the *New York Herald* until 1914. Whilst working for the *Herald*, he began to receive commissions to produce illustrations for magazines such as the *Illustrated Sunday Magazine* and *Judge*. Later in his career, he would also produce illustrations for *College Humor*, *Cosmopolitan* and *Life*.

Johnny Gruelle's most famous creation, 'Raggedy Ann', was inspired by a rag doll discovered in an attic by his daughter, Marcella, upon which he had drawn a face. After naming the doll 'Raggedy Ann', he was delighted by how much his daughter loved and played with her and, on 7 September 1915, registered a patent for the doll. He created adventures for Raggedy Ann to entertain Marcella, who had contracted diphtheria. The tragedy of her death in 1916, aged just 13, resolved Johnny Gruelle to create further stories and adventures of the doll in her memory. In 1918, the publishing company PF Volland published these as *Raggedy Ann Stories*. The same year, a Raggedy Ann doll was produced to accompany the book, to great commercial success. Between 1918 and 1926 alone, over 75,000 handmade dolls were produced. In 1920, a sequel, *Raggedy Andy Stories*, was published, introducing Raggedy Ann's brother, Raggedy Andy. From 1922, the serialised 'Adventures of Raggedy Ann and Andy' appeared in newspapers across the country. In addition to his own creations, Johnny Gruelle also illustrated a volume of *Grimm's Fairy Tales* in 1914, as well as other children's books such as *Nobody's Boy* (1916) and J P McEvoy's *The Bam Bam Clock* (1920).

Having suffered for much of his life with a heart condition, Johnny Gruelle died of a heart attack in Miami Beach, Florida, on 8 January 1938.

197 NOW, FREDDIE – START UP THE ONE MAN BAND!
Signed, inscribed 'To Fred Myers with all sorts of good wishes' and dated 'Nov 1 1932'
Pen ink and coloured pencil
8 x 6 inches

WALTER BERNDT

Walter Berndt (1899-1979)

The Brooklyn-born cartoonist, Walter Berndt, is best known for the well-loved comic strip 'Smitty', which first appeared in the *Chicago Tribune* in 1923 and was syndicated to numerous newspapers across America for over 50 years.

Walter Berndt was born in Brooklyn, New York, on 22 November 1899. His career as a cartoonist began at the age of 16 as an office boy in the art department of the *New York Journal*. Here, he was influenced by the numerous cartoonists whom he met, including E C Stegar, Winsor McCay and George Herriman. In 1915, he began drawing sports cartoons for the *Journal* and by 1919 he had taken over the gag panel, 'Then the Fun Begins', from Milt Gross. He left the *Journal* in 1920, moving to the *World Telegram* for a year.

After leaving the *Journal*, Berndt also began working on his own strip, titled 'That's Different'. However, it lasted just a year before he joined *The New York World* in 1922, working on the strip, 'Billy the Office Boy'. He worked on this cartoon for just a few weeks before he was fired for insubordination. However, this allowed him to refocus on his own comic strip. Under the

new title 'Smitty', he sent the cartoon to the *Chicago Tribune*, where it would become a mainstay. Through the Chicago Tribune-New York News Syndicate, 'Smitty' appeared in numerous newspapers across the country for over 50 years, before its final appearance in 1973.

'Smitty' told the story of a typical American Office Boy, just how Berndt had been at the start of his career. In the strip, Smitty's stratified existence in a bureaucratic world is a form of security, much like Frank Dickens' Bristow. Though Smitty grew up from 13 to about 23 over the course of the strip's run, and got married in the process, the little corner of the world that he occupies does not change. Berndt also produced the strip 'Herby', starring Smitty's brother, from 1938 to 1960. In 1969, he won the Reuben Award for Cartooning for the 'Smitty' strip.

During the 1960s, Walter Berndt began to join the Long Island branch of the National Cartoonists Society, including DC Comics cartoonist Creig Flessel and Marvel cartoonist Frank Springer, at a monthly lunch. After his death in Port Jefferson, New York, on 15 August 1979, the monthly lunch was renamed the Berndt Toast Gang in his honour.

143

198 SMITTY, WHEN YOU GO OUT FOR LUNCH, WILL YOU GET ME TWO SANDWICHES?
Signed
Pen and ink with pencil
6 x 20 inches
Probably drawn in 1931

AL HIRSCHFELD

Albert Hirschfeld (1903-2003)

Al Hirschfeld had the first and last word on New York theatre for nearly 80 years. Heralding the arrival of virtually every show on Broadway with a caricature each Sunday in *The New York Times*, he has as his legacy the longest-standing eyewitness record of the most elusive of art forms. With seemingly few strokes of ink, he captured all that is enthralling about one genre while demonstrating an unmatchable talent in another.

For a biography of Al Hirschfeld, please refer to *The Illustrators*, 2007, pages 325-326.

144

'Still possessed of the demons, Tennessee Williams has written another vivid play. "Sweet Bird of Youth" he calls it with ironic pity. Under Elia Kazan's direction it is brilliantly acted at the Martin Beck, where it opened last evening.'

(Brooks Atkinson, 'Portrait of Corruption: Williams' "Sweet Bird of Youth" Opens', *The New York Times*, 11 March 1959)

Sweet Bird of Youth
Sweet Bird of Youth by Tennessee Williams opened on 10 March 1959 at the Martin Beck Theatre in New York. It centres on the disintegrating relationship between the gigolo, Chance Wayne (Paul Newman), and the alcoholic film star, Alexandra Del Lago (Geraldine Page). Though Chance plans to blackmail Del Lago with a secret tape recording in order to get a part in a film, his concentration is diverted by the presence of Heavenly Finley, the only daughter of a powerful and wealthy businessman and politican.

199 A COUPLE OF SELF-STYLED MONSTERS:- PAUL NEWMAN & GERALDINE PAGE IN 'SWEET BIRD OF YOUTH'
Signed and inscribed 'Philadelphia' and 'The props – family size oxygen tank and respirator – a tape recorder (hidden under bed) for blackmail – marijuana and whiskey for kicks – a cool love scene'
Pen and ink
19 ¼ x 17 ¼ inches
Illustrated: *The New York Times*, 8 March 1959

'Ernest Thompson has written a tired play in "The West Side Waltz", which opened at the Barrymore last night, but be assured that his star goes ahead and puts on her own vital show without him. Katharine Hepburn is at hand here, and Katharine Hepburn, in all her wonder, is what you'll get.'

(Frank Rich, 'Stage: Miss Hepburn Saves Us a "Waltz"', *The New York Times*, 20 November 1981)

The West Side Waltz
The writer, actor and director, Ernest Thompson, is probably best known for his play, *On Golden Pond* (1978), which, in 1981, was made into a successful film starring Katharine Hepburn and Henry Fonda. Its successor, *The West Side Waltz*, opened at the Ethel Barrymore Theatre, in New York, on 19 November 1981. The play concerns Margaret Mary Elderdice (Katharine Hepburn), an ageing, widowed pianist living in an apartment on the Upper West Side of New York, and her relationship with a younger violinist, Cara Varnum (Dorothy Loudon).

The notes on Sweet Bird of Youth *and* The West Side Waltz *are written by David Wootton.*

200 KATHARINE HEPBURN AND DOROTHY LOUDON – THE WEST SIDE WALTZ
Signed and inscribed 'Philadelphia 5'
Pen and ink
25 x 17 ¾ inches
Provenance: The Estate of Katharine Hepburn
Illustrated: *The New York Times*, 15 November 1981

CHARLES ADDAMS
Charles Samuel Addams (1912-1988)

The cartoonist, Charles Addams, became a master of American Gothic as the result of his dry sense of humour and creation of a cast of delightfully macabre characters – including Morticia, Pugsley and Wednesday – who first appeared in *The New Yorker*, **and later gained fame on television as** *The Addams Family.*

Charles Addams was born in Westfield, New Jersey, on 7 January 1912. He attended Westfield High School and, encouraged by his father to draw, contributed cartoons to its literary magazine, *Weathervane*. In 1929, he enrolled at Colgate University, Hamilton Village, NY, but transferred to the University of Pennsylvania after a year, and then, just a year later, left to study Art at the Grand Central School of Art in New York City.

Addams began his career as an artist, in 1933, in the layout department of the magazine, *True Detective*. However, he contributed his first drawing to *The New Yorker* in 1932, and worked regularly, on a freelance basis, for that magazine from 1938, when it published the first cartoon containing examples of his immortal cast of characters, which would eventually be known as the Addams Family. He would also contribute to *Collier's*, *Town & Country* and *TV Guide*, among other periodicals. The first of several anthologies, *Drawn and Quartered*, appeared in 1942.

During the Second World War, Addams served at the Signal Corps Photographic Center in Astoria, Long Island City, Queens, New York, where he made animated training films for the United States Army. In 1946, his illustration to a short story by the science fiction writer, Ray Bradbury, was published in *Mademoiselle* magazine, and led to the development of a close friendship and collaboration.

In the post-war period, the work of Addams proved to be phenomenally popular and critically successful. He received the Yale Humor Award in 1954 and a special Edgar Award from the Mystery Writers of America in 1961, and was the subject of a solo exhibition at the Museum of the City of New York in 1956. Merchandising and spinoffs included, most notably, *The Addams Family* television series, which ran on ABC for two seasons, from 1964 to 1966, and crystallised his imagination.

While retaining an apartment in midtown Manhattan, the Addams family moved to Sagaponack, New York, in 1985, giving their estate the appropriate name of The Swamp. Addams died at St Clare's Hospital and Health Center, New York, following a heart attack, on 29 September 1988.

Further reading:
Robert C Harvey, 'Addams, Charles Samuel (7 Jan 1912-29 Sept 1988)', John A Garraty and Mark C Carnes (eds), *American National Biography*, Oxford University Press, 1999, vol 1, pages 138-139

The biography of Charles Addams *is written by David Wootton.*

146

201 PUGSLEY ADDAMS
Signed
Pen and ink
1 ¾ x 4 inches
Drawn on a printed card for the New Yorker's 25th Anniversary Party
Exhibited: 'The Americans are Coming', 5-30 May 2015

202 BE THE BEST BACK IN THE BUSINESS IF HE COULD KEEP HIS MIND ON THE GAME
Signed
Inscribed with title below mount
Pen ink and monochrome watercolour on board
17 x 13 inches
Possibly illustrated for *Town & Country*, circa 1950
Exhibited: 'The Americans are Coming', 5-30 May 2015

DAVID LEVINE

148

203 OSCAR WILDE
BETTER DEADING THAN READING
Signed and dated 64
Inscribed 'Oscar Wilde' on reverse
Pen and ink
9 ½ x 3 ¼ inches
Illustrated: The New York Review of Books,
23 January 1964, 'The Agony of Oscar Wilde'
by Sybille Bedford (a review of H Montgomery
Hyde's Oscar Wilde: The Aftermath)

204 LORD ALFRED DOUGLAS
Signed and dated 64
Inscribed 'Bosie-Wilde' on reverse
Pen and ink
4 ½ x 3 inches

DAVID LEVINE
David Julian Levine (1926-2009)

David Levine was widely acknowledged as one of the greatest, and most influential, caricaturists of the second half of the twentieth century. Best known as the staff artist of *The New York Review of Books*, he revived the tradition of American political caricature that originated in the nineteenth century with Thomas Nast, and has been frequently described as equal to Honoré Daumier. However, he sustained an equally distinguished career as a painter, producing figurative oils and watercolours in a poetically naturalistic style. His love of Corot and Vuillard, Eakins and Sargent, pervades his studies of Coney Island and the Garment District. But more fundamental to both his paintings and his caricatures is the fact that he said, 'I love my species'.

For a biography of David Levine, please refer to *The Illustrators*, 2010, pages 277-278.

His work is represented in numerous public collections, including the National Portrait Gallery; and Brooklyn Museum, the Cleveland Museum of Art, the Library of Congress (Washington DC), the Metropolitan Museum of Art (New York), the National Portrait Gallery (Smithsonian Institution, Washington DC) and The Morgan Library & Museum (New York).

Further reading (including collections of caricatures):
Thomas S Buechner (foreword), *The Arts of David Levine*, New York: Alfred A Knopf, 1978; Thomas S Buechner, *Paintings and Drawings by David Levine and Aaron Shikler*, New York: Brooklyn Institute of Arts and Sciences, 1971; John Kenneth Galbraith (intro) *No Known Survivors. David Levine's Political Prank*, Boston: Gambit, 1970; David Leopold (ed), *American Presidents*, Seattle: Fantagraphics, 2008; Malcolm Muggeridge (intro), *The Man from M.A.L.I.C.E.*, New York: Dutton, 1960; John Updike (intro), *Pens and Needles. Literary Caricatures by David Levine*, Boston: Gambit, 1969; Ian McKibbin White, *The Watercolors of David Levine*, Washington DC: The Phillips Collection, 1980

'there is no doubt that Byron is one of the five great English Romantic poets. The moment of transition from the poet of the dressing rooms to the poet to whom even Goethe accorded a superiority therefore deserves a closer attention than it has received——and above all the reasons and causes underlying that transition.'

(F W Bateson, 'Byron's Baby',
The New York Review of Books, 22 February 1973)

205-217 were all exhibited in 'The Americans are Coming', 5-30 May 2015

205 LORD BYRON
Signed and dated 72
Inscribed 'Byron' on reverse
Pen and ink
13 ½ x 9 ½ inches
Illustrated: *The New York Review of Books*, 22 February 1973, 'Byron's Baby' by F W Bateson (a review of Byron's *Hebrew Melodies*, edited by Thomas L Ashton, and two books about Byron)

150

206 RUDYARD KIPLING
Signed and dated 73
Inscribed 'Kipling' on reverse
Pen and ink
12 ½ x 9 inches
Illustrated: The New York Review of Books, 8 March 1973, 'The Insider'
by Noel Annan (a review of The Age of Kipling edited by John Gross)

207 E M FORSTER
Signed
Inscribed with title on reverse
Pen and ink
13 ½ x 9 inches
Illustrated: E M Forster, Aspects of the Novel, Harmondsworth:
Pelican Books, front cover

'Books on Kipling these days are usually elegant apologia … Kipling's imperialism is taken for granted, and his text is then – very properly – combed
for all the qualifications and modifications he made of imperialism and for his dire warnings against the folly of hubris. So in this collection of essays
which Mr Gross has edited, Philip Mason points out how ambivalent Kipling was toward the Indian Civil Service; Robert Conquest remarks how Kipling
combined romanticism in his verse with colloquial matter-of-fact language; and Eric Stokes reminds us that Kipling's hatred of white men who
exploited natives surpassed his contempt for the inability of the natives to govern themselves.'

(Noel Annan, 'The Insider', The New York Review of Books, 8 March 1973)

208 GRAHAM GREENE
Signed and dated 73
Inscribed with title on reverse
Pen and ink
12 ½ x 9 inches
Illustrated: *The New York Review of Books*, 18 October 1973, 'A Funny
Sort of God' by Conor Cruise O'Brien (a review of Graham Greene's
The Honorary Consul and *Collected Stories*)

209 SALMAN RUSHDIE
Signed and dated 96
Inscribed 'S Rushdie' on reverse
Pen and ink
13 ¾ x 10 inches
Illustrated: *The New York Review of Books*, 21 March 1996, 'Palimpsest
Regained' by J M Coetzee (a review of Salman Rushdie's *The Moor's Last
Sigh*); *The New York Review of Books*, 4 October 2001, 'Puppet Show' by
John Leonard (a review of Salman Rushdie's *Fury*); *The New York Review of
Books*, 6 October 2005, 'Massacre in Arcadia' by Pankaj Mishra (a review
of Salman Rushdie's *Shalimar The Clown*); *The New York Review of Books*,
12 June 2008, 'In the Emperor's Dream House' by Joyce Carol Oates
(a review of Salman Rushdie's *The Enchantress of Florence*)

152

210 AUGUST STRINDBERG
Signed twice and dated 66
Signed and inscribed 'Strindberg' and 'ink drawing' on reverse
Pen and ink
12 ½ x 8 inches
Illustrated: *The New York Review of Books*, 7 July 1966, 'Young Strindberg'
by Michael Meyer (a review of August Strindberg's *The Son of a Servant*,
translated by Evert Sprinchorn)

211 LLOYD GEORGE
Signed and dated 72
Inscribed with title on reverse
Pen and ink
12 ½ x 8 inches
Illustrated: *The New York Review of Books*, 10 February 1972,
'The Goat' by Noel Annan (a review of Frances Stevenson's
Lloyd George: A Diary)

153

212 JOSEPH STALIN
Signed and dated 95
Inscribed 'Ol' Joe' on reverse
Pen and ink
13 ¾ x 10 inches
Illustrated: *The New York Review of Books*, 16 February 1995,
'The Chechen Tragedy' by Jack F Matlock Jr

213 NIKITA KHRUSHCHEV
Signed and dated 71
Pen and ink
12 ½ x 10 inches
Illustrated: *The New York Review of Books*, 25 February 1971, 'Dead Souls' by
George F Kennan (a review of *Khrushchev Remembers*, translated and edited by
Strobe Talbot); *The New York Review of Books*, 1 May 2003, 'L'homme Nikita' by
Robert Cottrell (a review of three books on Russia)

Lloyd George (opposite)

*'In his Preface to these diaries, A J P Taylor remarks that Lloyd George was called the Welsh Wizard by his admirers and the Goat by those who
mistrusted him. It may be so. Taylor is the doyen of modern British history and no one is better able to distinguish fact from legend. But I was brought
up to believe that just as Asquith's enemies called him Squiff because he was so often squiffy, or tipsy, in the evening, so Lloyd George's enemies called
him the Goat in their disgust with (or envy of) his inexhaustible sexual appetite.'*

(Noel Annan, 'The Goat', *The New York Review of Books*, 10 February 1972)

214 LYNDON JOHNSON AND DEAN RUSK
AS BONNIE AND CLYDE
Signed and dated 67
Inscribed 'Bonnie & Clyde' and 'N Y Review of Books'
and dated 1967 on reverse
Pen and ink
10 x 9 inches
Illustrated: *The New York Review of Books*, 7 December 1967,
front cover

215 RICHARD NIXON
Signed
Pen and ink
10 ½ x 8 ½ inches
Illustrated: *New York* magazine, 10 June 1968,
front cover [in a modified form]
The image illustrates Dick Schaap's article, 'Will Richard Nixon
Trip Over Himself Again on His Way to Victory?', pages 25-29

*'Nixon has risen intact from the political ashes … and is once more bidding seriously to become
president of his country. Yet, now, as he campaigns across the nation, inhaling delegates and voters,
exhaling his square-and-pious philosophy, he realizes, perhaps better than anyone else, that at any
moment he could, like the Phoenix-man, sink suddenly back into ashes.'*

(Dick Schaap, 'Will Richard Nixon Trip Over Himself Again on His
Way to Victory?', *New York* magazine, 10 June 1968)

216 GORE VIDAL
Signed and dated 73
Inscribed with title twice on reverse
Pen and ink
9 ½ x 7 inches

217 GEORGE W BUSH
PRESIDENT PINOCCHIO
Signed and dated 03
Inscribed 'President Pinocchio' on reverse
Pen and ink
12 x 9 inches
Illustrated: *The New York Review of Books*,
18 December 2003, 'Health for Sale' by
Jeff Madrick (a review of four books on
the Welfare State)

MILTON GLASER

Milton Glaser (born 1929)

Undoubtedly one of America's greatest graphic designers, Milton Glaser is best known as the creator of one of the most iconic images of the twentieth century, the 'I ♥ NY' logo.

Milton Glaser was born in New York City on 26 June 1929. He was educated first at the High School of Music and Art in New York, then at the Cooper Union School of Art, graduating in 1951. He obtained a Fulbright Scholarship to study at the Academy of Fine Arts in Bologna, Italy, where he worked with the painter, Giorgio Morandi.

In 1954, Glaser co-founded Pushpin Studios, an illustration and design studio along with Seymour Chwast, Reynold Ruffins, and Edward Sorel. In 1968, he co-founded *New York* magazine with the journalist Clay Felker, working as President and Design Director until 1977. In 1974, he opened his own design studio, Milton Glaser Inc, in Manhattan. Still in operation today, Milton Glaser Inc, has been responsible for numerous famous designs and logos, such as the Brooklyn Brewery logo in 1987 and the 'DC Bullet' used by DC Comics between 1977 and 2005. In 1975, he was commissioned to complete the full graphic and decorative programs for the restaurants in the World Trade Center, as well as the design of the building's Observation Deck.

Glaser's most famous design was created in 1976, when he was commissioned by the state of New York to come up with a design to improve the image of New York City. His simple 'I ♥ NY' design became one of the most famous, copied and reproduced logos ever created. Inspired by the sculpture 'Love' by the artist Robert Indiana, the logo ensured Glaser's reputation as America's leading graphic designer. He formed the publication design firm, WBMG, with Walter Bernard in 1983, which has been responsible for design projects on over 50 newspapers and magazines worldwide, including the *Washington Post*, the *Los Angeles Times* and Rio de Janeiro's *O Globo*.

Milton Glaser has been presented with numerous awards throughout his career, such as lifetime achievement awards from the Cooper Hewitt National Design Museum, in 2004, and the Fulbright Association, in 2011. In 2009, he became the first graphic designer to receive the National Medal of the Arts. He has held solo shows at the Museum of Modern Art, New York, in 1975, and the Centre Pompidou, Paris, in 1977.

His work is represented in numerous public collections including the Cooper Hewitt National Design Museum (New York), the Museum of Modern Art (New York) and the National Archives (Smithsonian Institution, Washington DC); and The Israel Museum, Jerusalem.

156

'What is [Peer Gynt], we say, except a kind of Norwegian roaring boy, marvelously attractive to women, a kind of bogus poet, a narcissist, absurd self-idolator, a liar, seducer, bombastic self-deceiver? But this is paltry moralizing ... Peer the scamp bears the Blessing: more life'

(Harold Bloom, *The Western Canon*, San Diego CA: Harcourt Brace, 1994, page 357)

Peer Gynt

Henrik Ibsen wrote his satirical verse play, *Peer Gynt*, during the course of 1867. It was given its premiere at the Mollergaden Theatre in Christiania (now Oslo) on 24 February 1876, with incidental music by Edvard Grieg. The incidental music is now considered to be among Grieg's greatest works.

The Columbia Records LP for which Milton Glaser designed the sleeve – featuring an imaginary portrait of Peer Gynt – included the two suites drawn from that music. Glaser designed a number of other sleeves for Columbia Records, and also a celebrated poster of Bob Dylan, showing the musician in silhouette with psychedelic hair (1966).

The note on Peer Gynt *is written by David Wootton.*

218 PEER GYNT
Signed
Acrylic and bodycolour with collage
14 x 15 inches
Design for the sleeve for the LP record, *Andrew Davis Conducts Grieg*, Columbia Records, 1976

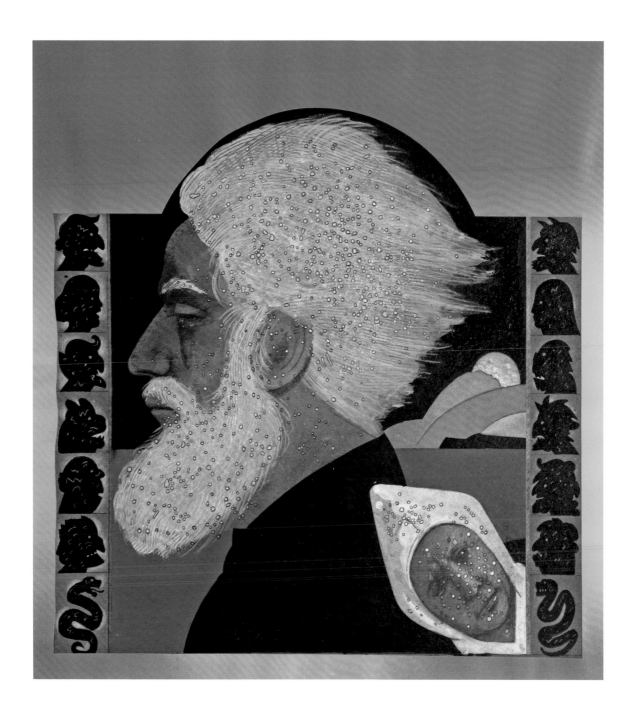

ARNOLD ROTH

Arnold Roth (born 1929)

'Arnold Roth is surely the most imaginative and humorous graphic artist of this or any other day. Even Max Beerbohm at his best would have to take a back seat.' (George Plimpton, *Paris Review*)

Arnold Roth was born in Philadelphia, Pennsylvania, on 25 February 1929. One of six children, he was encouraged to draw from an early age and, at the age of seven, began attending art classes at the Graphic Sketch Club, a philanthropic school at which children could learn from some of the city's finest artists. He studied art under Frederick Gill at Central High School in Philadelphia, where he was awarded a scholarship to study at the Philadelphia Museum School of Industrial Art (now The University of the Arts).

Arnold Roth's early career was interrupted when he contracted tuberculosis and spent over a year in a sanitarium in Brown Mills, New Jersey, before he returned to art school in 1950. However he was forced to quit just a few months later to take care of his terminally ill mother.

In 1952, the year that he married his wife Caroline, Arnold Roth began producing monthly drawings for *Holiday* magazine and illustrations for the debut issues of *TV Guide*. In 1956, he met cartoonist and editor Harvey Kurtzman, with whom he went on to collaborate on the satirical magazines, *Trump* (which closed before its first issue), *Humbug* (1957-58), which he co-edited, and *Help!* (1960-65). In 1959, he began *Poor Arnold's Almanac*, a full-colour Sunday cartoon strip for the New York Herald Tribune Syndicate which ran until May 1961. It was revived for a second run from September 1988 to January 1990.

In August 1960, Roth and his wife moved to London. In the late 1950s, Roth had had his first drawings accepted by *Punch* and whilst in London produced work for virtually every issue, while also producing a large amount of work for *Esquire*. He returned to the United States in 1962, settling first in Princeton and later in New York City. In 1965, he took over the *Punch* feature, 'Report from America', from PG Wodehouse, producing a two-page drawing each month until 1988.

Since the 1950s to the present day, Roth's cartoons and illustrations have appeared in magazines and periodicals from *Playboy* to *Sports Illustrated*, *GQ* to *Entertainment Weekly* and *Time* to *The New Yorker*. He has provided the illustrations to numerous books, including *Grimm's Fairy Tales* (1966), in addition to his own publications, such as *Arnold Roth's Crazy Book of Science* (1971).

Throughout his career, Arnold Roth has received a great deal of recognition for his work. The National Cartoonist Society, of which he served as President from 1983 to 1985, presented him with the Reuben Award for Cartoonist of the Year in 1984, Best Sports Cartoonist in 1976 and 1977, and Best Illustrator Cartoonist 13 times between 1976 and 1989. He entered the National Cartoonist Hall of Fame in 2001. That year also saw the launch of the touring exhibition, 'Arnold Roth: Free Lance, A Fifty Year Retrospective' which ran between 2001 and 2004 and was shown in Philadelphia, Columbus, San Francisco, New York, London and Basel.

219 FOILED BY THE RAIN
Signed
Pen ink and watercolour, 15 ½ x 12 ½ inches
Illustrated: *Punch's Almanack*, circa 1960
Exhibited: 'The Americans are Coming', 5-30 May 2015
This image was Arnold Roth's first colour piece to appear on the inside pages of *Punch*.

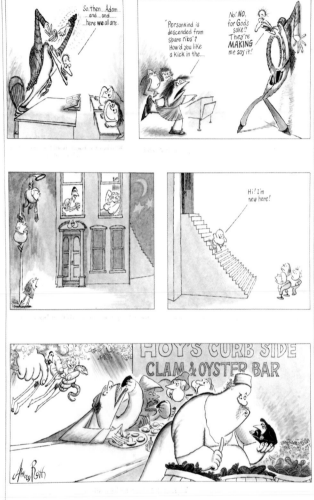

220 COMES THE EVOLUTION
OR MANKIND DESCENDING
Signed and inscribed with title
Pen ink and monochrome watercolour
15 x 24 ¼ inches
Illustrated: *Punch*, 25 February 1981, page 305

160

221 AS YOU BIKE IT
Signed and inscribed with title
Pen ink and watercolour
14 ¼ x 23 inches
Illustrated: *The New Yorker*, 4 September 2000, page 96,
'The back page by Arnold Roth', [in a modified form]

222 THE ART OF THE TATTOO
Signed and inscribed with title
Pen ink and watercolour
15 x 10 ¼ inches
Illustrated: *The New Yorker*, 10 November 2003, page 130,
'The Art of the Tattoo by Arnold Roth'
Exhibited: 'The Americans are Coming', 5-30 May 2015

223 HAUTE TIPLING
Signed
Inscribed with title below mount
Pen ink and watercolour
14 x 10 ¾ inches
Illustrated: *The New York Times*, 1 August 2007, 'Fine Diner to Riffraff:
Tipsy Tales of Four-Star Benders' by Frank Bruni

"It's Spring!"

"Some spring! Ahm freezin'."

"Spring? Already it's spring, already?"

"Mother of Mercy! Can this be the end of winter, Ricco?"

"Grandma, is that spring, too?"

"Tommy, come see what's spring."

224 IT'S SPRING!
Signed and inscribed with captions
Pen ink and watercolour
14 ¼ x 21 ½ inches
Illustrated: *The New Yorker*, 3 May 2004, page 112 [in a modified form]
Exhibited: 'The Americans are Coming', 5-30 May 2015

225 THE HELL OF IT
Signed
Inscribed with title below mount
Pen ink and watercolour
16 ½ x 10 inches
Drawn for but not illustrated in *The New Yorker*, 2010

226 LADY GODIVA VISITS TIMES SQUARE
Signed
Inscribed with title below mount
Pen ink and watercolour with bodycolour
14 ¼ x 10 ½ inches
Drawn for but not illustrated in *The New Yorker*, circa 2012
Exhibited: 'The Americans are Coming', 5-30 May 2015

ARNOLD ROTH

227 'CAN'T YOU SEE, YOU SILLY LITTLE FOOL? IT'S
YOU I REALLY WANT!':
EVERY ROMANTIC COMEDY EVER WRITTEN
Signed
Inscribed with title below mount
Pen ink and watercolour
17 ½ x 12 inches
Illustrated: *Southampton Review*, 2012

ED SOREL
Edward Sorel (born 1929)

Edward Sorel's clever and unforgiving satire is the product of a lifetime spent observing and criticising the unpleasant reality of the American Dream. His experiences of recent history from the Great Depression to Al-Qaeda, and his disdain for the greasy politics in between, have lent his cartoons a formidable bite that those his junior rarely match.

For a biography of Ed Sorel, please refer to *The Illustrators*, 2014, pages 248-250.

228-231 & **233-235** were all exhibited in 'The Americans are Coming', 5-30 May 2015

229 GEORGE
WASHINGTON AND
ABRAHAM LINCOLN
Pen and ink
13 ½ x 13 ½ inches
Advertisement for the bank
holding company, Manufacturers
Hanover

230 BULL MARKET
Signed
Pen and ink
13 x 16 ½ inches
Illustrated: *The New York Times*

228 ELECTION 1996 (opposite)
Signed, inscribed 'For Alan
on his 60th birthday with lots of
good wishes from his fan' and
dated 7/98
Pen ink and watercolour
16 ½ x 12 ½ inches
Similar to *The New Yorker*,
11 November 1996, front cover

166

231 JOSEPH CONRAD AND
LADY OTTOLINE MORRELL
Signed
Pastel
19 x 25 inches
Illustrated: *The Atlantic Monthly*, March 1986,
page 81; 'First Encounters. Joseph Conrad and
Lady Ottoline Morrell' by Nancy Caldwell Sorel;
Nancy Caldwell Sorel & Edward Sorel, *First
Encounters: A Book of Memorable Meetings*,
New York: Alfred A Knopf, 1996, page 40

232 RAINING DOLLAR BILLS
ON FIFTH AVENUE
Signed with initials
Watercolour with pen and ink
10 x 15 inches
Illustrated: *The New Yorker*, 24 April 2000,
pages 170-171

233 RUDYARD KIPLING
YOUR CHUMS ARE FIGHTING
WHY AREN'T YOU?
Signed
Pen ink and watercolour
14 x 10 inches
Illustrated: Adam Begley, *Certitude. A Profusely
Illustrated Guide to Blockheads and Bullheads,
Past & Present*, New York: Harmony Books,
2009, page 98

234 BERTOLT BRECHT
Signed
Pen ink and watercolour
18 ½ x 21 inches
Illustrated: *The Atlantic Monthly*, September 2002; Edward Sorel,
Literary Lives, London: Bloomsbury, 2006, [unpaginated]

169

235 MARCEL PROUST
Signed
Pen ink and watercolour
18 x 21 inches
Illustrated: Edward Sorel, *Literary Lives*, London: Bloomsbury, 2006, [unpaginated]

EDWARD KOREN

Edward Benjamin Koren (born 1935)

Edward Koren is undoubtedly one of the most loved and revered cartoonists in the history of *The New Yorker*. With his first cartoon appearing in 1962, he has since produced over one thousand cartoons, illustrations and covers for the magazine. Famous for his wonderfully fuzzy beasts, Koren delights in making, in his own words, 'the ordinary and mundane hairy and unshorn'.

Edward Koren was born in New York City on 13 December 1935. As a child, Edward attended the Horace Mann School in the Bronx, New York, where he first indulged in his love of painting and cartooning, working on the school's yearbook and literary magazine.

Initially enrolling as a pre-medical freshman at Columbia University, Edward Koren quickly found himself focusing on more artistic pursuits, contributing regularly to the Columbia's humour magazine *The Jester* and becoming its editor in his senior year. After graduating in 1957, he was accepted into Yale for an MFA in graphic design but decided to put it off for a year, instead choosing to work at a city-planning firm. Six months later and disillusioned with his career path, he was recommended by a professor at Columbia to work with painter and printmaker Stanley William Hayter at his prestigious studio, Atelier 17, in Paris. Travelling first to Cambridge with a friend, he spent a year and a half studying and working with Hayter in Paris, returning to the United States in 1959.

Upon his return, Edward Koren joined the US Army Reserves, spending six months stationed at Fort Dix, Texas. After completing his basic training, he attended the Pratt Institute in Brooklyn, New York, obtaining an MFA degree in art education. Although he took a job first at the Abelard-Schuman publishing company and then at Columbia University Press,

236-239 were all exhibited in 'The Americans are Coming', 5-30 May 2015

170

236 AT WHAT DO YOU TOIL?
Signed
Inscribed with title and publication details, and dated
'Dec 25, 2000'/Jan 1, 2001' on reverse
Pen and ink
20 ½ x 22 ½ inches
Illustrated: *The New Yorker*, 25 December 2000, page 122;
The New Yorker, 1 January 2001

237 THANK YOU, HONEY, FOR YOUR VOTE OF CONFIDENCE IN OUR PARENTING DECISIONS
Signed
Inscribed with title and publication details, and dated
'October 10, 2011' on reverse
Pen and ink
18 x 19 inches
Illustrated: *The New Yorker*, 10 October 2011, page 76

Koren was resolved to succeed as an artist. His first cartoon appeared in *The New Yorker* on 26 May 1962, beginning an association with the magazine that continues to this day. In the autumn of 1964, he took up a teaching position at Brown University, which he held until 1977.

In addition to his contributions to *The New Yorker*, Edward Koren's cartoons and illustrations have appeared in numerous other newspapers and magazines, including *The New York Times*, *Newsweek*, the *Boston Globe*, *GQ*, *Esquire*, *Sports Illustrated*, *Vogue*, *Fortune*, *The Nation* and *Vanity Fair*. He has illustrated numerous books, including *How to Eat Like a Child* (1978) by Delia Ephron, *A Dog's Life by Peter Mayle* (1996), *The New Legal Seafoods Cookbook* by Roger Berkowitz and Jane Doerfer (2003), *Thelonius Monster's Sky-High Fly Pie* (2006) and *Poems I Wrote When No One Was Looking* by Alan Katz (2011). He has also written and illustrated a number of children's books, including *Don't Talk to Strange Bears* (1969) and *Very Hairy Harry* (2003).

171

238 LISTEN UP, EVERYBODY – CHARLES IS GOING TO FILL US IN ABOUT THE GRENACHE GRAPE
Signed
Inscribed with title and publication details, and dated 'June 13/20 - 05' on reverse
Pen and ink
18 x 24 inches
Illustrated: *The New Yorker*, 13 & 20 June 2005, page 151

239 COULD WE SKIP THE PROSECUTION AND GET ON TO THE SENTENCING PHASE?
Signed
Inscribed with title and publication details and dated 3/20/06 on reverse
Pen and ink
18 ½ x 26 ½ inches
Illustrated: *The New Yorker*, 20 March 2006, page 97

KAL

Kevin Kallaugher (born 1955), known as 'Kal'

Kal is the international award-winning editorial cartoonist for *The Economist* and the *Baltimore Sun*. In a distinguished career that spans 35 years, he has created more than 8,000 cartoons and 140 magazine covers. His résumé includes six collections of his published work, international honours, awards in seven countries and one-man exhibitions in six.

For a biography of Kal, please refer to *The Illustrators*, 2014, page 266

In 2015, Kal was awarded the Herblock prize for Editorial Cartooning for a collection of work in the *Baltimore Sun* and *The Economist*. He was recently named as a finalist for the 2015 Pulitzer Prize for editorial cartooning.

240 UNWINNABLETON
Signed, inscribed 'The Economist' and dated 2006
Pen and ink
8 ¼ x 12 ¾ inches
Illustrated: *The Economist*, 8 July 2006

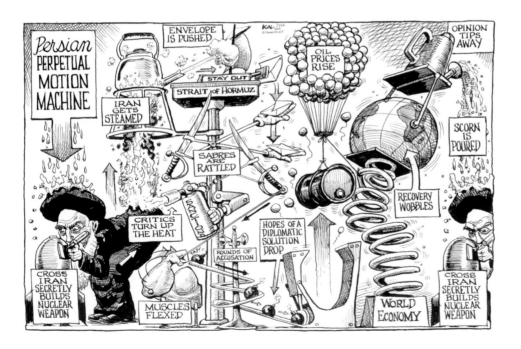

241 PERSIAN PERPETUAL MOTION MACHINE
Signed, inscribed 'The Economist' and dated 2012
Pen and ink
8 ¼ x 12 ¾ inches
Illustrated: *The Economist*, 7 January 2012

242 PLEASE WELCOME TO THE HISTORIC FIGURE SOCIETY ...
Signed, inscribed 'The Economist' and dated 2013
Pen and ink
7 ¾ x 12 ¼ inches
Illustrated: *The Economist*, 13 April 2013

243 I THINK WE HAVE STUCK THE RIGHT BALANCE
Signed, inscribed 'The Economist' and dated 2013
Pen and ink
8 x 12 ¾ inches
Illustrated: *The Economist*, 15 June 2013

173

244 IT'S HARD FOR A COUNTRY TO TURN THE CORNER
WHEN IT'S STUCK ON A ROUNDABOUT ...
Signed, inscribed 'The Economist' and dated '2014'
Pen and ink
8 ¼ x 12 ½ inches
Illustrated: *The Economist*, 1 March 2014

245 I AM LOOKING TO ARM MODERATE SYRIAN REBELS ...
Signed, inscribed 'The Economist' and dated 2014
Pen and ink
8 x 12 inches
Illustrated: The *Economist*, 20 September 2014

10

ILLUSTRATORS BETWEEN THE WARS

MABEL LUCIE ATTWELL
(1879-1964)

MARGARET TARRANT
(1888-1959)

EDWARD ARDIZZONE
(1900-1979)

S R BADMIN
(1906-1989)

174

246 I'SE BEEN A LONG TIME
BUT I JUST HAD TO LOOK
TO SEE IF I'SE TIDY,
TO COME IN YOUR BOOK!
Signed and inscribed with title
Watercolour and pencil, 8 ½ x 5 inches

247 OLIVE'S NIGHT-TIME VIGIL WITH THE FAIRIES
Signed and inscribed 'Olive'
Pen ink and watercolour with pencil on board
Decorative pen and ink border on supporting board below mount
17 x 13 ½ inches

MABEL LUCIE ATTWELL

Mabel Lucie Attwell, SWA (1879-1964)

Mabel Lucie Attwell developed her own imaginative, and often amusing, imagery through annuals and postcards. Then, as her popularity increased, she applied it to a wide range of products. She was a household name by the 1920s, by which time no home was complete without an Attwell plaque or money-box biscuit tin.

For a biography of Mabel Lucie Attwell, please refer to *The Illustrators*, 2009, page 55.

Chris Beetles' biography of Mabel Lucie Attwell, published by Pavilion Books in 1985, sold out in hardback, and is now published in paperback by Chris Beetles Ltd.

Further reading:
Brian Alderson (*rev*), 'Attwell [married name Earnshaw], Mabel Lucie (1879-1964)', H C G Matthew and Brian Harrison (eds), *Oxford Dictionary of National Biography*, Oxford University Press, 2004, vol 2, pages 885-887

248 FAIRY FAIR PLAY
Signed
Watercolour with pen ink and pencil, 11 ¼ x 8 ½ inches
Provenance: The Estate of Mabel Lucie Attwell
Illustrated: Mabel Lucie Attwell, *Fairy Book*, London: S W Partridge & Co, 1932, page 52

249 THE ANGEL'S VISIT
Signed
Watercolour with pencil
16 ¼ x 12 inches

175

251 THE FAIRY SONG
Pen ink, watercolour and bodycolour with pencil
9 ¾ x 8 ½ inches

250 LITTLE OLE LADY!
Signed
Inscribed 'All dressed up – S'only me/but not so
old-fashioned as I 'pears to be' on reverse
Watercolour and bodycolour
12 x 7 ½ inches
Illustrated: Design for a postcard, no 4187, for Valentine
of Dundee; Calendar, 1949
Literature: Chris Beetles, *Mabel Lucie Attwell*, London:
Pavilion Books, 1988, page 93; John Henty, *The Collectable
World of Mabel Lucie Attwell*, London: Richard Dennis,
1999, page 66

252 ALL SWEET – SAME AS YOU!
Inscribed with title
Watercolour and bodycolour with pencil
8 ¼ x 6 ¾ inches

253 THE TRULY FRIEND I'VE HEARD FOLKS SAY
WILL HELP YOU LAUGH OR DANCE OR PLAY,
OR HELP YOU DRY YOUR TEARS AWAY
AN' THAT'S ME!
Inscribed 'Poor, Poor Elizabeth Jane' on backboard
Watercolour
11 x 9 ¼ inches
Illustrated: Design for a postcard, no 2651, for Valentine
of Dundee
Literature: John Henty, *The Collectable World of Mabel
Lucie Attwell*, London: Richard Dennis, 1999, page 61

MABEL LUCIE ATTWELL

254 EVERY NIGHT-TIME THIS I SAY, BEFORE I SNUGGLE DOWN
Signed
Watercolour with pen ink and bodycolour on board, 14 x 13 inches
Provenance: The Estate of Mabel Lucie Attwell
Probably a design for a wall plaque for Valentine of Dundee

MARGARET TARRANT

Margaret Winifred Tarrant (1888-1959)

From the late 1900s, Margaret Tarrant was preoccupied with chronicling innocent childhood in its many moods and its great variety of activities. From 1920, her talents were channelled by her most important business relationship, with the Medici Society, which still publishes her books, cards and calendars today. Though her approach could seem highly idealised, even romanticised, its success lies in the degree to which it was grounded in close observation and the discipline of drawing from life.

For a biography of Margaret Tarrant, please refer to *The Illustrators*, 2014, page 162.

Further reading:
John Gurney, *Margaret Tarrant and Her Pictures*, London: The Medici Society, 1982; Claire Houghton, 'Tarrant, Margaret Winifred (1888-1959)', H C G Matthew and Brian Harrison (eds), *Oxford Dictionary of National Biography*, Oxford University Press, 2004, vol 53, pages 791-792

255 THE RAINBOW
Signed
Watercolour with bodycolour
6 ¼ x 6 ¼ inches
Provenance: The Medici Society

MARGARET TARRANT

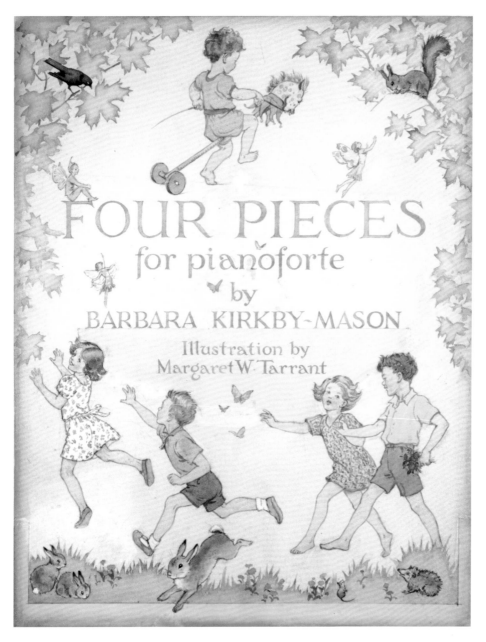

256 FOUR PIECES FOR PIANOFORTE
Signed
Watercolour with bodycolour
13 x 10 inches
Illustrated: Barbara Kirkby-Mason,
Four Pieces for pianoforte, London:
Bosworth & Co, 1932, front cover

EDWARD ARDIZZONE

Edward Ardizzone, CBE RA RDI (1900-1979)

Highly observant and immensely humane, the work of Edward Ardizzone is in direct descent from the finest French and English illustrators of the nineteenth century. Developing as an artist from 1930, Ardizzone made his name as an illustrator through his contributions to *The Radio Times* and then with *Little Tim and the Brave Sea Captain*, which proved to be one of the most significant picture books published between the wars. Soon considered one of the greatest illustrators of his generation, he also gained a reputation as a distinguished Official War Artist, through his record in word and image of action in Europe and North Africa. Versatile and productive, he produced paintings, sculptures, etchings and lithographs, and worked as a designer.

For a biography of Edward Ardizzone, please refer to *The Illustrators*, 2007, page 313; for an essay on Ardizzone's illustrations to Cyril Ray's *Merry England*, see *The Illustrators*, 1999, pages 193-195.

Key works written and illustrated: *Little Tim and the Brave Sea Captain* (1936); *Tim All Alone* (1956)

Key works illustrated: Contributed to *The Radio Times* (from 1932) and *The Strand Magazine* (from 1942); H E Bates, *My Uncle Silas* (1939); *Poems of François Villon* (1946); Walter de la Mare, *Peacock Pie* (1946); Anthony Trollope, *The Warden* (1952) and *Barchester Towers* (1953); William Thackeray, *The Newcomes* (1954); Eleanor Farjeon, *The Little Bookroom* (1955); Cervantes, *Exploits of Don Quixote* (1959)

His work is represented in numerous public collections, including the British Museum, the Imperial War Museums, Tate and the V&A; and the Ashmolean Museum (Oxford).

Further reading:
Brian Alderson, *Edward Ardizzone: A Bibliographic Commentary*, Pinner: Private Libraries Association, in association with the British Library and Oak Knoll Press, 2003; Nicholas Ardizzone, *Edward Ardizzone's World. The Etchings and Lithographs. An Introduction and Catalogue Raisonné*, London: Unicorn Press and Wolseley Fine Arts, 2000; Gabriel White, *Edward Ardizzone*, London: Bodley Head, 1979

181

257 LITTLE TIM & THE SHIP CAT
Signed and inscribed with title
Pen and ink
4 ½ x 5 ½ inches

258 COUPLE ON A BENCH
Signed with initials and dated 1935
Watercolour
4 ¾ x 6 ½ inches

182

259 ST PAUL'S SCHOOL – THE FRONT
Signed, inscribed 'St Paul's School from the
North' and numbered '1/100'
Lithograph
15 ½ x 21 ½ inches
From an edition of 100
Literature: Nicholas Ardizzone, *Edward
Ardizzone's World. The Etchings and Lithographs.
An Introduction and Catalogue Raisonné*, London:
Unicorn Press and Wolesley Fine Arts, 2000,
no 42 (suite viii: Public Schools)

260 THE LADIES' BAR (opposite)
Signed with initials
Inscribed with title below mount
Pen ink and watercolour
11 x 13 inches
Provenance: John Bell, editor at the Oxford
University Press
Exhibited: Royal Society of Painters in
Water-Colours, by 1955

S R BADMIN

Stanley Roy Badmin, RE RWS AIA FSIA (1906-1989)

One of Britain's foremost illustrators, watercolourists and printmakers, S R Badmin defined the way that Britain looked at itself for more than a generation.

Stanley Roy Badmin was born at 8a Niederwald Road, Sydenham, South London, on 18 April 1906, the second of three sons of Charles James Badman, a teacher, and his wife, Margaret (née Raine), both from Somerset. He and his brothers changed their surname to Badmin to avoid being teased at school. Educated at Sydenham School, he won a scholarship to Camberwell School of Arts & Crafts (1922-24), and then a studentship to the Royal College of Art, where he studied under Randolph Schwabe and E W Tristram, among others, and specialised in book illustration (1924-27). In 1928, he qualified as a teacher, and supplemented his income by teaching part-time at Richmond School of Art (1934) and St John's Wood School of Art (1936).

Badmin contributed his first illustrations to *The Graphic* (1927) and *The Tatler* (1928). However, he worked increasingly as an etcher and watercolourist. He had his first solo show at the Twenty-One Gallery (1930), and was elected to the Royal Society of Painter-Etchers and Engravers (ARE 1931, RE 1935, resigned 1939) and the Royal Society of Painters in Water-Colours (ARWS 1932, RWS 1939). As a result of developing a greater political awareness, he also became a member of the Artists' International Association (1936).

After the first of two exhibitions at the Fine Art Society, in 1933, Badmin received his first major commission – from the American magazine *Fortune* – to depict various towns in the United States; the results were exhibited at M A McDonald in New York (1936). Equally important developments in his illustrative style were marked soon after his return to England by the

Puffin Picture Book, *Village and Town*, and *Highways and Byways of Essex*, a collaboration with F L M Griggs (both 1939).

Even before the Second World War, Badmin made a mark as an important educational illustrator and was particularly admired for his accurate depiction of trees. Making a major contribution to the Pilgrim Trust's Recording Britain Scheme, in 1940, he went on to work for the Ministry of Information (1941) and serve in the Royal Air Force as an operational model-maker (1942-45).

From 1945, Badmin worked increasingly as a commercial artist and, three years later, began to receive regular and frequent commissions as a result of his joining the agency of Saxon Artists. He designed series of advertisements for Fisons and Bowater Paper, and produced posters for transport and travel companies. He was also patronised by Royle, one of the largest manufacturers of greeting cards and calendars. In 1950, he would be elected a Fellow of the Society of Industrial Artists.

Equally in demand as an illustrator of books and periodicals, Badmin published *Trees for Town and Country* (1947) and contributed to *Radio Times*. Only from the mid 1950s was he able to paint two or three major pieces for each RWS exhibition, and hold a solo show at the Leicester Galleries (1955). Even then, he found time to embark on projects for Shell: Geoffrey Grigson's *The Shell Guide to Trees and Shrubs* (1958) and four volumes of the series of 'Shell Guides to the Counties'. In addition, he taught General Drawing one day a week at the Central School of Art between 1947 and 1964.

In 1959, Badmin and his second wife, Rosaline, moved to Bignor, near Pulborough, West Sussex, with their children. There he continued to paint and exhibit, becoming a member of the Sussex Society of Painters and holding a solo show at Worthing Art Gallery (1967). In 1984, the Royal Society of Painters in Water-Colours honoured his achievement by devoting a part of its autumn exhibition to his work. He died at St Richard's Hospital, Chichester, West Sussex, on 28 April 1989.

Chris Beetles has been the leading authority on S R Badmin for the last 30 years, since he published his major monograph, *S R Badmin and The English Landscape* (Collins 1984) and mounted a large-scale exhibition at his Ryder Street Gallery (1985).

Earlier this year, Chris celebrated his championship of Badmin with 'S R Badmin RWS: Paintings, Drawings & Prints', a new exhibition of over 200 unseen works, mostly from the Badmin Estate. A 48-page catalogue, including a second edition of the catalogue raisonné of the prints, accompanied it.

Both the book and the exhibition catalogue are available for sale.

261 MANUDEN (opposite)
Signed with initials and inscribed 'Church Row Manuden, Essex'
Signed and inscribed with title and artist's address on reverse
Pen and ink
3 ¾ x 5 ½ inches
Illustrated: page 70

261-266 are all illustrated in Clifford Bax, *Highways and Byways in Essex*, London: Macmillan and Co, 1939

262 APPROACHING HIGH EASTER
Signed with initials and inscribed 'High Easter, Essex'
Pen and ink
4 ¾ x 5 inches
Illustrated: page 39

263 THAXTED
Signed and inscribed with title and 'Essex'
Signed and inscribed with title, artist's address and publishing details
on reverse
Pen and ink
8 ¼ x 5 inches
Illustrated: page 91
Exhibited: LSA, 1944

264 STANSTED HALL
Signed with initials and inscribed 'Stansted Hall, Essex'
Pen and ink
4 ½ x 7 inches
Illustrated: page 72

265 FINCHINGFIELD
Signed and inscribed with title
Signed and inscribed with title, 'Essex' and with artist's address on reverse
Pen and ink
5 ½ x 8 ¼ inches
Illustrated: page 102

266 HELION BUMPSTEAD
Signed and inscribed with title
Inscribed with title and 'Essex'
below mount
Pen and ink
5 ¼ x 8 ¼ inches
Illustrated: page 114

E H SHEPARD
Ernest Howard Shepard, MC OBE (1879-1976)

While Shepard is now best remembered for his immortal illustrations to *Winnie-the-Pooh* and *The Wind in the Willows*, he was a wide-ranging illustrator, with an unsurpassed genius for representing children, and an underrated talent for political cartoons.

For a biography of E H Shepard, please refer to *The Illustrators*, 2007, page 199; for essays on various aspects of the artist's achievements, see *The Illustrators*, 1999, pages 151-152; *The Illustrators*, 2000, pages 28-32; and *The Illustrators*, 2007, pages 199-200.

Key works illustrated: contributed *to Punch* from 1907, becoming second cartoonist in 1935, and chief cartoonist from 1945 until 1949; A A Milne, *When We Were Very Young* (1924); E V Lucas, *Playtime and Company* (1925); A A Milne, *Winnie-the-Pooh* (1926); *Everybody's Pepys* (1926); *The House at Pooh Corner* (1928); Kenneth Grahame, *The Wind in the Willows* (1931); Richard Jeffries, *Bevis* (1932); E V Lucas, *As the Bee Sucks* (1937)

His work is represented in the collections of the V&A; and the Shepard Archive at the University of Surrey (Guildford).

Further reading:
Arthur R Chandler, *The Story of E H Shepard: the man who drew Pooh*, West Sussex: Jaydem, 2001; Rawle Knox (ed), *The Work of E H Shepard*, London: Methuen, 1979; C A Parker (rev), 'Shepard, Ernest Howard (1879-1976)', H C G Matthew and Brian Harrison (eds), *Oxford Dictionary of National Biography*, Oxford University Press, 2004, vol 50, pages 230-231

267 LITTLE BO PEEP AND LITTLE BOY BLUE
Pencil with watercolour
9 x 7 ¾ inches
Possibly a preliminary drawing for *Punch*, 16 April 1924, page 413, 'Little Bo Peep and Little Boy Blue' by A A Milne; A A Milne, *When We Were Very Young*, London: Methuen & Co, 1924, pages 76-78

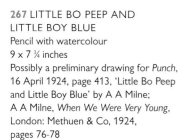

268 POLITENESS
Inscribed with title below mount
Extensively inscribed and dated 'Jan 1959' on reverse
Pen and ink
4 ¼ x 2 ¼ inches
Similar to A A Milne, *When We Were Very Young*, London: Methuen & Co, 1924, page 41

'E H Shepard: An Illustrator's War' –
the first ever exhibition of E H Shepard's
illustrations from the trenches of the Great
War – runs at House of Illustration until
10 January 2016.

Chris Beetles Gallery has loaned a number
of works to the show, including *Vespers*.

269 VESPERS
Signed with initials and inscribed with title
and poem text
Pen ink and pencil
11 ¼ x 7 ½ inches
Similar to A A Milne, *When We Were Very Young*,
London: Methuen & Co, 1924, pages 99 & 100
Exhibited: 'E H Shepard. An Illustrator's War',
House of Illustration, 9 October 2015-
10 January 2016

'Up, and again to look after the setting things right against dinner, which I did to very good content. So to the office, where all the morning till noon, when word brought me to the Board that my Lord Sandwich was come; so I presently rose, leaving the Board ready to rise, and there I found my Lord Sandwich, Peterborough, and Sir Charles Harbord; and presently after them comes my Lord Hinchingbroke, Mr Sidney, and Sir William Godolphin. And after greeting them, and some time spent in talk, dinner was brought up, one dish after another, but a dish at a time, but all so good; but, above all things, the variety of wines, and excellent of their kind, I had for them, and all in so good order, that they were mightily pleased, and myself full of content at it'

(*Everybody's Pepys*, London: G Bell and Sons, 1926, page 521)

189

270 DINNER WAS BROUGHT UP
Signed
Inscribed 'The Dinner Party' below mount
Pen and ink on board
11 x 7 ¼ inches
Illustrated: Samuel Pepys, *Everybody's Pepys.*
The Diary of Samuel Pepys 1660-1669, London:
G Bell and Sons, 1926, facing page 521

271-275 are all illustrated in E V Lucas, *Mr Punch's County Songs*, London: Methuen & Co, 1928

COUNTY SONGS

XVIII.—NORTHUMBERLAND

THE proud Northumbrian's constant lot
It was to fight the hardy Scot,
Who, flouting law and order,
But two ambitions had in life :
To dwell consistently in strife,
And get across the Border.
A vain attempt to keep at bay
The race that owns the earth today.

No longer now from Tweed to Tyne
Does rivalry incarnadine
The pastures of the PERCYS :
And on his lawn at Fallodon
Northumberland's most famous son
Cons Mr WORDSWORTH'S verses :
The Border sips the loving-cup,
And not a drawbridge now is up.

E.V.L.

271 COUNTY SONGS
XVIII – NORTHUMBERLAND
Pen and ink
12 ¾ x 9 ½ inches
Illustrated: *Punch*, 6 October 1926, page 389, 'Northumberland' by E V Lucas; *Mr Punch's County Songs*, page 55

272 COUNTY SONGS
XXV – CUMBERLAND
Pen and ink
12 ½ x 9 inches
Illustrated: *Punch*, 11 January 1928, page 53,
'Cumberland' by E V Lucas;
Mr Punch's County Songs, page 13

273 COUNTY SONGS
XXVI – DURHAM
Pen and ink
12 ¾ x 9 ½ inches
Illustrated: Punch, 25 January 1928, page 109,
'Durham' by E V Lucas;
Mr Punch's County Songs, page 21

274 COUNTY SONGS
XXIX – NOTTINGHAMSHIRE
Pen and ink
12 x 8 ¾ inches
Illustrated: *Punch*, 21 March 1928,
page 333, 'Nottinghamshire' by E V Lucas;
Mr Punch's County Songs, page 57

275 COUNTY SONGS
XL – SHROPSHIRE
Pen and ink
12 ½ x 8 ½ inches
Illustrated: *Punch*, 22 August 1928,
page 221, 'Shropshire' by E V Lucas;
Mr Punch's County Songs, page 63

Pooh and Piglet Go To War
This drawing originally formed part of a tribute by members of
the Savage Club to the baritone, George Baker (1885-1976), who
was both honorary secretary and trustee of the club. He was best
known for his contribution to recordings of the Savoy Operas of
Gilbert and Sullivan.

276 POOH AND PIGLET GO TO WAR
Signed
Pen and ink on paper laid on board
4 x 3 ¾ inches
Provenance: George Baker

277 POOH AND PIGLET IN A SNOWSTORM
Signed and dated '12 March 1955'
Pen and ink
3 ¼ x 4 inches
Taken from an autograph book belonging to Rosemary Smith,
goddaughter of Norah Shepard, the second wife of E H Shepard

278 POOH AND PIGLET STRUGGLING WITH A
SEWING MACHINE
Signed and dated 'Nov 14: 1951'
Pen and ink
3 x 4 ½ inches
Taken from an autograph book belonging to Rosemary Smith,
goddaughter of Norah Shepard, the second wife of E H Shepard

193

279 'NEARLY ELEVEN O'CLOCK', SAID POOH HAPPILY
Signed
Pen and ink
4 ¾ x 6 inches
Illustrated: A A Milne, *The House at Pooh Corner*, London: Methuen & Co, 1928, page 3

280 REACHING FOR HONEY
Signed, inscribed 'Replica drawing for Leif Dahlberg' and
dated '28 January 1970' below mount
Pen ink and coloured pencil
4 ¾ x 6 inches

196

281 SHE HABITUALLY WENT INTO AN ENGAGEMENT ON THE QUARTER-DECK
Signed
Signed, inscribed with title and artist's address on reverse
Pen and ink
11 x 7 ¼ inches
Illustrated: Kenneth Grahame, *Dream Days*, London: The Bodley Head, 1930, page 7

'Monsieur Pierre [a beekeeper] regarded me with a look of amused contentment. He is proud of his banksia roses; he adores flowers and birds, and has gained the reputation of a miser because, although he has many sous in his stocking, he does not spend them on gaieties of the town, but finds happiness pottering among his flowers, his fruit trees, his few vegetables, his bees, and his birds. He showed me a little rustic seat whereon he sits when eating his simple déjeuner, and told me proudly that a nightingale sang to him while he ate (they sing day and night in Provence), and had actually made her nest only three feet away.'

(The Honourable Lady Fortescue, *Perfume in Provence*, Edinburgh: W Blackwood & Sons, 1935, pages 48-49)

282 A NIGHTINGALE SANG TO HIM WHILE HE ATE HIS SIMPLE DEJEUNER
Signed and inscribed with title
Pen and ink
10 x 8 inches
Illustrated: The Honourable Lady Fortescue, *Perfume in Provence*, Edinburgh: W Blackwood & Sons, 1935, page 50

197

198

284 MR PUNCH AND HIS DOG
Signed and dated 'July 1943'
Pen and ink
4 ½ x 2 ¾ inches
Taken from an autograph book belonging to
Rosemary Smith, goddaughter of Norah
Shepard, the second wife of E H Shepard

283 NEW GAME FOR NEPTUNE
BRING 'EM DOWN BOYS. I'LL COLLECT THE PIECES
Signed and inscribed with title
Signed and inscribed with artist's address, 'RAF scheme unframed cartoon no 8'
on label on reverse
Pen ink and bodycolour on board, 14 x 10 inches
Illustrated: *Punch*, 28 August 1940, page 215

New Game for Neptune
Here E H Shepard provides a propagandist allegory of the
Battle of Britain, during which the Royal Air Force defended
our shores against the German Luftwaffe. The critical phase
of the battle took place between 24 August and 6 September
1940, when many Luftwaffe pilots were captured or killed,
often as a result of parachuting into the English Channel.
When the battle ended on 31 October, it proved to be a
decisive British victory, and a significant turning point in the
Second World War.

The Vicious Spiral

The term, 'The Vicious Spiral', has been used in discussions of American economics since the early twentieth century. On 7 September 1942, President Franklin D Roosevelt employed it in one of his famous radio 'Fireside Chats' – that concerning 'the Cost of Living and the Progress of War'. About halfway through, he stated:

> If the vicious spiral of inflation ever gets under way, the whole economic system will stagger. Prices and wages will go up so rapidly that the entire production program will be endangered. The cost of the war, paid by taxpayers, will jump beyond all present calculations.

During the following year, he attempted to control wartime inflation, signing Executive Order 9328 on 8 April 1943, which froze prices nationwide on anything that could affect the cost of living, and prohibited wage increases and employment changes except in special circumstances.

As this cartoon indicates, the control of inflation continued to be an issue for Roosevelt. However, he became more preoccupied by the postwar future, as it became clear to him that the United States and its allies would ultimately win the Second World War. As a result, he attended both the Cairo Conference (alongside Churchill and Chiang Kai-shek) and the Tehran Conference (alongside Churchill and Stalin) during November 1943.

Shepard represents Roosevelt's concerns as a confrontation between Uncle Sam and a rattlesnake. While snakes eating their own tails had long been used to denote the circle of life and death, here the snake is coiled to suggest the downward spiral of inflation.

285 THE VICIOUS SPIRAL
HULLO! YOU AGAIN. ALWAYS THE SAME OLD RATTLE
Signed
Inscribed with title below mount
Signed and inscribed with artist's address on reverse
Pen ink and bodycolour on board
11 ½ x 9 inches
Illustrated: *Punch*, 10 November 1943, page 389

199

THE WIND IN THE
TELEGRAPH WIRES

THROUGH these outstretched
aërial wires
That cross the desert dune
I hear the sound of heavenly choirs
That sing a heavenly tune.

What they may say I dare not ask,
Nor ever may divine
From out what transcendental cask
They draw such holy wine.

The telegrams along those wires
Tell tales of woe or bliss
But never telegram inspires
Tune that was like to this.

Locked in their narrow metal shell
Fly round the waiting earth
Tidings from those that buy and sell
And news of death and birth;

But never rumour of these things
Leaks from the pendant wire,
Through whose vibration strangely sings
The high and heavenly choir.

R. P. LISTER

286 THE WIND IN THE TELEGRAPH WIRES
Signed
Inscribed with title and 'Punch' below mount
Pen ink and collage with bodycolour and pencil on board
11 ½ x 17 ¾ inches
Illustrated: *Punch*, 19 April 1950, pages 434-435,
'The Wind in the Telegraph Wires' by R P Lister

The Wind in the Telegraph Wires

Through these outstretched aërial wires
That cross the desert dune
I hear the sound of heavenly choirs
That sing a heavenly tune.

What they may say I dare not ask,
Nor ever may divine
From out what transcendental cask
They draw such holy wine.

The telegrams along those wires
Tell tales of woe or bliss
But never telegram inspires
Tune that was like to this.

Locked in their narrow metal shell
Fly round the waiting earth
Tidings from those that buy and sell
And news of death and birth;

But never rumour of these things
Leaks from the pendant wire,
Through whose vibration strangely sings
The high and heavenly choir.

(R P Lister)

THE ENCHANTED STEED

AN ARTHURIAN LEGEND

FAR in the western woods, unbreathed and rusting, lies
   The ancient steed we rode when we were young.
At the which time we pyghte, in knightly wise,
   Our fair pavilion, of a meagre size,
     The woods among.

One day a damosel we spied, richly bisene,
   Who on a fine two-seater palfrey rode.
So seemly was, and semblant to a queen,
   That we sterte up among the dapple-green
     Of our abode.

Drove she unwarly through the shaws, until at last
   She turned, to spere what venture lay at hand.
And, spying us, was stonied and aghast,
   For that an errant knight could ride so fast
     Across the land.

And walloped she away, and walloped yet amain,
   Till came a time when wallop could no more.
Needless she pulled upon her palfrey's rein,
   And turned, and spered. And there we were again.
     Whereat she swore,

For she was orgulous, and swore a grimly oath,
   Full of despite, and sharper than sharp need.
From which we understood that she was loth
   Ever again for to behold us both.
     Knight and his steed.

Think no mal engyn, damosel, nor shrewd intent,
   Quoth we. For that repenteth us, indeed.
Your gears are all to-brast, your palfrey shent,
   The night draws on, and it is time we went,
     That is our rede.

For noyous paynim woneth in this holty brake,
   And would embushment make of passing wight
Disparpled on the rivage of the lake.
   In such a place it were a great mistake
     To spend the night.

Then made that damosel unmeasurable grame,
   And took the siege behind me, there to sit
And speak in angry steven of the same.
   So, sadly, to a hermitage we came,
     Where she alit.

And from that place we had betimes most stiffly sped,
   But that our boteless steed lacked any spark.
Then laughed she wonderly, and reared her head.
   Enter this hermitage, Sir Knight, she said,
     For it grows dark.

So were we made accord, and of this enterprise
   Made much good chere, for we were young and gay.
Meseems that steed were Merlin in disguise,
   For start it never wold, and there it lies
     Sythen that day.
                R. P. LISTER

287 THE ENCHANTED STEED
Signed
Pen and ink
12 x 9 ¼ inches
Illustrated: *Punch*, Summer Number,
22 May 1950, page 19, 'The
Enchanted Steed: An Arthurian
Legend' by R P Lister

201

202

288 FARM KITCHEN
Signed
Pen and ink on board
11 x 18 ¼ inches
Illustrated: *Punch*, 2 May 1951, pages 550-551,
'Farm Kitchen' by Jesse Baggaley

Farm Kitchen

At thrashing-time men thin and fat
came slowly in and scraped the mat;
and, after hours on drum and ricks
the first they saw was well – scrubbed bricks;
and then the men came from the stable
and all got round the kitchen table.

The spit turned slowly; new bread rose
warm in the pancheon; every nose,
though oily – grimy – full of dust,
became aware of home-made crust!
The day-old chicks cheeped in the grate –
red flannel warming up the crate.

The bacon hanging on the hooks
meant more than pictures, more than books;
the old steel fender winked and shone;
the clock tick-tocked (with one hand gone),
and, dragging chairs, the men sat down –
in the one room they called their own.

And, I'll be bound, I'm with the rest;
of all the rooms the kitchen's best!

(Jesse Baggaley)

289 FOUNTAINS OF ROME
Signed, inscribed with title and dated 1949
Pen and ink on board
13 ¾ x 21 ¾ inches
Illustrated: *Punch*, 19 December 1951,
pages 706-707, 'Fountains of Rome'
by P M Hubbard

Fountains of Rome

Let there be running water near, said Virgil,
And sunlit stones for them to dry their wings;
And even now, two thousand summers later,
The Roman bees rejoice in just these things.

With white stone bees awash with silver water
And brown bees flying live above the foam,
Bees, live and dead, are the familiar spirits
Of half the fountains of much-fountained Rome.

Men come from all the world; they see the fountains
And go. The fountains and the bees remain;
And he who drops his penny into Trevi,
He willy-nilly comes to Rome again;

He smells again sweet water dried in sunlight
He hears the timeless monotone; he sees
The flying silver of the driven waters
Shot with the flying gold of dipping bees.

(P M Hubbard)

E H SHEPARD

204

MIRAGE

WITH traffic rolling like the sea behind me
And grey stone hot beneath like yellow sand,
I used to stand
Long days ago—and let the bright show blind me
To all the dusty horrors of the Strand—
Before each window where a master-hand
Had coiled a virgin rope, in dreams to bind me,
Or scattered great smooth pebbles to remind me
Or rolled a yard of grass—enough to stand
Exultant on and let the cool breeze find me.

And I alone
Among the gazers never once, believe me,
Thrilled to the urgency that bade me own
The shoes or shirts or shorts: commerce had thrown
Her subtle net in vain, could not deceive me:
Out of its strands I was content to weave me
A dream of holiday.
                              Now I atone.
Fresh from my swim each morning I have seen
A bland shop window with a dictaphone
And filing cabinets in olive-green . . . .
The sea is grinding heavy gears to grieve me:
The sand beneath is hot as city stone.

290 MIRAGE
Signed
Pen and ink
13 x 9 ½ inches
Illustrated: *Punch*, 6 August 1952, page 203, 'Mirage'

KEITH HENDERSON

Alan Keith Henderson, OBE RSW RWS ROI RP (1883-1982)

Keith Henderson was a wide-ranging and sometimes idiosyncratic Scottish artist, who was equally skilled as a painter and illustrator. His black and white book illustrations, his posters for the Empire Marketing Board and his commissions as an Official War Artist all show him to have been a master of design.

Keith Henderson was born in Kensington, London, on 16 April 1883, one of the three children of George MacDonald Henderson, barrister-at-law, and Constance Helen (née Keith). His father worked at Lincoln's Inn, and Keith grew up between 18 Kensington Gardens Square, in London, and Campfield House, near Glassel, in Aberdeenshire. He was educated at Orme Square School and Marlborough College, and then studied art, against his father's wishes, at the Slade School of Art and the Académie de la Grande Chaumière, Paris. While in Paris, he shared a studio with Maxwell Armfield, Norman Wilkinson 'of Four Oaks' and the French sculptor, Gaston Lachaise. He and Wilkinson collaborated on his first work as a book illustrator, an elegant edition of Geoffrey Chaucer's translation of *The Romaunt of the Rose* (1908).

Working in London as a portrait painter early in his career, he exhibited at various venues, and was elected to the membership of the Royal Society of Portrait Painters in 1912.

During the First World War, Henderson served in the Royal Wiltshire Yeomanry, rising to the rank of Captain. While on the Western Front, he produced a number of remarkable pastels, which his friend, Ernest Gowers, suggested that he publish with letters that he had written to his fiancée, Helen Knox-Shaw, as an accompanying text. The volume, entitled *Letters to Helen: Impressions of an Artist on the Western Front*, appeared in 1917, the year in which he and Helen married at St Martin-in-the-Fields. The pastels, some of the most beautiful images of war ever made, were Henderson's last illustrations in his earlier style. He was awarded an OBE for his reconnaissance during the war.

From the 1920s, Henderson worked increasingly as an illustrator and poster artist, and made an extensive use of scraperboard. Many of his illustrations reflect his sympathy for the landscapes, wildlife and cultures of non-European civilizations, which he developed through wide travels and study in the British Museum and at London Zoo.

The two-volume edition of W H Prescott's *The Conquest of Mexico* (1922), which is represented here, is his greatest published achievement of this period, matched only in invention by the unpublished drawings for his own project, 'Creatures and Personages: A Book of Assyrian, Egyptian and Greek Mythologies'. His other publications between the wars include several collaborations with his brother-in-law, Eric Rücker Eddison, who was a friend of C S Lewis and J R R Tolkien, and wrote similar kinds of fantasy.

As an advertising artist, Henderson worked especially for the Empire Marketing Board, which sent him to paint in Cyprus for a year and a half. The results were exhibited in 1929, at his dealer, the Beaux Arts Gallery, in Bruton Street. Other paintings were shown at the leading exhibiting societies of which he became a member: the Royal Society of Painters in Water-Colours (ARWS 1930, RWS 1937), the Royal Institute of Painters in Oils (1934) and the Royal Scottish Society of Water-Colour Painters (1936).

Despite the wide exposure of his work in London, Henderson lived mainly in Scotland, sharing his time between Eoligarry, on the Isle of Barra, in the Outer Hebrides, and Achriabhach,

205

291-300 are all illustrated in W H Prescott, The Conquest of Mexico, London: Chatto & Windus, 1922

291 MONTEZUMA OFFERING INCENSE TO QUETZALCOATL
Inscribed with title below mount
Pen and ink with bodycolour
12 ½ x 12 inches
Illustrated: vol one, book ii, chapter vi, page 185

Glen Nevis, by Fort William, Inverness-shire. In 1942, he and Helen moved north from Achriabhach to Chorriechoille, Spean Bridge.

With the outbreak of the Second World War, Henderson became one of the first two painters to be appointed as Official War Artist to the Air Ministry, the other being Paul Nash. Sent to RAF bases in Scotland, he was frustrated to find that William Rothenstein had already made many portrait drawings at the same bases, even though not contracted to the War Artists' Advisory Committee. So Henderson instead concentrated on ground crew, aircraft hangars, repair shops and runways, and among other paintings produced *An Improvised Test of an Under-carriage*. This proved so controversial with the Air Ministry that his contract was not extended. Nevertheless, it was included in the first of the WAAC 'Britain at War' exhibitions, held at the Museum of Modern Art in New York in May 1941, and he continued to paint military subjects throughout the war.

Following the end of the war, Henderson continued to paint, refining his style, so that by the 1970s, he was painting figure groups in minimal settings, often against all-white backgrounds. On the death of his wife in 1971, he sold their Scottish home, and most of their pictures, and moved to London. He died in hospital in South Africa, on 24 February 1982, following an accident in Cape Province. He was 98 years old. In 1970, he had published *Till 21*, a memoir of his earliest years.

His work is represented in numerous public collections, including Imperial War Museums and the Royal Air Force Museum; Manchester Art Gallery and Worthing Museum and Art Gallery; Newport Museum and Art Gallery; and Inverness Museum and Art Gallery and Perth Museum and Art Gallery.

292 MARINA HAD DONE MUCH TO FORTIFY THE DROOPING SPIRITS OF THE SOLDIERS
Pen and ink with bodycolour
5 ½ x 12 inches
Illustrated: vol one, book iii, chapter iii, page 264

The Conquest of Mexico
Originally published in 1843, *The History and Conquest of Mexico* was written by the great American historian and Hispanist, William H Prescott (1796-1859). It was extremely well received, both critically and by the general public, and is considered to be a pioneering and classic work in the field, which has greatly impacted on the study of Spain and Mesoamerica. In his illustrated edition of the work, published in 1922, Keith Henderson did all that he could to match the scholarship of Prescott, and his images complement the text in remarkable ways (as suggested by Benjamin Keen in *The Aztecs in Western Thought*, which is quoted below).

'Keith Henderson made large and imaginative use of Aztec materials in his illustrations for the edition of Prescott's Conquest of Mexico published by Holt in 1922. In his preface Henderson wrote that his edition was the result of his obsession with the idea of making a picture book of the Conquest of Mexico. To master the material he spent weeks in study of the Aztec collections of the British Museum, being greatly aided by the curator, T A Joyce, who presided over those collections …

Henderson's artistic plan for Prescott's book reflected a fine inventive spirit. In Book I, dealing with pre-Cortesian Mexico … he annotated the pages with line drawings from native pictures. Beginning with Book II, Henderson imagined himself as having arrived with the Spaniards, "as a spy to begin with and eventually as a deserter." One does not know which to praise more highly, the charming, meticulously drawn figures taken from codices and other artifacts, in Book I, or the romantic, highly stylized portraits of Spaniards and Indians in action in the rest of the work, containing, in the words of T A Joyce, "the most correct interpretation of ancient Mexican costumes, ornaments, and warlike equipment which have yet supplemented the text of a history of that country."'

(Benjamin Keen, *The Aztecs in Western Thought*, New Brunswick NJ: Rutgers University Press, 1971, page 512)

The Conquest of Mexico in Summary

The Spanish conquest of the Aztec Empire in the early sixteenth century was one of the most significant events in the European colonisation of the Americas.

Montezuma II (or more properly Motehcuzoma) [291] had been ruling the Aztecs for 17 years when a second Spanish expedition, led by Hernándo Cortés, landed on the Gulf Coast in the spring of 1519. Before the Spaniards entered Mexico, Cortés enlisted the support of two valuable aides. A Spanish soldier called Aguilar, who had been taken captive by natives during the first, preliminary expedition, served as an interpreter and a native woman, whom he christened Marina, became both interpreter and mistress.

On arriving in Mexico, Cortés and his expedition found the empire to be in a state of disunity, a fact that they used to their advantage. Not only was there political unrest among the lesser kingdoms, but there was also a growing belief that the benevolent god, Quetzalcoatl (or 'feathered serpent'), was going to return to earth.

Leaving some men to protect the coastal settlement of Vera Cruz, the Spanish marched towards the island capital of Tenochtitlan (now Mexico City). They first experienced resistance from the Tlascalans, a people who were both farmers and warriors. However, after two indecisive battles, the Spaniards effected a victory on 5 September 1519. They then forged ahead, plundering as they went, and finally

293 ARRIVAL OF THE AZTEC TRIBUTE-COLLECTORS
Pen and ink with bodycolour
10 ½ x 12 ½ inches
Illustrated: vol one, book ii, chapter vii, page 205

294 ARREST OF THE EMPEROR MONTEZUMA
Pen and ink with bodycolour
12 ½ x 22 inches
Illustrated: vol one, book iv, chapter iii, page 394-395

207

295 MONTEZUMA WAS SPEECHLESS UNDER THE INFLICTION OF THIS LAST INSULT
Inscribed with title below mount
Pen and ink with bodycolour
12 ½ x 12 inches
Illustrated: vol one, book iv, chapter iii, page 400

296 THE BURNING OF QUAUPOPOCA
Pen and ink
10 ½ x 6 inches
Illustrated: vol one, book iv, chapter iii, page 402

arriving at Tlascala itself. At Cholula, Cortés learned through Marina that, with the support of Montezuma, the natives were planning a conspiracy. Playing on an old enmity between the Tlascalans and the Cholulans, Cortés placed the former people around the city and proceeded to massacre the latter.

As they experienced no further resistance, Cortés and his men advanced to the fertile valley of Mexico. Surprised by their advance and impressed by their power, Montezuma sent his nephew, Cacama, to welcome them. Then, on 8 November 1519, the conquistadors entered Tenochtitlan. Though Montezuma greeted them with ceremony and the Aztecs were outwardly friendly, Cortés remained suspicious of them, because he had received reports that Montezuma had instigated troubles close to Vera Cruz. He had Montezuma arrested [294] and Quaupopoca, governor of the coastal province, burned for his part in the disturbances [296].

In 1520, Montezuma formally announced his subservience to Spain, as did his nobles, and the legend of Quetzalcoatl was revived among the people. However, Cortés had to deal with the formation of a rival Spanish expedition under the leadership of Panfilo de Narvaez. Leaving the capital in the hands of an aide, Pedro de Alvarado, he marched to the coast with a detachment of troops and Indian allies. There he surprised Narvaez and took him prisoner. Meanwhile, with Cortés away, Alvarado so feared conspiracy that he arranged the slaughter of several hundred

208

297 THE PRIESTS, WITH FRANTIC GESTURES, ANIMATING THEM TO AVENGE THEIR INSULTED DEITIES
Pen and ink with bodycolour, 12 ½ x 22 inches
Illustrated: vol two, book v, chapter i, page 70

Aztec nobles, a decision that incited Montezuma's brother, Cuitlahuac, to lead a revolt.

Cortés returned to the capital, with his own band reinforced by two thousand Tlascalans. Montezuma attempted to intercede and pacify his people, but they then turned on him and fatally wounded him. Broken and despairing, he died on 30 June 1520 [**299**].

During the uprising, the Aztecs had destroyed all bridges leading from the island city of Tenochtitlan, so that the Spanish retreat from the city became chaotic, and led to significant losses (an event known as *la noche triste* or 'night of sorrows' [**298**]). However, once on the plains of Otumba, the Spaniards and their Tlascalan allies managed to put the Aztecs to flight. The Spaniards retreated into the territory of Tlascalans, who fortunately remained friendly; indeed, their chief became the first native to be successfully converted to Christianity, before he died of smallpox.

Montezuma's nephew and second successor, Guatemozin, had sworn to drive the Spaniards from his country. However, Cortés managed to gather more Indian auxiliaries from among the friendly tribes to lead against the Aztecs. Welcomed in Tezcuco by the new prince, Ixtlilxochitl, an enemy of Montezuma, Cortés' forces advanced for the final subjugation of the Aztec civilization (epitomized by the torture of Guatemozin [**300**]).

298 THE 'NOCHE TRISTE'
Pen and ink with bodycolour
11 x 12 ½ inches
Illustrated: vol two, book v, chapter iii, pages 110-111

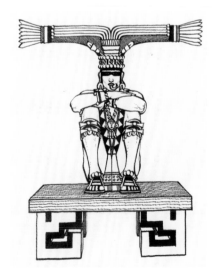

299 ON MONTEZUMA'S DEATH, HIS BROTHER, CUITLAHUAC, SUCCEEDED HIM
Pen and ink with bodycolour
8 x 7 inches
Illustrated: vol two, book v, chapter v, page 138

300 THE TORTURING OF THE EMPEROR GUATEMOZIN
Pen and ink with bodycolour
14 x 11 ½ inches
Illustrated: vol two, book vii, chapter i, page 311

209

13
HELEN JACOBS

HELEN JACOBS

Helen Mary Jacobs, BWS (1888-1970)

Talented in both draughtsmanship and watercolour painting, Helen Jacobs soon established herself as a children's illustrator. Though best known for the precision, energy and imagination of her early fairy subjects, she responded well to a variety of commissions; and, as a primary teacher, she seemed an ideal interpreter of textbooks and primers.

For a biography of Helen Jacobs, please refer to *The Illustrators*, 2007, page 11.

Nos **301** to **315** were all drawn for and probably illustrated in Constance M Martin, *The Wild Swans and Other Stories*, which is said to have been published in 'The Golden Readers' series, though the publisher has not been identified. Helen Jacobs collaborated with Constance M Martin on textbooks published by Philip & Tacey and Martins Press between the 1930s and the 1950s.

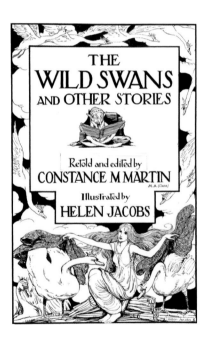

301 THE WILD SWANS AND OTHER STORIES FROM HANS ANDERSEN
TITLE PAGE
Signed
Pen and ink
12 x 7 ½ inches
Provenance: The Estate of Constance M Martin

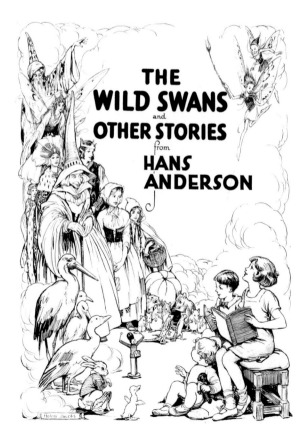

302 THE WILD SWANS AND OTHER STORIES FROM HANS ANDERSEN
FRONT COVER
Signed
Pen and ink
14 ½ x 10 ½ inches
Provenance: The Estate of Constance M Martin

The Wild Swans

For a summary of 'The Wild Swans', please see page 95.

303 ELEVEN PRINCES WALKING TO SCHOOL
Signed
Pen and ink with pencil
6 ½ x 7 ¾ inches

304 THEY FLEW OUT OF THE WINDOW
Signed
Pen and ink with pencil
11 x 8 inches

305 THE QUEEN AND THE THREE TOADS
Signed
Pen and ink
6 x 6 ¾ inches

212

306 THREE SCARLET POPPIES
FLOATED ON THE WATER
Signed
Pen and ink
11 x 8 inches

307 ELISE AND HER BROTHERS ON THE ROCK
Signed
Pen and ink with pencil
6 ¾ x 7 ¾ inches

214

309 ELISE AND THE FLUTTERING BIRDS
Signed
Pen and ink with pencil
6 ¾ x 8 inches

310 THE KING ENTERED THE CAVE AND STOOD AMAZED
Signed
Pen and ink with pencil
11 x 8 inches

311 THE KING AND ELISE ON HORSEBACK
Signed
Pen and ink with pencil
4 ½ x 5 ¾ inches

312 ELISE AND WAITING-WOMEN
Signed
Pen and ink with pencil
6 ¼ x 7 ¾ inches

216

313 ELISE WORKED AT THE ELEVENTH SHIRT
Signed
Pen and ink with pencil
11 x 7 ¾ inches

314 AS THE SUN ROSE, ELEVEN SWANS FLEW AWAY
Signed
Pen and ink
6 x 7 ½ inches
Provenance: The Estate of Constance M Martin

315 ELISE PLUCKED
THE STINGING NETTLES
Signed
Pen and ink with pencil
10 ¾ x 7 ¾ inches

The Emperor's New Clothes

For a summary of 'The Emperor's New Clothes', please see page 91.

316 THE BOY CALLED OUT THAT THE EMPEROR
HAS NO CLOTHES
Signed
Pen and ink with pencil
10 ½ x 7 ½ inches

The Goblin and the Grocer

The Goblin and the Grocer
A goblin lives with a grocer, because the grocer gave him a bowl
of porridge at Christmas. One day, a student, lodging in the
grocer's attic, comes into the shop to buy cheese and candles.
On discovering that the grocer is wrapping cheese in pages from a
poetry book, he buys the book rather than the cheese, and jokes
that the grocer knows nothing about poetry. So offended is the
goblin by the joke that he uses magic to give voice to the things in
the room, all of which agree that poetry is useless. The goblin
goes to tell this to the student but, peeping through the keyhole,
sees the student reading the book, out of which is growing a
marvellous tree of light. The goblin has never seen anything so
splendid and, while he goes to the grocer in order to be fed,
returns to look at the effects of the book whenever possible.
When a fire breaks out in the town, the goblin runs to save the
book and realizes that he now thinks that it is the greatest
treasure in the house. However, he continues to divide his time
between the grocer and student, because the student has no
porridge to spare.

317 GOBLIN WITH A PLATE OF PORRIDGE
Signed
Pen and ink with pencil
6 ½ x 7 ½ inches

318 THE GOBLIN SKIPPED OUT
ON TO THE ROOF AND SAT THERE
Signed
Pen and ink with pencil
10 ¾ x 7 ¾ inches

14

POST-WAR CARTOONISTS

VICKY
(1913-1966)

NORMAN THELWELL
(1923-2004)

GERARD HOFFNUNG
(1925-1959)

LARRY
(1927-2003)

VICKY
Victor Weisz, FSIA (1913-1966), known as 'Vicky'

Four years after his arrival from Germany in 1935, Vicky prepared for his work as political cartoonist of the *News Chronicle* by making a year's study of English culture and society. Developing a brittle and biting pen line, he then drew for the *Daily Mirror* and the *Evening Standard*, for which he created 'Supermac', his highly memorable caricature of Harold Macmillan.

For a biography of Vicky, please refer to *The Illustrators*, 2011, page 196.

His work is represented in numerous public collections, including the National Portrait Gallery; and the British Cartoon Archive, University of Kent (Canterbury).

Further reading:
Ritchie-Calder (*rev*), 'Weisz, Victor [*pseud.* Vicky] (1913-1966)', H C G Matthew and Brian Harrison (eds), *Oxford Dictionary of National Biography*, Oxford University Press, 2004, vol 57, pages 958-959; Russell Davies and Liz Ottaway, *Vicky*, London: Secker & Warburg, 1987

'Vicky made himself the best cartoonist in the world'

(Michael Foot, *Debts of Honour*, London: Davis Poynter, 1980, page 158)

319 PORTER!
'MY BED OF NAILS' — MR RAY GUNTER OCT.17.1964
Signed and inscribed with title
Pen ink and crayon
13 ¾ x 18 ¾ inches
Probably drawn for but not illustrated in the *Evening Standard*, 6 September 1965

Porter!
Ray Gunter (1909-1977) was Minister of Labour between 1964 and 1968, as a member of the first ministry of the Labour Prime Minister, Harold Wilson. Having had a background in the railway industry, he was a member of the trades union, the Transport Salaried Staffs' Association, and had to compromise his union allegiance to fulfil his ministerial responsibilities. Deciding to support Wilson, in taking a hard line on wildcat strikes that threatened to damage the economy, he described his time as Minister of Labour as a 'bed of nails'.

A cartoon of a similar subject was published in the *Evening Standard* on 6 September 1965. It shows George Brown, the First Secretary for State, at the TUC Conference, introducing Ray Gunter, who is sitting, fakir-like, on a bed of nails.

320 LAURENCE OLIVIER AND VIVIEN LEIGH
Signed and inscribed with title
Pen ink and watercolour on board
15 x 10 inches

321 RALPH RICHARDSON
Signed and inscribed with title
Pen ink and watercolour on board
13 x 6 ½ inches

NORMAN THELWELL
Norman Thelwell (1923-2004)

Norman Thelwell is arguably the most popular cartoonist to have worked in Britain since the Second World War. Though almost synonymous with his immortal subject of little girls and their fat ponies, his work is far more wide ranging, perceptive – and indeed prescient – than that association suggests.

322 THELWELL ON HOLIDAY (top)
WHEN VISITING HISTORIC BUILDINGS DO NOT LET THE CHILDREN
INTERFERE WITH THE EXHIBITS
TRY NOT TO MISS ANY POINTS OF INTEREST ...
AND NEVER WANDER ROUND WITHOUT THE GUIDE
Pen and ink, 5 ¼ x 14 ¾ inches
Illustrated: *Sunday Express*, 23 August 1964, page 15

323 THELWELL ON HOLIDAY (above)
BEFORE STARTING THE JOURNEY HOME,
TAKE SOME ANTI-SICKNESS PILLS ...
YOU ARE GOING TO NEED THEM ...
WHEN YOU SEE THE STATE OF YOUR GARDEN
Pen and ink, 5 ¼ x 14 ¾ inches
Illustrated: *Sunday Express*, 6 September 1964, page 20

For a biography of Norman Thelwell, please refer to *The Illustrators*, 2009, page 25.

Having mounted major exhibitions of the work of Thelwell in 1989 and 1991, Chris Beetles encouraged further interest in the artist in 2009 with 'The Definitive Thelwell' and its accompanying catalogue. The 100 page catalogue surveys all aspects of his career, through 177 illustrations, an appreciation, a biographical chronology and a full bibliography.

324 BE MY VALENTINE
Signed
Pen ink and watercolour
6 ½ x 8 ¾ inches
Illustrated: *Daily Express*,
14 February 1965, page 20

223

325-329 are all inscribed with title below mount

325 OH HE SAW OUR PICNIC THINGS ALRIGHT! AND OUR TRANSISTOR
Signed
Pen and ink
7 x 10 ½ inches
Illustrated: *Daily Express*,
6 June 1965, page 20

326 THEY'RE ONLY GERMS, BUT HE GREW
THEM HIMSELF
Signed
Pen and ink
7 ¾ x 10 ¾ inches
Illustrated: *Daily Express*, 4 April 1965, page 20

327 I WISH THEY WOULD GET ON WITH
NATIONALISING LAND, LIKE THEY PROMISED
Signed
Pen and ink
7 x 9 ½ Inches
Illustrated: *Daily Express*, 5 June 1966, page 20

224

328 WHO PUT MY STAMP COLLECTION
ON THE CONVECTION HEATER?
Signed
Pen ink and watercolour
7 ½ x 10 ½ inches
Illustrated: *Daily Express*, 27 November 1966,
page 26

329 DIDN'T YOU HEAR THE SONIC
BANG MISTER?
Signed
Pen and ink
7 ½ x 10 ½ inches
Illustrated: *Daily Express*, 16 July 1967, page 4

225

GERARD HOFFNUNG

Gerard Hoffnung (1925-1959)

Gerard Hoffnung developed a unique vein of gentle, yet powerful humour through drawings, lectures and even concerts – for his favourite subject was music at its most delightful and daft.

For a biography of Gerard Hoffnung, please refer to *The Illustrators*, 2011, page 257.

Further reading:
Annetta Hoffnung, *Gerard Hoffnung*, London: Gordon Fraser, 1988; Richard Ingrams (rev), 'Hoffnung, Gerard [*formerly* Gerhardt] (1925-1959)', H C G Matthew and Brian Harrison (eds), *Oxford Dictionary of National Biography*, Oxford University Press, 2004, vol 27, pages 523-524

226

330 DON'T OPEN
TILL CHRISTMAS
Signed
Pen ink, watercolour
and bodycolour
8 ¼ x 8 ¼ inches
Design for a Gordon Fraser
greeting card

LARRY

Terence Parkes (1927-2003), known as 'Larry'

Larry was the cartoonist's cartoonist, highly respected by his peers for his consistently funny work, and cherished by them for his affability. In the autobiographical *Larry on Larry* (1994), he wrote, 'I seem to have the reputation for being a beer-swigging Brummie cartoonist', and while each particular of that statement may have been true, its overall spirit suggests an essential modesty. He even expressed some reservations about the increasing seriousness with which cartooning was being taken, and yet was steeped in the history of his profession and, more widely, in the history of art. This combination of the easy-going and the erudite informed much of his work, in content and draughtsmanship, and he will long be remembered for both his frequent depiction of an Everyman figure, 'Larry's man', and his parodies of famous works of art.

For a biography of Larry, please refer to *The Illustrators*, 2014, page 226.

His work is represented in the collections of the British Museum and the V&A; and the British Cartoon Archive, University of Kent (Canterbury), and the University of Essex.

227

331 OVERMANNING
BY FORD MADOX BROWN
Signed
Pen ink and watercolour
10 ½ x 14 ¾ inches

332 SANDERSON
WILLIAM BLAKE PATTERN
Signed
Pen ink and watercolour
7 ½ x 10 inches

333 ASSOCIATION FOOTBALL
BY ROY LICHTENSTEIN
Signed
Pen ink and watercolour
11 x 14 inches

334 THE PEASANT WEDDING
WITH BANANA SKIN
Signed
Pen ink and watercolour
12 x 14 ¼ inches

335 NIGHT WATCH (opposite)
MEMBERS OF THE AMSTERDAM ALLOTMENT HOLDERS GUILD
ON GUARD DUTY 1642
Signed
Pen ink and watercolour
15 x 14 inches

NIGHT WATCH
MEMBERS OF THE AMSTERDAM ALLOTMENT HOLDERS GUILD ON GUARD DUTY 1642

15
HARGREAVES DRAWS PADDINGTON

HARRY HARGREAVES

Harry Hargreaves, MSIAD (1922-2004)

The artist, animator and writer, Harry Hargreaves, was the finest British animal cartoonist of his generation, with 'outstanding skill at drawing movement' and 'real knowledge of how animals move' (William Hewison). His abilities are seen to their best both in his own creations, 'The Bird' and 'Hayseeds', and in his interpretations of Michael Bond's Paddington Bear for the *Blue Peter* annuals.

Harry Hargreaves was born in Manchester on 9 February 1922, the elder son of Harry Hargreaves, a civil servant in the Ministry of Labour, and Eugenie (née Ince). He became a choirboy at Manchester Cathedral at the age of eight (1930-33), and began to teach himself to draw cartoons at the age of nine. Then, in 1936, at the age of 14, and while still at Chorlton High School, he published his first cartoon in the *Manchester Evening News*.

Following the divorce of his parents, Hargreaves left school at the age of 16, in 1938, and joined a local interior design company – while, in his spare time, he studied architecture, furniture design and mechanical drawing at Manchester School of Art. Within a year, he was working as a trainee engineer, and gaining experience with such companies as Rolls-Royce, Ford and Kestrel Engines. But soon after, he was hired by the Manchester art agency, Kayebon Press, and began assisting Hugh McNeil with his strips for *The Beano* and *The Dandy*.

During the Second World War, Hargreaves served in the RAFVR Signals, first in the United Kingdom (1940-41), and later in the Far East (1941-45). While in service, he contributed to *Blighty* (1940) and various air force magazines, and designed official Christmas cards for RAF Ceylon Postal Services (1942-43).

After the war, Hargreaves joined J Arthur Rank's Gaumont British Animation Ltd, in Cookham, Berkshire, as a cartoon animator (1946-50). While there, he met Penny Vickery, who was working at the company as an inker and painter, and they married in 1948. They would have two daughters.

When the Cartoon Unit disbanded, Hargreaves turned freelance for three years, creating and developing strips for Amalgamated Press comics, including 'Harold Hare' for *The Sun*, and producing advertising drawings for Dunlops, Pickering and Rowntrees.

In 1953, Hargreaves moved to Amsterdam to join Toonder Film Studios, working as a Master Cartoonist for Marten Toonder, the 'Dutch Disney'. While living there, he took over Toonder's cartoon strip, 'Panda', which was syndicated to 150 daily newspapers across Europe, including the London *Evening News*. Returning to England in 1954, he continued this strip until 1961, while contributing on a freelance basis to many national newspapers and magazines, including *The Christian Science Monitor*, *The Countryman*, *The Cricketer*, *Lilliput*, *Men Only*, *Punch* and *The Tatler*.

Hargreaves' best known creation is probably 'The Bird', an indeterminate scruffy little bird, which first appeared as a wordless strip in *Punch* on 29 October 1958, and later worldwide, including in colour on *TV-am* as 'Early Bird' (1985-87). Many of the cartoons were collected in four volumes between 1961 and 1967.

In 1961, Hargreaves created a fox called 'Gogo' for *Discs-a-Gogo*, a new pop music programme produced by Television Wales & West (TWW). The character proved so popular that the programme was syndicated throughout Europe between 1961 and 1965.

336-349 are all illustrated in *Blue Peter,* Eighth Book, London: British Broadcasting Corporation, 1971, 'Paddington Weighs In' by Michael Bond

336 PADDINGTON HEADED DOWN WINDSOR GARDENS AS FAST AS HIS LEGS WOULD CARRY HIM
Pen and ink
3 ¾ x 4 inches
Illustrated: page 58

Another major success was 'Hayseeds', which was inspired by 'Pogo', a strip by the American cartoonist, Walt Kelly. Containing British wildlife characters such as Toby the Badger, it ran in the *Evening News* between 1968 and 1970, was syndicated internationally and gave rise to two books.

Having produced so many original animal cartoons, it seems only proper that he should have turned to interpreting such a classic character as Michael Bond's Paddington Bear. Applying his characteristic vitality, he illustrated Bond's 'Paddington' stories for BBC TV's *Blue Peter* annuals between 1969 and 1980. He also illustrated a 1983 edition of Kenneth Grahame's *The Wind in the Willows*.

Hargreaves produced advertising drawings for Barclays Bank, Kelloggs, Guinness, Saxa Salt, the Coal Board, Walls and Post Office Telegrams; greetings cards for Sharpes (1987-88), and designs for mechanical and soft toys.

His extensive illustration work for the publications of the Army Air Corps and Wildlife and Wetlands Trust, led to an Honorary Membership of the former and an Honorary Life Fellowship of the latter. He was also a member of both the British Cartoonists' Association and the Society of Industrial Artists and Designers.

In 1989, Hargreaves suffered an aneurism, and his health never fully recovered. He died in Yeovil of cancer on 12 November 2004.

His work is represented in the British Cartoon Archive, University of Kent (Canterbury).

Further reading:
Mark Bryant, 'Harry Hargreaves', *Independent*, 22 November 2004 [obituary]; Paul Gravett, 'Harry Hargreaves', *Guardian*, 8 December 2004 [obituary]

231

Paddington Weighs In
Catching the end of *Blue Peter* on BBC television, Paddington believes that its presenters – Val, John and Peter – have been robbed of all their savings while staying at a new hotel near his home. He decides to investigate the robbery, and books into the hotel. Almost immediately the receptionist ushers him into a room where he receives a strenuous massage from Mr Constantine, followed by sessions in the steam bath and cold pool. This is enough to make him think that he has solved the mystery of the robbery, for if Val, John and Peter had 'spent only a quarter of the time he had with Mr Constantine they'd probably been in no fit state to resist any kind of attack'. He is then offered dinner, but is given just one small spoonful of carrot juice, so brings out the marmalade sandwich that he has been keeping under his hat. The other guests, who have been surviving on equally small rations, advance towards him. He is saved just in time by the arrival of the Browns, the family that looks after him. The receptionist then explains to him that the hotel is actually a health centre, and that Val, John and Peter had lost pounds in weight rather than in money.

337 PADDINGTON FALLS OFF HIS CHAIR IN ASTONISHMENT
Inscribed with artist's notes below mount
Pen and ink
5 x 4 ¾ inches
Illustrated: page 58

232

339 PADDINGTON MEETS MR CONSTANTINE II
Pen and ink
3 ¼ x 3 ¼ inches
Illustrated: page 60 [printed in green]

338 PADDINGTON CHECKS IN
Pen and ink
3 x 4 inches
Illustrated: page 59

340 PADDINGTON MEETS MR CONSTANTINE I
Pen ink and pencil on tracing paper
3 x 3 ¾ inches
Preliminary drawing for page 60

341 PADDINGTON LOOKS UP AT MR CONSTANTINE
Pencil on tracing paper
2 ¾ x 1 ¾ inches
Preliminary drawing

342 PADDINGTON ENTERS THE STEAM ROOM
Pen and ink
3 ¾ x 4 ¼ inches
Illustrated: page 61 [printed in green]

343 ICE COLD PADDINGTON
Pen and ink
3 ¼ x 3 inches
Illustrated: page 61 [printed in green]

233

344 OUT OF THE
COLD POOL
Inscribed with title below mount
Pen ink and pencil
3 x 3 ¼ inches
Preliminary drawing for page 61

345 PADDINGTON
HEADS HOME TO
WINDSOR GARDENS
Signed
Pen and ink
5 ½ x 5 inches
Illustrated: page 63
[printed in purple]

HARRY HARGREAVES

234

346 THE SPOON OF
ORANGE COLOURED
LIQUID
Pen and ink
2 ¾ x 2 ¾ inches
Illustrated: page 62
[printed in purple]

347 SECONDS!
Inscribed 'Level measure
of orange coloured liquid to
combine with P's emotional
outburst about "seconds!"'
below mount
Pen ink and pencil on
tracing paper
2 ¾ x 2 ¾ inches
Preliminary drawing
for page 62

348 PADDINGTON'S
SANDWICH BLISS
Pen and ink
3 ½ x 3 inches
Illustrated: page 62
[printed in purple]

349 PADDINGTON
EATS A MARMALADE
SANDWICH
Inscribed with title and with
artist's notes below mount
Pen ink and pencil on
tracing paper
3 ¾ x 4 ¼ inches
Preliminary drawing
for page 62

16
RONALD SEARLE

350-356 are taken from a sketch book of theatre drawings, circa 1950-55

RONALD SEARLE

Ronald William Fordham Searle, CBE (1920-2011)

Equally inspired by a wide range of experience and a great knowledge of the history of caricature, Ronald Searle honed an incisive graphic skill to develop an unparalleled graphic oeuvre, an oeuvre that made him the most popular and influential cartoonist-illustrator of his time.

For a biography of Ronald Searle, please refer to *The Illustrators,* 2007, pages 355-356; for essays on various aspects of the artist's achievements, see *The Illustrators*, 1999, pages 228-230; and *The Illustrators*, 2000, pages 40-42.

Key works illustrated: Contributed to *Punch* (from 1946); *Hurrah for St Trinian's* (1948); Geoffrey Willans, *Down with Skool!* (1953)

His work is represented in numerous public collections, including the British Museum and the V&A; and the Bibliothèque Nationale (Paris).

Further reading: Russell Davies, *Ronald Searle*, London: Sinclair Stevenson, 1990

Chris Beetles Gallery held the major tribute exhibition, 'Ronald Searle Remembered', in May-June 2012. It was accompanied by a 200 page fully illustrated catalogue, containing newly researched essays and notes.

Ring Round the Moon

No **350** is one of a number of studies that Ronald Searle made at the first night of *Ring Round the Moon* in preparation for a caricature that appeared in *Punch* on 8 February 1950.

Ring Round the Moon is a translation by Christopher Fry of Jean Anouilh's *L'Invitation au Château*, which had premiered in Paris in 1947. Fry's version opened three years later at the Globe Theatre (now known as the Gielgud) in a production directed by Peter Brook.

As Eric Keown explained in his *Punch* review, 'What I shall chiefly remember, apart from a certain airy charm that hangs indefinably about the evening, will be Miss Margaret Rutherford [as Madame Desmortes], cheroot in mouth and snuff in nostril, booming with malice from a bathchair …' (*Punch*, 8 February 1950, page 161)

350 MARGARET RUTHERFORD
Sketch of Margaret Rutherford and Claire Bloom on reverse
Pencil
9 ½ x 7 ¾ inches

351 ARTHUR ASKEY
Inscribed 'White shirt, belt, golden silk tie, egg blue apron, pink edged, fawn trs, brown shoes'
Pencil
8 ½ x 7 ½ inches

236

(reverse)

352 JOHN NEVILLE AS RICHARD II
Pencil sketches of Eric Porter on reverse
Pencil
9 ½ x 6 inches
Preliminary drawing for *Punch*, 26 January
1955, page 157

(reverse)

353 JOHN NEVILLE AS RICHARD II
Inscribed 'John Neville'
Pencil sketches of the head of Eric Porter on reverse
Pencil, 7 ½ x 7 inches
Preliminary drawing for *Punch*, 26 January
1955, page 157

Richard II

These are two of a number of studies that Searle made at the first night of a production of Shakespeare's *Richard II* in preparation for a caricature that appeared in *Punch* on 26 January 1955.

Writing in *Punch*, Eric Keown stated positively that

> Michael Benthall's *Richard II* is the most complete expression of Shakespeare given us by the [Old Vic] for quite a long time …

> Since I first saw John Neville nearly three years ago in the Bristol Old Vic's *The Two Gentlemen of Verona* I have thought him a very interesting young actor, who was taking the trouble to learn to speak verse, and wasn't content with a presence and profile which suggested a comfortable passage to Hollywood …

> His Richard is a delicate and consistent piece of work, that balances the king's character between the weakness of a playboy and the imagination of a man so gifted that but for the accident of the throne he might have made something of his life.

The production was such a success that it was taken, with other plays by Shakespeare, to New York in October 1956, and ran at the Winter Garden Theatre until 12 January 1957.

A Kind of Folly

These are three of a number of studies that Searle made at the first night of *A Kind of Folly* in preparation for a caricature that appeared in *Punch* on 23 February 1955.

Premiering at the Duchess Theatre, *A Kind of Folly* by Owen Holder was described by *Punch* theatre critic, Eric Keown, as 'a comedy of manners' inspired by Wilde and Maugham, but 'weighed down by juvenile jokes'. At its heart is the question, 'Shall this middle-aged play-boy (an intolerably dull dog) take back his wife, or shall he marry his mistress?' Unfortunately, 'As the wife, a thin part, Flora Robson is miscast and sadly wasted', while 'Wilfrid Hyde White gives his own casual edge to irresponsible cynicism, but with heavy repetition it grows blunted' (*Punch*, 23 February 1955, page 272).

While Flora Robson and Wilfrid Hyde-White had glittering careers on stage and screen, Owen Holder developed more quietly as a writer – and actor – for television. He also appeared in *A Kind of Folly* as 'a very tiresome boy' (loc cit).

237

354 FLORA ROBSON
Pencil
9 ¾ x 7 ½ inches
Preliminary drawing for *Punch*,
23 February 1955, page 272

355 FLORA ROBSON
Pencil sketch of a profile of Jean Kent's head on reverse
Pencil
10 ½ x 6 inches
Preliminary drawing for *Punch*,
23 February 1955, page 272

356 WILFRID HYDE-WHITE
Pencil
9 ½ x 6 inches
Preliminary drawing for *Punch*,
23 February 1955, page 272

357 FANNY'S FIRST PLAY
PUNCH THEATRE – EDINBURGH
FESTIVAL – LYCEUM THEATRE
JUGGINS ... ROBIN BAILEY
DORA DELANEY ... BRENDA BRUCE
Signed and inscribed with title and
'Edinburgh'
Pen and ink
15 ½ x 16 inches
Illustrated: *Punch*, 12 September 1956,
page 318

'Those of us who saw Village Wooing [1933] a few years ago in London were the less surprised that at seventy-seven Shaw should have written such a crackling little comedy, which says with absolute economy so much that he said elsewhere at greater length about sex …

This sparkling curtain-raiser over, the curtain rose on a patchy production of Fanny's First Play [1911]. In any case it is poor Shaw. His tilt at respectability, by upsetting the household gods of two appalling families, does produce a certain comic dividend in the third act, but in the meantime we have had to pay heavily in forced facetiousness. As the butler who settles everything by being a Duke's broker, Robin Bailey gave a performance of polished green-baize authority. After him Miss Bruce and Mr Denison were the best of a cast whose tail was [an Edinburgh Festival] surprise. Edwardian décor is unyielding, I know, but if the colours here were supposed to be part of the joke they hurt too much to be funny.'

(Eric Keown, 'At the Play', *Punch*, 12 September 1956, page 318)

358 DONALD WOLFIT AS MALATESTA I
Pencil sketch of Donald Wolfit on reverse
Pencil
8 x 5 inches
Preliminary drawing for *Punch*, 3 April 1957, page 454
Taken from a sketch book of Paris, circa 1957-59

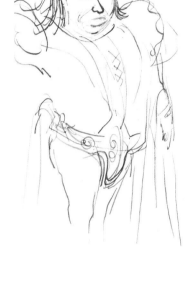

(reverse)

Malatesta

These are two of a number of studies that Searle made of the first night of *Malatesta* in preparation for a caricature that appeared in *Punch* on 3 April 1957.

Henry de Montherlant's *Malatesta*, premiered in Paris in 1950, and received its London debut, in a translation by Jonathan Griffin, at the Lyric Hammersmith seven years later. *Punch* theatre critic, Eric Keown, considered the play

(reverse)

> to have scenes of considerable excitement in its study of a full-blooded Renaissance lord fencing for power with a cunning and able Pope. *Malatesta* is an outsize animal, has respect for nothing except beauty, and his plan to stab the Pope is completely in character. As Tamburlaine did, he suits Donald Wolfit, always prepared for a tremendous expenditure of nervous energy. Much of the performance is good, though at times Mr Wolfit drives it a little far, when *Malatesta* becomes slightly a caricature, drawing laughs surely not intended by his austere author.
> (*Punch*, 3 April 1957, pages 453-454)

239

359 DONALD WOLFIT AS MALATESTA II
Pencil
Pencil sketch of Donald Wolfit's head on reverse
8 x 5 inches
Preliminary drawing for *Punch*, 3 April 1957, page 454
Taken from a sketch book of Paris, circa 1957-59

240

Long John's other Leg

Sea dogs along the Thames tell of the time when Long John Silver lost his leg in a bloody brawl, shortly after his ladylove had presented him with a pair of Allen Solly hose. To please her—and his vanity—he thenceforth wore the extra sock on his head—which, they solemnly say, is the origin of the pirate's stocking-hat.

360 LONG JOHN'S OTHER LEG
Signed
Inscribed with title below mount
Pen and ink
12 x 6 inches
Design for an advertisement for the clothing company, Allen Solly & Co, which appeared in *The New Yorker*, on 17 November 1951, among other publications

361 EUNICE! HOW MANY TIMES MUST I TELL YOU – TAKE THE BAND OFF FIRST!
Signed, inscribed with title and dated 1951
Pen and ink
11 ½ x 7 ½ inches
Illustrated: *Lilliput*, April 1951; Ronald Searle, *Back to the Slaughterhouse and Other Ugly Moments*, London: Macdonald, 1951, page 50; Ronald Searle, *The Curse of St Trinian's*, London: Pavilion Books, 1993, page 49

**362 EXPORTING FOR THE SMALLER
BUSINESS**
Signed and inscribed with title and 'Lloyds Brochure'
Stamped with artist's agent stamp and copyright
stamp and dated 1981 on reverse
Pen ink and watercolour with crayon
16 ½ x 11 ½ inches
Drawn for a Lloyds Bank Brochure, 1981,
'Exporting for the Smaller Business'

363 LLOYDS BANK TRUST DIVISION
Signed
Inscribed 'Money Management' below mount
Stamped with agent's label and copyright label and
dated 1981 on reverse
Pen ink and watercolour with pencil
16 ½ x 10 ¾ inches
Drawn for a Lloyds Bank Brochure, 1981

364-367 are from the series of medals, 'Six Fathers of Caricature', commissioned and struck by the French Mint, 1976-77

'In 1973, Pierre Dehaye, Director of the French Mint (La Monnaie), had asked Searle in the aftermath of his Bibliothèque Nationale exhibition to design a self-portrait medal for the eventual issue to subscribers. In Britain, where the concept "medal" is almost entirely bound up with the monarchy, patronage and the approval of the state, the tradition of the art-medal is very weak; but the continent of Europe has kept alive the Renaissance practice of striking medals as personal expressions of the urge to commemorate and celebrate. Searle's auto-médaille, struck in June 1974 as a limited edition and subsequently issued as a general release, displayed his most famous self-portrait sketch of that period, a quite unjustly cruel three-quarter profile … Dehaye went on to approve a whole series of Searle medals in honour of 'Six Fathers of Caricature', none of whom (Carracci, Ghezzi, Hogarth, Gillray, Rowlandson and George Cruikshank) belonged to the French tradition at all … Searle's early medals were drawn rather than modelled: incised, that is, as designs in the flat medal rather than upheavals of it in relief … Following the flight from Paris, however, Searle did progress to three full worked dimensions, submitting each medal in the form of a clay maquette, and these were a literally outstanding success.'

(Russell Davies, *Ronald Searle*, London: Chris Beetles Ltd, 2003, pages 166 & 167)

242

(reverse)

364 WILLIAM HOGARTH 1697-1764
PHIZ-MONGER
Signed
Bronze medal
3 ¼ inches diameter

(reverse)

(reverse)

365 JAMES GILLRAY 1756-1815
CARICATURISTE
Signed on reverse
Bronze medal
3 ¼ inches diameter

366 THOMAS ROWLANDSON 1756-1827
CARICATURISTE
Signed
Bronze medal
3 ¼ inches diameter

(reverse)

(reverse)

367 GEORGE CRUIKSHANK 1792-1878
CARICATURISTE
Signed on reverse
Bronze medal
3 ¼ inches diameter

368 GEORGE GROSZ 1893-1959
CARICATURISTE
Signed
Bronze
3 inches diameter

(reverse)   (reverse)

369 EDWARD LEAR 1812-1888
PERE DU NON-SENS
Signed
Bronze, 3 inches diameter
Commissioned and struck by the French Mint, 1979-83

370 JAMES THURBER 1894-1961
Signed
Bronze
3 inches diameter
Commissioned and struck by the French Mint, 1979-83

17
ROY GERRARD

246

ROY GERRARD
Roy Gerrard (1935-1997)

Roy Gerrard was best known for his delightful picture books, which 'charmed children with … bouncy rhymes and thumb-shaped characters acting out their adventures – and misadventures – in sumptuous period settings' (Wolfgang Saxon, *The New York Times*, 13 August 1997, 'Obituary').

The son of a coal miner, Roy Gerrard was born in Atherton, Lancashire, on 25 January 1935. His artistic talent was recognised at an early age and, in 1948, at the age of 13, he won a scholarship to train at Salford School of Art. Focusing on etching and lithography, among other subjects, he received a National Diploma in Art and Design in 1954. While working as an abstract oil painter in his spare time, he taught Art at Egerton Park County Secondary School, in Denton, rising to become head of the department. He then held the equivalent position at Hyde Grammar School, Hyde (1966-80).

An enthusiastic cyclist and rock climber, Gerrard suffered a climbing accident in 1972 and, while laid up, began to paint in watercolour. Realising that this was his 'true medium', he abandoned oil, which he had grown to dislike, and destroyed his work to date. He came to the attention of an interior designer, Glynn Stockdale, who collected his pictures. This led to him leaving his teaching career, in 1980, to paint full time. He exhibited at the Royal Academy, and had solo shows at the Seen Gallery, London, between 1978 and 1985, and also at the Crescent Gallery, New Orleans, and in Atlanta, Georgia.

In 1981, Gerrard illustrated his first book for children, *Matilda Jane*, written by his wife, Jean, head of the lower school at Marple Ridge High School, Stockport, Cheshire. His visual contribution was essential to communicate this story of a Victorian seaside holiday, and spurred him to produce his own texts. Having been encouraged by his father to develop a love of poetry from an early age, he developed a style of amusing, jaunty narrative verse to tell historical tales, in a variety of settings from the Stone Age to the Wild West. Proving very popular, they were translated into most European languages. (A list of the dozen volumes appears opposite.)

Gerrard and his family lived in Chinley, in the Peak District, in Derbyshire. He died on 5 August 1997 of a heart attack, while cycling in the countryside near his home. He had delivered his artwork for his final book, *The Roman Twins*, to Hamish Hamilton just three weeks before.

With thanks to Jean Gerrard for her help in compiling this entry.

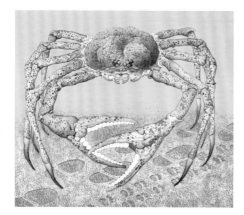

371 SPIDER CRAB
Signed
Inscribed 'Spider Crab II' below mount
Watercolour and bodycolour
8 ¾ x 10 inches

372 DONKEY & DAISIES
Signed and dated 77 twice
Inscribed with title on reverse
Pen ink and watercolour
10 ½ x 13 ½ inches

**Checklist of books written and
illustrated by Roy Gerrard**
1981
Jean Gerrard, *Matilda Jane*, London:
Victor Gollancz (In 1989, this was reissued
in miniature form as *Beside the Sea:
An Edwardian Summer*, London: Victor
Gollancz.)
1982
Roy Gerrard, *The Favershams*, London:
Victor Gollancz (1982 The New York Times
Best Illustrated Book of the Year; 1983
Bologna Children's Book Fair Graphics Prize
for Younger Children)
1984
Roy Gerrard, *Sir Cedric*, London: Victor
Gollancz (1984 The New York Times Best
Illustrated Book of the Year)
1986
Roy Gerrard, *Sir Cedric Rides Again*, London:
Victor Gollancz
1988
Roy Gerrard, *Sir Francis Drake. His Daring
Deeds*, London: Victor Gollancz (1988 The
New York Times Best Illustrated Book of
the Year)
1989
Roy Gerrard, *Rosie and the Rustlers*, London:
Gollancz Children's
(Parents' Choice for Picture Book award)
1990
Roy Gerrard, *Mik's Mammoth*, London:
Victor Gollancz
(1991 Irma S and James H Black Book
Award, Honor Book)
1991
Roy Gerrard, *A Pocketful of Posies*, London:
Victor Gollancz
1992
Roy Gerrard, *Jocasta Carr: Movie Star*,
London: Victor Gollancz
1994
Roy Gerrard, *Croco'nile*, London: Gollancz
(1995 Bologna Children's Book Fair
Graphics Prize for Younger Children)
1996
Roy Gerrard, *Wagons West!*, London: Victor
Gollancz (International Reading Association-
Children's Book Council Children's Choices)
1998
Roy Gerrard, *The Roman Twins*, London:
Hamish Hamilton

373 THE TRAM
Signed and dated 77
Inscribed with title on reverse
Watercolour
15 x 13 ½ inches

374 THE AUTHOR
Signed and dated 77
Inscribed with title below mount
Pen and ink sketches of cats below mount
Watercolour
14 ½ x 9 inches

375 THE MELANCHOLIC SYNCOPATORS
Signed and dated 78
Inscribed with title below mount
Watercolour
13 ½ x 10 inches

Sir Cedric Rides Again

376 SIR CEDRIC PUREHEART
Signed
Inscribed with title below mount
Watercolour with pencil
10 x 10 ½ inches
Illustrated: Roy Gerrard, *Sir Cedric Rides Again*,
London: Victor Gollancz, 1986, title page

377 THE LONG JOURNEY
Signed
Inscribed the title below mount
Watercolour with bodycolour and pencil
10 ¼ x 18 ½ inches
Illustrated: Roy Gerrard, *Sir Cedric Rides Again*,
London: Victor Gollancz, 1986, [unpaginated]

Mik's Mammoth

Sir Francis Drake. His Daring Deeds

378 THEN, SAFE WITHIN THEIR BARRICADE
THEY FELT COMPLETELY UNAFRAID
Signed
Pen ink and watercolour with bodycolour
9 ¼ x 7 ¼ inches
Illustrated: Roy Gerrard, *Mik's Mammoth*, London:
Victor Gollancz, 1990, [unpaginated]

379 THE ENGLISH SAILORS, PLEASED
AND PROUD,
SPED HOME TO FACE A JOYFUL CROWD
Signed
Watercolour with pencil
8 ¾ x 9 ¾ inches
Illustrated: Roy Gerrard, *Sir Francis Drake. His Daring
Deeds*, London: Victor Gollancz, 1988, [unpaginated]

380 JO'S FINAL JOURNEY PROVED TO BE
ACROSS A SHARK-INFESTED SEA (detail)
Signed; Watercolour with pen ink and bodycolour
10 ½ x 17 ½ inches

Illustrated: Roy Gerrard, *Jocasta Carr: Movie Star*,
London: Victor Gollancz, 1992, [unpaginated]

Jocasta Carr: Movie Star

381 'CHOCKS AWAY' FOR WANGALOO
(detail)
Signed twice
Watercolour with pen and ink
9 ¾ x 8 ¾ inches
Illustrated: Roy Gerrard, *Jocasta Carr: Movie Star*,
London: Victor Gollancz, 1992, [unpaginated]

251

382 SO OVERJOYED WAS BELLE TO SEE
HER MISTRESS COME TO SET HER FREE
Signed
Watercolour with pen and ink
9 ¾ x 8 ¾ inches
Illustrated: Roy Gerrard, *Jocasta Carr: Movie Star*, London:
Victor Gollancz, 1992, [unpaginated]

Croco'nile

383 EGYPTIANS STOOD AROUND HER
TO ADMIRE AND GASP IN AWE
Signed
Watercolour with pen ink and bodycolour, 9 ¼ x 8 ¼ inches
Illustrated: Roy Gerrard, *Croco'nile*, London: Victor Gollancz, 1994, [unpaginated]

384 EGYPTIAN DECORATION
Signed
Watercolour with ink
9 ¾ x 8 ¾ inches
Illustrated: Roy Gerrard, *Croco'nile*, London: Victor Gollancz, 1994, [unpaginated]

The Roman Twins

385-402 are all illustrated in Roy Gerrard, *The Roman Twins*, London: Hamish Hamilton, 1998, [unpaginated]

385 MAXIMUS AND VANILLA
WITH POLYDOX
Inscribed 'Roman Twins front cover'
below mount
Watercolour with pen ink and bodycolour
10 ½ x 9 ¼ inches
Front cover

386 MAXIMUS
AND VANILLA
Inscribed 'Title page'
below mount
Watercolour with pen
ink and bodycolour
4 x 4 inches
Title page

387 YOUNG
MAXIMUS, THOUGH
JUST A BOY, WAS
DOOMED TO BE
A SLAVE …
VANILLA, HIS TWIN
SISTER, WORKED
FOR LADY POMPIUS
Signed
Watercolour with pen
ink and bodycolour
8 ¼ x 17 ½ inches

388 THE TASK
WHICH THEY MOST
HATED AND WHICH
REALLY WORE
THEM DOWN
WAS CARRYING
THE LITTER WHEN
THEIR OWNERS
WENT TO TOWN
Signed
Watercolour with pen
ink and bodycolour
8 ¼ x 17 ½ inches

389 THEY LEFT THEIR LAZY MASTER AT THE PUBLIC BATHS EACH DAY
WHERE HE WOULD GORGE AND GOSSIP, JUST TO PASS THE TIME AWAY
Signed
Watercolour with pen ink and bodycolour
7 ¼ x 17 ½ inches

256

390 NOW, ONE DAY SLOBBUS WENT TO BUY
A CHARIOT AND HORSE
IMAGINING THE NEIGHBORS WOULD BE MOST
IMPRESSED, OF COURSE
Signed
Watercolour with pen ink and bodycolour
6 x 7 ¼ inches

391 THOUGH POLYDOX, THE TRUSTY STEED,
WAS GENTLE WITH EACH SLAVE,
WHEN SLOBBUS POMPIUS APPROACHED, HE'D
SNORT AND MISBEHAVE
Signed
Watercolour with bodycolour
6 x 7 ¼ inches

392 SO INTO THE FIELD THAT NIGHT
THE DARING TWOSOME CREPT
AND STOLE AWAY WITH POLYDOX,
WHILE NASTY SLOBBUS SLEPT
Signed
Watercolour with pen ink and bodycolour
7 ¼ x 8 inches

393 NEXT MORNING WHEN THEIR MASTER FOUND
THEIR COLD AND EMPTY BEDS,
HE FLEW INTO A TEMPER AND DECLARED HE'D HAVE
THEIR HEADS
Signed
Watercolour with pen ink and bodycolour
7 ¼ x 8 inches

394 FOR NOW THE SLAVES AND POLYDOX WERE
SNUGLY BEDDED DOWN,
WELL HIDDEN IN A STABLE IN THE HUMBLEST PART
OF TOWN
Signed
Pen ink and watercolour with bodycolour
6 ½ x 9 inches

395 SLOBBUS ASKED HIS COUSIN, WHO WAS CAPTAIN
OF THE LEGION,
TO SEND HIS MEN FORTHWITH ON A SEARCH
THROUGHOUT THE REGION
Signed
Watercolour with pen ink and bodycolour
6 ½ x 8 inches

396 NOW, ONCE THE RACE BEGAN, BEFORE THE VAST AND CHEERING CROWD, THEIR HORSE'S SPEED AND DARING MADE THE PAIR OF THEM FEEL PROUD
Signed
Watercolour with pen ink and bodycolour
8 ¼ x 18 inches

397 WHEN TAKEN TO THE PALACE TO RECEIVE THE WINNER'S PRIZE, THEY ENTERED WITH THEIR KERCHIEFS OFF, NO LONGER IN DISGUISE
Signed
Watercolour with pen and ink
8 x 18 inches

398 THEN OUT SPOKE
BOLD SPONTANIUS
AND GAVE THE
PEOPLE HOPE
BY POINTING OUT
THAT ... THE BRIDGE
WAS ONLY HELD WITH
ROPE
Signed
Watercolour with pen and ink
9 ½ x 18 inches

399 THE OSTROGOTHS ALL LAUGHED TO SEE
SPONTANIUS ALONE;
IT TICKLED THEM TO THINK ONE MAN WOULD
FACE THEM ON HIS OWN
Signed
Watercolour with pen ink and bodycolour, 8 x 9 inches

259

400 WHEN THE GOTHS SAW WULFUS FLATTENED
WITH A SINGLE BLOW,
NO OTHER FROM THAT ARMY WAS PREPARED
TO HAVE A GO
Signed
Watercolour with pen ink and bodycolour, 8 x 9 inches

401 TO SHOW THE FOUR
HIS GRATITUDE,
HE GAVE THEM GIFTS OF GOLD
Signed
Watercolour with pen and ink
7 x 9 inches

402 TRIUMPHANTLY THE
FAMOUS FOUR PARADED THROUGH
THE STREETS
Signed
Watercolour with pen ink and bodycolour
9 ½ x 18 inches

THE
TWENTY-
FIRST
CENTURY

QUENTIN BLAKE

Quentin Saxby Blake, CBE (born 1932)

Quentin Blake is the most popular of contemporary illustrators, with an instantly recognisable line and a back catalogue that includes some of the great children's books of the last 50 years. For an extensive chronology of Quentin Blake, including exhibitions at Chris Beetles Gallery, please refer to *The Illustrators*, 2007, pages 383-385.

Key works written: *Words and Pictures* (2000); *Laureate's Progress* (2002); *Beyond the Page* (2013)

His work is represented in the collections of House of Illustration and the V&A.

Further reading:
Douglas Martin, *The Telling Line*, London: Julia MacRae Books, 1989, pages 243-263; Joanna Carey, *Quentin Blake*, London: Tate Publishing, 2014

403-413 were all drawn for Apuleius, *The Golden Ass*, London: The Folio Society, 2015

262

403 THE GOLDEN ASS
Signed
Ink
10 ½ x 7 ¼ inches
Similar to front cover

404 A BACCHIC FRENZY OF LOVE
Signed
Pen ink and watercolour
4 x 4 ½ inches
Drawn for but not illustrated in Book Three, page 66

'The Folio Society have just published my illustrated edition of Apuleius's The Golden Ass. Alma Books have brought out an illustrated collection of stories by Saki called Gabriel-Ernest and Other Stories.

Frances Lincoln have re-issued four of Joan Aiken's Arabel and Mortimer stories.

This Summer, I had an exhibition of work at the Jerwood Gallery in Hastings called "Life Under Water – a Hastings Celebration". In July, Chris Beetles Gallery staged "A Quentin Blake Summer. With Wing, Dogs, Kites, and Extra Ducks", which was one of my most popular shows ever.

I was admitted as an Honorary Freeman of the City of London in February. Also, importantly for me, the French Institute opened the Bibliothèque Quentin Blake in September.

The year ends with "Quentin Blake & Friends", an event with readings, live illustration and a live auction, which I will be co-hosting for House of Illustration in December.'

(Quentin Blake writes about his latest activities)

263

405 THE TRANSFORMATION OF LUCIUS
Signed
Pen ink and watercolour
Two images measuring 3 ¼ x 4 ¾ inches and
3 ¾ x 4 ¾ inches
Alternative version for Book Three, pages 70-71

406 THE ANTIQUE JAR
Signed
Pen ink and watercolour
4 ½ x 5 inches
Alternative version for Book Nine, page 174

407 THE SHEPHERD
Signed
Pen ink and watercolour
9 x 6 ¾ inches
Drawn for but not illustrated

408 STIRRING THE POT
Signed
Pen ink and watercolour
4 ½ x 4 ½ inches
Alternative version for Book Two, page 42

'The Golden Ass [is] the only Latin novel that has survived complete and whole ... it has a real picturesque energy, and delights, like Don Quixote, in outlandish adventures ... [it] is a work of genius that burts out of its historical moment; one that has had an enormous influence on the history of the novel, and which continues to influence contemporary literature.'

(James Wood, Introduction to Apuleius, *The Golden Ass*, London: The Folio Society, pages 11-12)

409 A GARLAND OF BLOSSOMS
Signed
Pen ink and watercolour
10 x 6 inches
Similar to Book Two, page 46

410 PHAMPHILE'S MAGIC ARTS
Signed
Pen ink and watercolour
9 ¼ x 6 ½ inches
Similar to Book Three, page 68

266

412 YOU'RE THE
ONLY ONE I LOVE
Signed
Pen ink and
watercolour
8 ½ x 6 ¼ inches
Similar to Book Ten,
page 207

411 THE GODDESS OF PROVIDENCE
Signed
Pen ink and watercolour
10 ½ x 6 inches
Alternative version for Book Eleven, page 220

413 FLUTTERING
HER EYELIDS
SEDUCTIVELY
Signed
Pen ink and
watercolour
9 ¼ x 5 ¾ inches
Alternative version for
Book Ten, page 209

414 THE BIRD BALANCER
Signed and dated 1974
Inscribed with title on reverse
Pen ink and watercolour
9 x 13 ¼ inches
Exhibited: 'A Quentin Blake
Summer. With Wind, Dogs,
Kites, and Extra Ducks', July
2015, no 101

415 CELEBRATING
THE OWL
Signed and dated 1974
Inscribed with title on reverse
Pen ink and watercolour
15 x 23 inches
Exhibited: 'A Quentin Blake
Summer. With Wind, Dogs,
Kites, and Extra Ducks', July
2015, no 17

19

CONTEMPORARY ILLUSTRATORS

BARRY LEITH
(born 1943)

JANE PINKNEY
(born 1948)

PETER CROSS
(born 1951)

EMMA CHICHESTER CLARK
(born 1955)

AMANDA HALL
(born 1956)

PAUL COX
(born 1957)

GILLIAN TYLER
(born 1963)

416-432 are all illustrated in Elisabeth Beresford, *The Wombles*, London: Ernest Benn, 1975

416 'WAIT AND SEE,' SAID TOBERMORY, AND BEGAN PUTTING A CAMERA TOGETHER ON HIS WORKBENCH
Inscribed with artist's notes below mount
Pen and ink on board
4 ½ x 7 inches
Illustrated: page 25, 'Orinoco and the Black Umbrella'

BARRY LEITH
Barry Edward Leith (born 1943)

The distinguished puppet animator, Barry Leith, not only helped create the animated television series, *The Wombles*, but illustrated editions of the books on which it was based.

Barry Leith studied graphic design at Hornsey College of Art, and then took a post-graduate course in film and photography. He soon moved into animation, and worked for a while with the French animator, Jacques Forgeot. He then joined FilmFair and, becoming a director of animation, contributed to some classic children's animated television series.

In 1973, the BBC commissioned FilmFair to produce a series of 30 five-minute films based on Elizabeth Beresford's *The Wombles*. In addition to his role as cinematographer, Barry Leith designed the sets and collaborated with the director, Ivor Wood, on the development of the puppets. They so changed the initial look of the Wombles, as established by their original illustrator, Margaret Gordon, that, in 1975, Leith produced a new set of illustrations for the reissue of Beresford's first book (as shown here) and the publication of its sequels. A second television series, of another 30 episodes, appeared in that year.

From 1975 to 1979, FilmFair took up a suggestion by Ivor Wood and followed *The Wombles* with 56 five-minute films based on Michael Bond's stories about Paddington Bear, also made for the BBC. Leith worked as its director of animation. In 1984, he was nominated for a BAFTA for the 12-minute special, *Paddington goes to the Movies*, which includes the bear reprising Gene Kelly's famous dance routine from *Singin' in the Rain*.

From 1983 to 1986, Leith helped make *The Adventures of Portland Bill*, a third children's programme with FilmFair, though this time for ITV. It consisted of two series, each of thirteen 5-minute episodes.

In 1987, Leith founded his own company, Puppetoon Productions, which, for about a decade, made commercials, often at the premises of FilmFair. He and his second wife, Jayne, then settled in Norfolk, where they brought up their two daughters. He now teaches on the BA (Hons) Animation course at Norwich University of the Arts.

Further reading:
Geir Madland, 'Basil, Model Citizen', *YLM: Your Lifestyle Magazine for Norfolk & Suffolk*, August 2014, pages 6-7

417 ORINOCO AND THE DALMATIAN
Pen and ink on board, 10 ½ x 7 ¾ inches
Illustrated: Frontispiece

418 BUNGO DRESSED FOR THE RAIN
Pen and ink on board, 10 x 7 ½ inches
Illustrated: page 41, 'The Tree that Moved'

419 GREAT UNCLE BULGARIA PICKED UP THE TIMES
AND SHOOK OUT THE PAGES AND BEGAN TO READ
Pen and ink on board, 4 ½ x 6 ½ inches
Illustrated: page 13, 'Bungo'

420 HE BENT DOWN AND PICKED UP THE WHOLE
BUCKET-LOAD AND THREW THAT AT BUNGO
Pen and ink on board
4 ½ x 6 inches
Illustrated: page 49, 'Tomsk Hangs On'

421 LET'S GO AND CLEAR UP THAT MESS WE MADE
IN THE WORKSHOP
Pen and ink on board
4 ½ x 6 ½ inches
Illustrated: page 58, 'Tomsk Hangs On'

422 SHE WAS SENT OFF WITH THE TROLLEY PILED HIGH
WITH CAKES, BUNS AND BISCUITS AND A BIG STEAMING
URN OF BRACKEN JUICE
Pen and ink on board
4 x 9 inches
Illustrated: page 62, 'Bungo and the Concrete Mixer'

423 YOU SHALL TOP AND TAIL THE HAWTHORN BERRIES
Pen and ink on board
4 ½ x 5 ½ inches
Illustrated: page 79, 'Orinoco and the Rabbit Hole'

424 THE RESCUE OF TOMSK
Pen and ink on board
9 ¾ x 7 inches
Illustrated: page 55, 'Tomsk Hangs On'

425 CHRISTMAS CAROLS
Pen and ink on board
7 x 10 ½ inches
Illustrated: page 103, 'The Christmas Party
and Mr D Smith'

426 IT WAS QUITE A LONG WALK
TO GET TO THE UNDERGROUND
Pen and ink on board
5 ½ x 7 inches
Illustrated: page 141, 'Bungo's Great Adventure'

427 BUNGO IN PICCADILLY
Pen and ink on board
10 ½ x 7 ½ inches
Illustrated: page 145, 'Bungo's Great Adventure'

428 BUILDING THE SNOW WOMBLE
Pen and ink on board
10 x 7 ½ inches
Illustrated: page 107, 'The Snow Womble'

429 HE FAILED TO NOTICE THAT A HUMAN BEING
WAS FOLLOWING HIM
Pen and ink on board
5 x 6 inches
Illustrated: page 167, 'Great Uncle Bulgaria's Day Out'

430 OH WELL PLAYED SIR!
Pen and ink on board
5 x 6 inches
Illustrated: page 173, 'Great Uncle Bulgaria's Day Out'

432 THE SILVER WOMBLE
Pen and ink on board
4 x 9 inches
Illustrated: page 183, 'Tobermory's Surprise and the Midsummer Party'

431 THE PRESENTATION TO COUSIN YELLOWSTONE (opposite)
Pen and ink on board
4 x 9 inches
Illustrated: page 176, 'Great Uncle Bulgaria's Day Out'

JANE PINKNEY
Lesley Jane Pinkney (née Magee) (born 1948)

Jane Pinkney's finely rendered depictions reveal a variety of anthropomorphic narratives steeped in nostalgia and charm. Her work can be firmly situated within the tradition of illustrative art, and her name comfortably coupled with those of Beatrix Potter, Edmund Dulac and Arthur Rackham.

For a biography of Jane Pinkney, please refer to *The Illustrators*, 2011, pages 338-340.

433 CHRISTMAS SONGS
Signed
Watercolour
3 ½ x 3 ¼ inches

434 TOPSY
Signed and inscribed with title
Watercolour
3 ¼ x 2 ¾ inches

435 THE DANCER
Signed
Watercolour with
pen and ink
2 ¾ x 2 inches

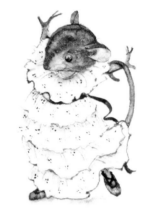

436 NIGEL
Signed, inscribed with title and dated 1991
Watercolour
3 ½ x 3 inches

437 THE JUGGLER
Signed and dated 1993
Watercolour with bodycolour
3 ½ x 2 ½ inches

438 THE WALKING STICK MAKER
Signed and dated 95
Watercolour
3 ½ x 3 inches

439 PLAYTIME
Signed
Watercolour
5 ½ x 5 ¾ inches

440 KNITTING
Signed
Watercolour
3 ½ x 2 ¾ inches

441 DRESSING UP
Signed
Pencil
6 x 7 ¾ inches

442 THE RIGHT KEY
Signed
Pencil
6 ½ x 5 ½ inches

443 DISTRACTING THE CHICKENS
Signed
Pencil
7 x 9 inches

444 SPRING CLEANING
Signed
Pencil
10 ½ x 10 inches

PETER CROSS
Peter Cross (born 1951)

From 1975, Peter Cross began to emerge as an illustrator of great originality, making his name with books that continue to delight children and adults alike. Unwilling to restrict his fertile imagination to two dimensions, he also created a series of eccentric cabinets of curiosities. Such richness and variety were then directed towards advertising and, in particular, to delightful work for the company Wine Rack. Cross's dry, yet charming visual-verbal wit has reached a wide international public through designs for greetings cards, first for Gordon Fraser (Hallmark 1995-2000) and then for The Great British Card Company.

For a biography of Peter Cross, please refer to *The Illustrators*, 2007, page 403

Since 2008, Peter Cross has been building his card range – providing some of the National Trust's bestselling designs. More recently, he has returned to making 'boxes', unique mixed-media cabinets of curiosity, which allow him to express his scintillating imagination to its fullest. He now also has his own website: www.petercrossart.com

Over the last year, he has continued to build work for a major retrospective book and exhibition planned by Chris Beetles Gallery. As he explains:

'I am continuing to work on my Cross-Country project, which chronicles a life spent drawing, painting in watercolour and pursuing various other creative endeavours. The book and accompanying exhibition will tell a story as well as display a body of work not seen before. By exploring and developing various themes – landscape, satire and the whimsically eccentric, I have attempted, to the best of my ability, to forge an identity as an artist as well as make an enduring statement. This is what I do.'

445 LOUD SPEAKERS
Signed with initials
Pen ink and watercolour with pencil
7 x 8 inches

A modified version is illustrated on the title page of this catalogue.

EMMA CHICHESTER CLARK

Emma Chichester Clark (born 1955)

In **1988**, Emma Chichester Clark won the Mother Goose Award as the most exciting newcomer in children's book illustration. Since then she has written and illustrated many acclaimed picture books, including the series, 'Blue Kangaroo' and 'Melrose and Croc'. The hallmark of her work is her sensitive and convincing portrayal of human feelings and foibles, even within the most fantastic situations.

For a biography of Emma Chichester Clark, please refer to *The Illustrators*, 2008, page 135.

281

446 THE SLEEPING PRINCESS
Signed with initials
Watercolour and coloured ink with bodycolour and pencil
12 ¼ x 11 inches
Illustrated: Saviour Pirotta, *The Sleeping Princess and Other Fairy Tales from Grimm*, London: Orchard Books, 2002, front cover

'Since 2012, I have been publishing a blog online – Plumdog Blog – an illustrated diary, as told by my dog, Plum. It was published in book form by Jonathan Cape in 2014, and we have also created two picture books for children about Plum. The first, Love is My Favourite Thing, *published by Jonathan Cape, came out in September this year. The blog continues to record Plum's thoughts and feelings about life. You can find it at: emmachichesterclark.blogspot.com*

I have also written and illustrated the ninth book in the "Blue Kangaroo" series. It is a prequel about how Lily and Blue Kangaroo found each other – When I First Met You, Blue Kangaroo!, *published by HarperCollins.*

Just before that I wrote and illustrated a story about a large brown bear called George who was fortunate enough to meet a little girl called Clementine. Its title – Bears Don't Read!, *published by HarperCollins – is something George refuses to believe and Clementine shows him that it's perfectly possible, with a little determination.'*

(Emma Chichester Clark writes about her latest activities)

447-463 are all illustrated in Martin Waddell, *The Orchard Book of Hans Christian Andersen's Fairy Tales*, London: Orchard Books, 2010

A Little Love Story
[based on 'The Steadfast Tin Soldier']

447 'A SOLDIER!' ONE SAID. 'LET'S MAKE HIM A BOAT TO SAIL IN.'
Signed with initials
Watercolour and coloured ink with coloured pencil
4 x 9 ½ inches
Illustrated: page 75

448 THE WATER FLOWED INTO A DRAIN, AS DARK AS THE TIN BOX HE'D LIVED IN
Signed with initials
Watercolour and coloured ink with coloured pencil
4 x 9 ½ inches
Illustrated: page 76

449 THE LITTLE TIN
SOLDIER HAD BEEN
SWALLOWED BY A FISH
Signed with initials
Watercolour and coloured ink
with coloured pencil
4 ¼ x 9 ½ inches
Illustrated: page 78

450 THE FISH HAD BEEN
CAUGHT, TAKEN HOME
AND CUT OPEN IN A
KITCHEN
Signed with initials
Watercolour and coloured ink
with coloured pencil
5 x 9 ½ inches
Illustrated: page 79

The Princess and the Pigman

451 MY ROSE BUSH AND MY NIGHTINGALE! WHAT MORE COULD ANY GIRL ASK FOR!
Signed with initials
Watercolour and coloured ink with coloured pencil
5 ¼ x 9 ½ inches
Illustrated: page 83

452 HE PACKAGED HIS TWO GIFTS IN BIG SILVER CRATES AND SENT THEM TO HER BY SPECIAL MESSENGER
Signed with initials
Watercolour and coloured ink with coloured pencil
5 ½ x 9 ½ inches
Illustrated: page 84

284

453 THE PRINCESS'S PUG
Signed with initials
Watercolour and coloured ink
with coloured pencil
2 ½ x 2 ½ inches
Illustrated: page 87

454 SHE GAVE THE PIGMAN HIS TEN KISSES
AND THEN WALKED AWAY, CLUTCHING
THE MUSICAL BOX
Signed with initials
Watercolour and coloured ink with coloured pencil
5 ¼ x 9 ½ inches
Illustrated: page 90

455 HE CHANGED INTO HIS HANDSOME
PRINCE CLOTHES
Signed with initials
Watercolour and coloured ink with
coloured pencil
4 ¼ x 9 ½ inches
Illustrated: page 92

285

Sweet Song of the Forest
[based on 'The Nightingale']

456 A GOLD AND SILVER
CLOCKWORK NIGHTINGALE
Signed with initials
Watercolour and coloured ink with
coloured pencil
5 ¾ x 5 ¾ inches
Illustrated: page 102

457 SHE BROUGHT THEM
TO THE TREE WHERE THE
NIGHTINGALE SAT
Signed with initials
Watercolour and coloured ink with
coloured pencil
4 ¼ x 9 ½ inches
Illustrated: page 99

458 THE LITTLE MAID
STILL HEARD
THE BIRD SING
EVERY DAY
Signed with initials
Watercolour and coloured
ink with coloured pencil
10 ¾ x 9 ½ inches
Illustrated: page 113

459 DEATH'S COLD
EYES SHONE
GREEDILY AS THE
EMPEROR'S LIFE
EBBED AWAY
Signed with initials
Watercolour and
coloured ink with
coloured pencil
10 ¾ x 9 ½ inches
Illustrated: page 109

Daughter of
the Sea
[based on 'The
Little Mermaid']

460 SHE SWAM
DOWN INTO THE
DEPTHS AND
SAVED HER DARK-
EYED PRINCE
Signed with initials
Watercolour and
coloured ink with
coloured pencil
10 ¾ x 9 ½ inches
Illustrated: page 117

461 'YOU'D SWAP YOUR BEAUTIFUL SILVERY TAIL FOR THE
TWO STUMPY THINGS HUMANS CALL LEGS?' CROWED THE SEA WITCH
Signed with initials
Watercolour and coloured ink with coloured pencil
4 x 19 inches
Illustrated: pages 120-121

Daughter of the Sea

290

462 THE POOR
GIRL SAID THAT
SHE WAS A
PRINCESS
Signed with initials
Watercolour and
coloured ink with
coloured pencil
10 ½ x 9 ½ inches
Illustrated: page 11

A Very Princessy Princess
[based on 'The Princess and the Pea']

463 THE QUEEN'S
REAL PRINCESS
TEST
Signed with initials
Watercolour and
coloured ink with
coloured pencil
11 x 9 ¾ inches
Illustrated: page 13

464-468 are all illustrated in Colin McNaughton, *Have You Ever Ever Ever?*, London: Walker Books, 2011, [unpaginated]

291

464 INCY-WINCY SPIDER
Signed with initials
Watercolour, coloured ink and bodycolour
with coloured pencil
10 x 11 ½ inches

465 BOBBY SHAFTOE
Signed with initials
Watercolour, coloured ink and bodycolour
with coloured pencil
10 x 11 ¾ inches

466 PETER PIPER
Signed with initials
Watercolour, coloured ink and bodycolour
with coloured pencil
10 x 11 ½ inches

467 YANKEE DOODLE DANDY
Signed with initials
Watercolour, coloured ink and bodycolour
with coloured pencil
10 x 11 ½ inches

468 LET ME INTRODUCE –
THE FRIENDS OF MOTHER GOOSE!
Signed with initials
Inscribed 'Friends of Mother Goose'
below mount
Watercolour, coloured ink and
coloured pencil
9 ¾ x 22 ½ inches

469 THE LION AND THE UNICORN
Signed with initials
Watercolour and coloured ink with coloured pencil
11 ¾ x 18 ¾ inches
Drawn for but not illustrated in *Alice Through The Looking Glass*, London: Harper Collins, 2013

AMANDA HALL
Amanda Hall (born 1956)

Amanda Hall is an award-winning contemporary illustrator, particularly renowned for her wonderfully decorative and colourful children's book illustrations, as well as her work for educational publications both in Britain and America.

For a biography of Amanda Hall, please refer to *The Illustrators*, 2011, page 356

470-479 are all illustrated in Dawn Casey, *Babushka*, Oxford: Lion Children's Books, 2015

470 THE CLOUDS PARTED AND A BRIGHT STAR SHONE
Signed
Watercolour ink, pencil crayon and chalk
9 x 17 inches
Illustrated: pages 8-9

471 A NEWBORN KING
Signed
Watercolour ink, pencil crayon and chalk
10 x 8 inches
Illustrated: page 13

'I have two new books out this autumn:

Brother Giovanni's Little Reward: How the Pretzel Was Born, *written by Anna Egan Smucker,*
and published by Eerdmans Books for Young Readers in August 2015;

Babushka, *written by Dawn Casey, and published by Lion Hudson in September 2015.*

I am currently working on a children's picture book for PJ Library, which is a Jewish family engagement programme
implemented on a local level throughout North America. This new title will be out in September 2016.

I also begin work soon on my new picture book collaboration with writer Michelle Markel. This second book with Michelle will be another artist's
biography for children, and follows the success of The Fantastic Jungles of Henri Rousseau, *written by Michelle Markel, and published by*
Eerdmans Books for Young Readers. The book will be published by Balzer & Bray in the United States in the winter of 2017-18.

During 2015, The Fantastic Jungles of Henri Rousseau *featured in the Ten Artistic Reads of the Scottish Book Trust.'*

(Amanda Hall writes about her latest activities)

472 'WHAT,' SAID BABUSHKA, 'WITHOUT WASHING THE DISHES?'
Signed
Watercolour ink, pencil crayon and chalk, 8 ½ x 16 ½ inches
Illustrated: page 14-15

473 THAT NIGHT BABUSHKA HAD A DREAM
Signed
Watercolour ink, pencil crayon and chalk
5 x 6 inches
Illustrated: page 16

474 SHE DREAMED OF A BABY, WITH EYES DARK AND BRIGHT AS THE STARRY NIGHT
Signed
Watercolour ink, pencil crayon and chalk, 11 x 9 inches
Illustrated: page 17

475 BABUSHKA LOOKED UP AT THE STAR. THE STAR LOOKED DOWN AT BABUSHKA
Signed
Watercolour ink, pencil crayon and chalk, 11 x 8 ½ inches
Illustrated: page 19

296

476 AND, IN THE MORNING, SHE OPENED AN OLD CHEST
Signed
Watercolour ink, pencil crayon and chalk
11 x 8 inches
Illustrated: page 21

477 THE GIRL FLUNG HER ARMS AROUND BABUSHKA
Signed
Watercolour ink, pencil crayon and chalk
11 x 8 ½ inches
Illustrated: page 25

298

478 AND SHE TOOK FROM
HER BASKET A THICK
SLICE OF GINGERBREAD
Signed
Watercolour ink, pencil crayon
and chalk
10 ½ x 8 inches
Illustrated: page 27

479 SHE MET GIRLS AND BOYS WITH NO TOYS TO PLAY WITH
Signed
Watercolour ink, pencil crayon and chalk
12 x 17 inches
Illustrated: cover and pages 28-29

PAUL COX
Paul William Cox (born 1957)

Paul Cox's fluid, immediate draughtsmanship and vibrant colour make him one of the most enjoyable, versatile and sought-after of contemporary illustrators. Well known for his warm and witty contributions to books and magazines, he has ranged in his work as a designer from stamps to stage sets.

For a biography of Paul Cox, please refer to *The Illustrators*, 2009, page 182.

480 WIMBLEDON
Signed
Watercolour
9 ¼ x 13 ¼ inches
Illustrated: *Ace*, the official magazine of the Lawn Tennis Association, June 2003

300

481 LE BEAUJOLAIS NOUVEAU EST ARRIVE
Signed
Pen ink and watercolour
15 ½ x 15 ½ inches
Drawn for a French Government brochure promoting food and wine in the Beaujolais Region, 1988

Chris Beetles Gallery has held a number of major solo shows of the work of Paul Cox since 1989. The latest, 'A Journey Through His Art', took place in 2013, and was accompanied by a comprehensively illustrated catalogue, which is still available for sale.

'I am preparing a collection of drawings for a book on London, including work made in the 1980s, showing how things have changed, and finding new and unusual contrasts both social and architectural.'

(Paul Cox writes about his latest activities)

301

482 LES FETES DU BEAUJOLAIS
Signed
Pen ink and watercolour
22 ½ x 16 ¼ inches
Drawn for a French Government brochure promoting food and wine in the Beaujolais Region, 1988

484 POLICEMAN ON A BICYCLE
Stamped '4 Jun 1991' on reverse
Pen ink and watercolour
8 ½ x 11 ½ inches
Drawn for a DDM Needham advertising brochure, Netherlands, 1991

483 CAWDOR CASTLE
Signed
Stamped '29 Sep 1989' on reverse
Pen ink and watercolour
23 x 17 ½ inches
Design for one of three promotional posters for the
British Tourist Board, 1989

485 NAPA VALLEY – WINE TASTING ON HORSEBACK
Stamped '23 Apr 1994' on reverse
Pen ink and watercolour
11 ½ x 10 inches
Illustrated: *Travel + Leisure*, New York, 1994

486 SKATERS, HYDE PARK
Signed
Stamped '23 April 1994' on reverse
Pen ink and watercolour
23 x 16 ½ inches
Drawn for an Alzheimer's Society charity
Christmas card, 1994

487-491 are all illustrated in
Jerome K Jerome, *Three Men on
the Bummel,* London: Reader's
Digest, 1998

487 WE STARTED
BICYCLING IN EARNEST
Signed
Pen ink and watercolour
17 ½ x 23 ¼ inches
Illustrated: title page

488 WE'VE FORGOTTON
THE BALLS!
Signed
Inscribed with title below mount
Pen ink and watercolour
11 ½ x 11 ½ inches
Illustrated: page 235

489 PRETTY LITTLE PLACE,
THAT TITISEE,
ACCORDING TO THE MAP
Signed
Inscribed 'We'll Stop At Titsee!'
below mount
17 x 12 ½ inches
Pen ink and watercolour
Illustrated: page 324

490 WHAT D'YE THINK I KEEP BOOTS FOR – TO SMELL 'EM?
Signed
Pen ink and watercolour
16 x 12 inches
Illustrated: page 253

491 THIS IS THE BEST VIEW WE'VE HAD OF IT AS YET
Signed
Inscribed with title below mount
Pen ink and watercolour
11 ½ x 11 ½ inches
Illustrated: page 341

492 A FLY ON THE WATER
Signed
Pen ink and watercolour
14 ½ x 20 ½ Inches
Illustrated: Patricia Wentworth, *Thornhill Square*,
London: Harper Collins, 1995

493 ARCH OF CONSTANTINE, ROME
Signed and dated 2011
Pen ink and watercolour
20 ½ x 29 ½ inches
Exhibited: 'Paul Cox. A Journey through his Art',
October 2013, no 125

306

494 SANT'IVO FROM
SANT'EUSTACHIO
Signed, inscribed 'Saint'Ivo and
Saint'Eustachio' and dated '11
Pen ink and watercolour
27 x 18 ¾ inches
Exhibited: 'Paul Cox. A Journey
through his Art', October 2013, no 116

GILLIAN TYLER
Gillian Mary Tyler (Born 1963)

Gillian Tyler began her career as a wildlife artist and etcher, but turned to illustrating children's books when she realised that bringing characters from stories to life was what she really enjoyed.

For a biography of Gillian Tyler, please refer to *The Illustrators*, 2012, pages 239-240.

495-505 are all illustrated in Michael Rosen, *The Bus is for Us!*, London: Walker Books, 2015, [unpaginated]

495 I REALLY LIKE TO RIDE MY BIKE
Signed
Pen ink and watercolour
10 x 19 inches

496 WHEN IT STARTS TO RAIN I LIKE THE TRAIN
Signed
Pen ink and watercolour
10 x 14 ¾ inches

'This April saw the publication of The Bus is for Us!, written by the former Children's Laureate, Michael Rosen, and published by Walker Books and Candlewick Press. A paperback edition is just being prepared for publication.

This Christmas, I am looking forward to the publication of The Fox at the Manger, written by P L Travers, author of Mary Poppins, and published by Virago.

I attended the Penistone Literary Festival alongside Carol Ann Duffy and Ian McMillan and donated artwork to the Bath Literature Festival.

I gave several talks to various arts societies to celebrate 'The Big Draw', and held workshops at the Cooper Gallery in Barnsley.

I have also been commissioned to design a set of four new cards for Barnsley museums celebrating various tourist attractions in the borough.

It's been a busy year for preparing new projects and work is underway on my next children's book, which will be published in Autumn 2016.'

(Gillian Tyler writes about her latest activities)

500 I LIKE TO FLOAT IN A LITTLE BOAT
Signed
Pen ink and watercolour
5 ½ x 4 ¾ inches

497 I DO OF COURSE LIKE RIDING A HORSE
Signed
Pen ink and watercolour
8 x 15 ½ inches

498 OR FOR A DARE RIDE ON A BEAR
Signed
Pen ink and watercolour
11 ½ x 16 inches

499 I'D LOVE TO PARAGLIDE HIGH IN THE SKY
Signed
Pen ink and watercolour
10 ¾ x 15 ½ inches

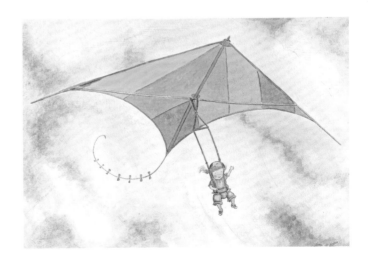

501 THE BUS IS FOR US
Signed
Pen ink and watercolour
9 ¼ x 14 inches

502 BUT BEST IS THE BUS.
THE BUS IS FOR US
Signed
Pen ink and watercolour
9 ½ x 19 inches

503 FLY TO THE MOON
IN A HOT-AIR BALLOON
Signed
Pen ink and watercolour
10 ¾ x 7 ¼ inches

504 BUT EVEN SO, THE
BUS IS THE BEST. BEST IS
THE BUS.
THAT'S BECAUSE THE BUS
IS FOR US!
Signed
Pen ink and watercolour
9 ¼ x 17 inches

312

505 DRIVING IN THE
MOONLIGHT
Signed
Pen ink and watercolour
9 ¼ x 19 inches

BILL TIDY

William Edward Tidy, MBE (born 1933)

Since selling his first cartoon almost 60 years ago, Bill Tidy has forged a reputation as one of Britain's best-loved and most prolific cartoonists. He is perhaps best known for his strip cartoons, 'The Cloggies' and 'The Fosdyke Saga'.

For a biography of Bill Tidy, please refer to *The Illustrators*, 2014, page 254.

506 START
MOVING ABOUT
YOU IDIOTS!
Signed
Pen and ink with
watercolour
6 ¾ x 6 inches

313

507 SORRY
I'M LATE JB!
Signed
Pen and ink with
watercolour
7 ¼ x 8 ¼ inches

BILL TIDY

314

508 YOU MUST WARN MI5 ... THE RUSSIANS HAVE
DISCOVERED A NEW ... PERFUME FOR MEN ...
Signed
Pen and ink with watercolour
7 ¼ x 9 ½ inches

509 MIGHT AS WELL SEE WHAT THE WEATHER'S GOING TO
BE LIKE WHILE WE'RE AT IT ...
Signed
Pen and ink with watercolour
7 ½ x 9 ½ inches

510 THAT LOT YOU'RE LOOKING AT WOULDN'T HAVE
LASTED FIVE MINUTES WITH: BEDE; DUNSTAN AND ALCUIN;
CUTHBERT, ALBAN AND ANSELM; ...
Signed
Pen and ink with watercolour
6 ½ x 9 inches

ED MCLACHLAN

Edward Rolland McLachlan (born 1940)

Ed McLachlan's cartoons offer a comical but often cutting commentary on modern life. From his gormless, baggy-suited businessmen to his ungainly bucktoothed women, his undeniably British sense of humour makes him a master of the macabre with an eye for the ridiculous. In every cleverly observed image, he takes the mundane and delivers the hilariously absurd.

For a biography of Ed McLachlan, please refer to *The Illustrators*, 2002, page 110

His work is represented in the collections of the British Cartoon Archive (University of Kent).

"All ready for the opening night, Mr Newton — the make-up people are here."

'During this year, I have produced a series of menu designs for the celebrity chef Angela Hartnett, a calendar for Saga Magazine for 2016, three large presentation drawings for the multinational property group, Inland plc, plus the usual work for The Oldie, Private Eye, Saga Magazine, The Salisbury Review and The Spectator. In addition, the four "Simon in the Land of Chalk Drawings" books have been reprinted in the USA'.

(Ed McLachlan writes about his latest activities)

315

511 ALL READY FOR THE OPENING NIGHT, MR NEWTON – THE MAKE-UP PEOPLE ARE HERE
Signed and inscribed with title
Pen and ink with coloured pen
9 x 12 inches
Illustrated: *Saga Magazine*

512 WHEN I TOOK YOU ON AS AN APPRENTICE, YOU DIDN'T TELL ME YOU ARE DYSLEXIC
Signed and inscribed with title
Pen and ink with coloured pen
9 ½ x 10 ¾ inches
Illustrated: *Saga Magazine*

513 RESERVED AND LOUTISH
Signed
Pen and ink
6 ½ x 12 ¾ inches
Illustrated: *Private Eye*

316

514 WHO'S LOOKING OVER
YOUR SHOULDER?
Signed
Pen and ink
8 x 7 inches
Illustrated: *The Oldie*, November 2010

515 HOW TO OVERCOME SHYNESS
Signed
Pen and ink
8 ½ x 12 inches
Illustrated: *The Oldie*, June 2005

516 NAKAHITO BACK PAIN CLINIC
Signed
Pen and ink with watercolour
8 ¼ x 12 inches
Illustrated: *The Oldie*, December 2007

517 THE NEIGHBOURS FROM HELL
ARE PLAYING UP AGAIN
Signed and inscribed with title
Pen and ink with coloured pen
9 ½ x 12 ¼ inches
Illustrated: *Saga Magazine*

" The neighbours from hell are playing up again."

MIKE WILLIAMS
Michael Charles Williams (born 1940)

Since his first cartoon was published in *Punch* in 1967, Mike Williams has contributed regularly to many a magazine. He has a particular interest in comic representations of animal life, calling this his 'Animalia'.

For a biography of Mike Williams, please refer to *The Illustrators*, 1999, page 245.

318

518 MR PRESIDENT! MR PRESIDENT! MAY I GO TO THE TOILET?
Signed and inscribed with title
Pen and ink with watercolour
13 x 8 ½ inches
Illustrated: *Playboy*

519 'THE BELL'S! THE BELL'S!"
Signed and inscribed with title
Pen ink and watercolour
10 ¾ x 13 ½ inches

520 I FLUNKED SANDPIT
Signed and inscribed with title
Pen ink and watercolour
11 x 14 inches

521 OHO, IT'S STARTED
Signed and inscribed with title
Pen ink and watercolour
10 ½ x 13 ¾ inches

522 OH NO! IT'S AN EAR! DIDN'T VINCENT GET THE LIST??
Signed and inscribed with title
Pen and ink with watercolour
11 x 14 inches

MIKE WILLIAMS

523 I'M AFRAID IT'S NOT A BATTLE OF BRITAIN FLY-PAST YOUR MAJESTY, IT'S YOUR AIR FORCE
Signed and inscribed with title
Pen ink and watercolour
13 ½ x 9 ¼ inches

524 WE JUST THOUGHT THAT WHILST YOUR MAJESTY IS LOOKING AT SOME NEW CLOTHES HE MIGHT JUST BE INTERESTED IN THIS EARLY EXAMPLE OF A STRADIVARIUS AIR GUITAR THAT HAS JUST COME INTO OUR POSSESSION?
Signed and inscribed with title
Pen ink and watercolour
13 ¾ x 9 ½ inches

PETER BROOKES

Peter Derek Brookes, FRSA RDI (born 1943)

Peter Brookes maintains the most consistently high standard of any editorial cartoonist working in Britain today. His daily political cartoons and regular 'Nature Notes', produced for *The Times*, are always inventive, incisive and confidently drawn. They are the fruit of wide experience as a cartoonist and illustrator, and of complete independence from editorial intrusion.

For a biography of Peter Brookes, please refer to *The Illustrators*, 2009, page 164.

His work is represented in the collections of the British Cartoon Archive (University of Kent).

525-531 were all exhibited in 'Testing Times', September 2015

Peter's activities and achievements over the last year include:
Testing Times was published by The Robson Press in October 2015.
Awards during 2014:
British Press Awards Cartoonist of the Year
Political Cartoon Society Cartoonist of the Year
Speaking engagements during 2014 included the Blenheim Literature Festival and the Cheltenham Literature Festival.

525 MAN LOST FOR 29 YEARS DIDN'T KNOW THE CLASS WAR HAD ENDED ...
Signed, inscribed with title and dated '18 i 14'
Pen ink and watercolour
8 x 11 inches
Illustrated: *The Times*, 18 January 2014
Literature: Peter Brookes, *Testing Times*, London: The Robson Press, 2015, page 23

526 TALIBAN VERMIN
Signed, inscribed with title and dated '19 xii 14'
Pen ink and watercolour
8 x 11 ¼ inches
Illustrated: *The Times*, 18 December 2014
Literature: Peter Brookes, *Testing Times*, London: The Robson Press, 2015, page 69

527 FARAGE THE WEASEL
Signed and dated '4 iii 15'
Pen ink and watercolour, 8 x 11 inches
Illustrated: *The Times*, 4 March 2015
Literature: Peter Brookes, *Testing Times*, London: The Robson Press, 2015, page 81

528 'THE SWING' AFTER FRAGONARD
Signed, inscribed with title and dated '12 v 15'
Pen ink and watercolour, 8 x 11 inches
Illustrated: *The Times*, 12 May 2015

322

529 I'M THE RIGHT MAN TO CLEAN IT UP!
Signed and dated '30 v 15'
Pen ink and watercolour, 8 x 11 inches
Illustrated: *The Times*, 30 May 2015
Literature: Peter Brookes, *Testing Times*, London: The Robson Press, 2015, page 101

530 NEW-STYLE PMQS ...
Signed, inscribed with title and dated '17 ix 15'
Pen ink and watercolour, 8 x 11 ¼ inches
Illustrated: *The Times*, 17 September 2015

531 TROPHY HUNTER
Signed and dated '30 vii 15'
Pen ink and watercolour
8 x 11 ¼ inches
Illustrated: *The Times*, 30 July 2015

323

532 ON THE RED PLANET...
Signed, inscribed with title and dated '29 ix 15'
Pen ink and watercolour
8 x 11 ¼ inches
Illustrated: *The Times*, 29 September 2015

BILL STOTT
William Stott (born 1944)

Bill Stott is one of the best-known of contemporary cartoonists, and his humour can be considered alongside that of fellow Merseyside draughtsmen, Bill Tidy, Pete and Mike Williams, and Albert Rusling.

For a biography of Bill Stott, please refer to *The Illustrators*, 2014, page 262.

324

533 SHE'S ON A DRIP
Signed
Pen ink and watercolour
8 ¼ x 11 ¾ inches

534 GOD! I'VE HAD IT WITH CHAMELEONS!
Signed
Pen ink and watercolour
11 ¾ x 8 ¼ inches

'Over the past year I seem to have fashioned an understanding with The Oldie *– which is far more ship-shape than in Mr Ingrams' day – and they've taken a few gags. I've also sold a few to* Private Eye, *although I suspect that happened when Mr Hislop was on holiday. As ever these days, if you're a gag merchant, new outlets are few and far between.*

As Chair of the Professional Cartoonists' Organisation, I work hard with the wonderful PCO Committee trying to fix the apparent cartoon disconnect between artists, editors and publishers. After the Paris murders in January, the PCO crowdfunded a book of anti-terrorism cartoons called Draw the Line Here. *Published by English Pen, it involved a lot of hard graft, but contains some cogent, and in many cases, despite its inspiration, very funny cartoons, mainly from PCO members.'*

(Bill Stott writes about his latest activities)

535 IT'S THE FEEDING OF THE FIVE THOUSAND AND YOU'VE GOT TO START SOMEWHERE
Signed
Pen ink and watercolour
8 ¼ x 11 ½ inches

536 YES – SOLD OFF THAT USELESS WATER MEADOW FOR AFFORDABLE HOUSING. BEEN DOWN TO MEET & GREET AND DO YOU KNOW? NOT ONE OF THEM SHOOTS!
Signed
Pen ink and watercolour
8 ½ x 12 inches

537 OK, YOU VARMINTS – I'M LOOKING FOR SOME FREAK CALLED COLOSSAL BOB ...
Signed
Title printed on attached label
Pen ink and watercolour
8 ½ x 12 inches

538 BUNFIGHT AT THE OK CORRAL
Signed
Title printed on attached label
Pen ink and watercolour
8 ½ x 12 inches

539 AND WATCH OUT FOR THE LOOSE CARPET
HALFWAY DOWN ...
Signed
Pen ink and watercolour
7 ¼ x 10 ¾ inches

540 FOR HEAVEN'S SAKE MURIEL – I'VE GOT A MAJOR
DERAILMENT GOING ON HERE!
Signed
Pen ink and watercolour
8 ¼ x 11 ¾ inches

541 LOOK – I'M TELLING YOU! THAT IS <u>NOT</u>
HOUSEHOLD WASTE!
Signed
Pen ink and watercolour
8 ½ x 11 inches

542 YOU KNOW THE RULES HUGO. PIANO PRACTICE FIRST.
THEN AND ONLY THEN YOU GO HANGIN' WID YO BRUVVAS
IN THE BUS SHELTER DRINKING CHEAP CIDER
Signed
Pen ink and watercolour
8 ¼ x 11 ¾ inches

MATT

Matthew Pritchett, MBE (born 1964), known as 'Matt'

Matt's much-loved pocket cartoons for the *Daily Telegraph* provide a consistently original take on the big news stories of the day.

For a biography of Matt, please refer to *The Illustrators*, 2009, page 185.

Our annual 'Evening with Matt Pritchett' and signing of the latest cartoon collection *The Best of Matt 2015* takes place this year on 8 December from 6-8pm.

'In March 2015 my downstairs loo was graced by the arrival of a new trophy, The Journalists' Charity Award.

News-wise it's been a quiet 12 months, apart from the Euro crisis, the general election, the Euro crisis, the FIFA scandal, the Euro crisis, the Labour leadership election, the Euro crisis, the Scottish referendum, the Euro crisis ...

In sport, we won the Ashes and lost the Rugby World Cup.

And the news event of the year was when Madonna fell down some stairs.'

(Matt writes about his latest activities)

543-557 were all illustrated either in the *Daily Telegraph* or the *Sunday Telegraph*

543 THE 8.35 IS DELAYED BECAUSE THE WOMEN'S CARRIAGE KEPT THE REST OF THE TRAIN WAITING
Signed and inscribed with title
Pen ink and watercolour
4 x 2 ¾ inches
Illustrated: Thursday 27 August 2015

544 HE'S A BRILLIANT MIMIC. HE SAW CORBYN ON TV AND NOW HE REFUSES TO SING THE NATIONAL ANTHEM
Signed and inscribed with title
Pen ink and watercolour
4 x 2 ¾ inches
Illustrated: Wednesday 16 September 2015

545 IF THE PUBLIC IS PROVIDING THE QUESTIONS, CAN WE CLAIM PARLIAMENTARY EXPENSES?
Signed and inscribed with title
Pen ink and watercolour
4 x 2 ¾ inches
Illustrated: Thursday 17 September 2015

546 I THINK MY HUSBAND'S HAVING AN AFFAIR. HE'S STARTED WEARING A VEST AND CALLING FOR RAIL NATIONALISATION
Signed and inscribed with title
Pen ink and watercolour
4 x 2 ¾ inches
Illustrated: Sunday 20 September 2015

547 WE'VE FOUND THE PROBLEM. YOU'RE LOOKING AT £18 BILLION PLUS PARTS AND LABOUR
Signed and inscribed with title
Pen ink and watercolour
4 x 2 ¾ inches
Illustrated: Wednesday 23 September 2015

548 DRIVERS OF ELECTRIC AND HYBRID CARS MAY BE 22 TIMES MORE SMUG THAN ORIGINALLY THOUGHT
Signed and inscribed with title
Pen ink and watercolour
4 x 2 ¾ inches
Illustrated: Friday 25 September 2015

549 IT SAYS 'CORBYN' SOME OF THE WAY THROUGH
Signed and inscribed with title
Pen ink and watercolour
4 x 2 ¾ inches
Illustrated: Sunday 27 September 2015

550 NASA FINDS WATER; MAN WALKS ON MARS – GETS VERRUCA
Signed
Pen ink and watercolour
4 x 2 ¾ inches
Illustrated: Tuesday 29 September 2015

551 NOW THAT I KNOW THIS CAR HAS BEEN LYING TO ME, I CAN'T EVEN TRUST THE SAT-NAV
Signed and inscribed with title
Pen ink and watercolour
4 x 2 ¾ inches
Illustrated: Wednesday 23 September 2015

552 DARLING, I HAVE TERRIBLE NEWS! MY VW GOLF HAS BEEN DECEIVING ME
Signed and inscribed with title
Pen ink and watercolour
4 x 2 ¾ inches
Illustrated: Thursday 24 September 2015

553 BE CAREFUL. MR MCDONNELL MIGHT SWOOP DOWN AND TAKE YOUR MONEY
Signed and inscribed with title
Pen ink and watercolour
4 x 2 ¾ inches
Illustrated: Tuesday 29 September 2015

554 HE FAILED TO EMBRACE THE KINDER, MORE CARING POLITICS
Signed and inscribed with title
Pen ink and watercolour
4 x 2 ¾ inches
Illustrated: Wednesday 30 September 2015

329

555 GO OUT THERE, AND IN THE WORDS OF JEREMY CORBYN, HAVE A HEALTHY, GROWN-UP DISAGREEMENT
Signed and inscribed with title
Pen ink and watercolour
4 x 2 ¾ inches
Illustrated: Saturday 3 October 2015

556 I'D LIKE TO JOIN THE PARISH COUNCIL. I WOULD BE WILLING TO PUSH THE NUCLEAR BUTTON
Signed and inscribed with title
Pen ink and watercolour
4 x 2 ¾ inches
Illustrated: Sunday 4 October 2015

557 WOULD YOU GIFT WRAP IT, PLEASE – IT'S A PRESENT
Signed and inscribed with title
Pen ink and watercolour
4 x 2 ¾ inches
Illustrated: Wednesday 7 October 2015

JONATHAN CUSICK

Jonathan Kristofor Cusick (born 1978)

Over the last decade, Jonathan Cusick has gained a strong reputation for his work as an illustrator, and particularly his arresting caricatures, which seem to hold a comically distorting mirror up to personalities who are prominent in the contemporary worlds of politics and entertainment.

For a biography of Jonathan Cusick, please refer to *The Illustrators*, 2010, page 275.

558 TOMMY COOPER
Signed
Acrylic on canvas
13 ¼ x 8 ¼ inches

559 GEORGE OSBORNE
Signed
Acrylic on canvas
8 ¾ x 4 ¼ inches

569 THE
SANCTIFICATION
OF LORD
BEAVERBROOK
BY A J P TAYLOR
Signed on reverse
Pen ink and bodycolour
on board
11 ½ x 9 ¼ inches
Illustrated: *Private Eye*

570 ANDRE PREVIN
Signed and inscribed
with title on reverse
Pen ink, bodycolour
and collage
13 ¾ x 9 ¼ inches
Illustrated: *Private Eye*

337

'Being a press baron of sorts, Ingrams, in the main an honest and basically good man, had little time for press barons who were crooks and liars. He hated Lord Beaverbrook for what he saw as his dishonesty, and hated equally the historian, A J P Taylor, for sucking up to him (the historian had just written yet another book saying how wonderful Beaverbrook was).

I did virtually all the illustrations for the Eye from the time I joined in 1961 until the 70s, when new faces knocked on the door. Willie Rushton was busy doing telly, and both Scarfe and Steadman both fell out of favour with Ingrams. They resented working in collaboration with him, that is, being given an idea and asked to draw it. I never had this problem, as the whole essence of working at Private Eye is one of collaboration, a team effort, like cricket and rugby. Beating the Hun and so on.'

(Barry Fantoni writes on *The Sanctification of Lord Beaverbrook by A J P Taylor*)

'Under Ingrams, the Eye attacked anyone who seemed not to have the right credentials for the job: Labour politicians who went to Public schools; Tories who were grammar boys. André Previn was best known as a jazz pianist who was given the job of conducting the LSO: red rag to the bull for Ingrams (who was born in 1937 – the Chinese year of the Ox, as it happens). The press as a whole saw young, easy going, smooth talking and super hip André a breath of fresh air. Putting him in a sports car and not on a rostrum was my take on the appointment. We then went on to feature him in a series by Sylvie Krin, in which the hapless Previn ruined every concert he conducted.'

(Barry Fantoni writes on *André Previn*)

'During the 50 years that I did portraits for illustration, I was never able to find a way of using anything other than a photo for reference. Obviously the dead can't sit and celebs would never dream of giving up their priceless time to come to my Clapham studio and sit still for a day. But after looking at pics of celebs for a long time, I gradually discovered that, when posing for a photo, a celeb would put on the professional face they wanted the world to see. So I figured I would use what they presented – the image they had of themselves – and develop it through my own vision. Adding a touch to the nose, a bit more to the ears if in a satirical mood. Copying exactly if not.'

(Barry Fantoni writes on his portraits and caricatures)

Observer Magazine

338

571 EISENHOWER,
MONTGOMERY
AND PATTON
Signed on reverse
Pen ink, watercolour
and bodycolour on board
13 ½ x 16 inches
Illustrated: *Observer Magazine*,
6 September 1964

'I produced an illustration for the very first copy of the Observer colour magazine and continued to illustrate for it for over ten years, working under some very fine and imaginative art directors. Ray Hawkey, who designed the iconic Len Deighton book jackets, was a great man to work for. The main point of an illustrator's work is to produce an image that cannot be obtained by any other source. The three Second World War generals never met in the circumstances of the article that I illustrated – Ike, Monty and Patton.'

(Barry Fantoni writes on *Eisenhower, Montgomery and Patton*)

'In 1967, I got a call from Geoffrey Cannon, an art director who had just been asked to redesign The Listener. Geoffrey later went on to redesign Radio Times and then edit it. He asked me to provide illustrations and cartoons. I then spoke to Karl Miller, the magazine's new editor, and we agreed a cartoon a week and an illustration as and when needed. I did the job for 21 years, until Alan Coren took over and saw the circulation drop to nothing. The Listener finally folded with Coren at the helm. Under editors Miller, Russell Twisk and George Scott and Anthony Howard, I did hundreds of portraits to illustrate features written by journalists who wrote for radio and TV as well as magazines and newspapers.

All the illustrations are from the early period – 1967 to 77 – after which the format of the paper altered slightly and I was given more time in advance to prepare larger images, some reproduced as a quarter page.'

(Barry Fantoni writes on *The Listener*)

The Listener

572 BASIL BRUSH
Signed on reverse
Pen ink and bodycolour on board, 9 ¼ x 8 ¼ inches
Illustrated: *The Listener*

'Basil Brush is the only puppet illustration I did for The Listener and apart from a painting of a cake I did to celebrate a Woman's Hour anniversary, I only illustrated living people. Although I did do a Dalek, come to think of it.'

(Barry Fantoni writes on *Basil Brush*)

573 EAMONN ANDREWS
Signed on reverse
Pen ink and bodycolour on board, 10 x 8 ½ inches
Illustrated: *The Listener*

'Eamonn Andrews was the best fight commentator I ever heard and was almost the worst TV presenter of his day. Since then, every TV interviewer I have seen seems more interested in themselves than their guests.'

(Barry Fantoni writes on *Eamonn Andrews*)

574 DAVID COLEMAN
Signed on reverse
Pen ink and watercolour on board
12 x 10 inches
Illustrated: *The Listener*

575 PETER O'SULLEVAN
Signed on reverse
Pen ink and bodycolour
7 ½ x 7 inches
Illustrated: *The Listener*

*'I enjoyed painting the horse racing
commentator, Peter O'Sullevan, as I
considered him to be as good in his
field (no pun intended) as it gets.'*

(Barry Fantoni writes on *Peter O'Sullevan*)

*'The sports commentator, David Coleman was a
very private man and disliked the fact I had
invented a column in* Private Eye *called
'Colemanballs'. I think his handling of the Munich
Olympics was nothing short of masterly.
Hour after hour with nothing happening and
trying to keep the viewer interested in an
exterior shot of the Israeli athletes camp using
the same technique as when commentating
on Stoke versus Bolton.'*

(Barry Fantoni writes on *David Coleman*)

*'I would say the same for John Arlott,
who also added poetry
to the art of commentary.'*

(Barry Fantoni writes on *John Arlott*)

576 JOHN ARLOTT
Signed on reverse
Pen ink and bodycolour on board
9 ¼ x 7 ¾ inches
Illustrated: *The Listener*

Daily Mirror Magazine

577 JACK LEMMON
Signed on reverse
Pen ink, watercolour and bodycolour on board
12 x 9 inches
Illustrated: *Daily Mirror Magazine*, 1968

578 WALTER MATTHAU
Signed on reverse
Pen ink, watercolour and bodycolour on board
10 ½ x 7 inches
Illustrated: *Daily Mirror Magazine*, 1968

'In 1968 the Daily Mirror produced a colour magazine. It was a trend started by The Sunday Times, *followed by the* Observer *and the* Sunday Telegraph, *which was printed in Germany and a far superior production than both its rivals, the content less so. Mike Malloy was the Mirror Magazine's editor. They had had a trial period producing a centre paper pullout in black and white. I also worked on that project, but the portraits of Jack Lemmon and Walter Matthau remain my major contribution to what was a very short lived adventure for the Mirror. The magazine did not take. The feature I illustrated was on* The Odd Couple *starring Lemmon and Matthau, which had just been released and considered their finest work to date.'*

(Barry Fantoni writes on *Jack Lemmon* and *Walter Matthau*)

The Sunday Times

579 KATHLEEN FERRIER
Signed on reverse
Pen ink and bodycolour on board
11 x 12 inches
Illustrated: *The Sunday Times*

580 OLIVIER MESSIAEN
Signed on reverse
Pen ink and bodycolour on board
11 x 12 inches
Illustrated: *The Sunday Times*

'In the late 70s and early 80s, I did illustrations for The Sunday Times. It was well paid and my work was given a key place in the paper.
It gave me a chance to work in great detail and I enjoyed painting the subjects, who were in the main people whose work I admired.
The idea was to find a background that reflected the subject's work. For the contralto, Kathleen Ferrier, I chose a Greek image of Orpheus, as her
big hit was from Gluck's opera about him. [The image is from the Orpheus vase, a red figure vase painted in circa 450 BC.]
For the French composer, Olivier Messiaen, I used a Braque painting, since they knew each other. At the time, the photo I used to copy from was the
only available image of Messiaen, who was very little photographed.'

(Barry Fantoni writes on *Kathleen Ferrier* and *Olivier Messiaen*)

The Times

581 MUST HAVE USED OUR PLUMBER
Signed, inscribed with title and dated 1988
Pen and ink
5 x 3 inches
Illustrated: *The Times*, April 1988

582 I HEAR THE CITY ARE TAKING IT
WITH A PINCH OF SALT
Signed, inscribed with title and dated 1989
Pen and ink
5 x 3 inches
Illustrated: *The Times*, November 1989

583 GOOD TO SEE THE
ARCHBISHOP'S REMARKS
ON FUNDAMENTALISM
ARE TAKING EFFECT
Signed, inscribed with title and dated 1989
Pen and ink
5 x 3 inches
Illustrated: *The Times*, 1989

584 DON'T TELL ME –
IN AN APPLE PIE
Signed, inscribed with title and dated 1990
Pen and ink
5 x 3 inches
Illustrated: *The Times*, February 1990

SELECT BIBLIOGRAPHY

Backemeyer 2005
Sylvia Backemeyer (ed), *Picture This: The Artist as Illustrator*, London: Herbert Press, 2005

Baker 2002
Martin Baker, *Artists of Radio Times. A Golden Age of British Illustration*, Oxford: The Ashmolean Press & Chris Beetles Ltd, 2002

Bryant 2000
Mark Bryant, *Dictionary of Twentieth-Century British Cartoonists and Caricaturists*, London: Ashgate, 2000

Bryant and Heneage 1994
Mark Bryant and Simon Heneage, *Dictionary of British Cartoonists and Caricaturists, 1730-1980*, Aldershot: Scolar Press, 1994

Clark 1998
Alan Clark, *Dictionary of British Comic Artists, Writer and Editors*, London: The British Library, 1998

Driver 1981
David Driver (compiler), *The Art of Radio Times. The First Sixty Years*, London: BBC, 1981

Feaver 1981
William Feaver, *Masters of Caricature. From Hogarth and Gillray to Scarfe and Levine*, London: Weidenfeld and Nicolson, 1981

Horne 1994
Alan Horne, *The Dictionary of 20th Century Book Illustrators*, London: Antique Collectors' Club, 1994

Houfe 1996
Simon Houfe, *The Dictionary of British Book Illustrators and Caricaturists, 1800-1914*, Woodbridge: Antique Collectors' Club, 1996 (revised ed)

Johnson and Gruetzner 1986
Jane Johnson and Anna Gruetzner, *The Dictionary of British Artists, 1880-1940*, Woodbridge: Antique Collectors' Club, 1986 (reprint)

Khoury 2004
George Khoury (ed), *True Brit. A Celebration of the Great Comic Book Artists of the UK*, Raleigh, NC: TwoMorrows Publishing, 2004

Lewis 1967
John Lewis, *The 20th Century Book*, London: Herbert Press, 1967

Mallalieu 1976
Huon Mallalieu, *The Dictionary of British Watercolour Artists, up to 1920*, Woodbridge: Antique Collectors' Club, 1976

Martin 1989
Douglas Martin, *The Telling Line. Essays on fifteen contemporary book illustrators*, London: Julia MacRae Books, 1989

Matthew and Harrison 2004
H C G Matthew and Brian Harrison (eds), *Oxford Dictionary of National Biography*, Oxford University Press, 2004 (61 vols)

Peppin and Mickelthwait 1983
Brigid Peppin and Lucy Mickelthwait, *The Dictionary of British Book Illustrators: The Twentieth Century*, London: John Murray, 1983

Price 1957
R G G Price, *A History of Punch*, London: Collins, 1957

Ray 1976
Gordon Norton Ray, *The Illustrator and the Book in England from 1790 to 1914*, New York: Pierpoint Morgan Library, 1976

Reid 1928
Forrest Reid, *Illustrators of the Sixties*, London: Faber & Gwyer, 1928

Souter 2007
Nick and Tessa Souter, *The Illustration Handbook. A Guide to the World's Greatest Illustrators*, Royston: Eagle Editions, 2007

Spalding 1990
Frances Spalding, *20th Century Painters and Sculptors*, Woodbridge: Antique Collectors' Club, 1990

Spielmann 1895
M H Spielmann, *The History of 'Punch'*, London: Cassell and Company, 1895

Suriano 2000
Gregory R Suriano, *The Pre-Raphaelite Illustrators*, New Castle: Oak Knoll Press/London: The British Library, 2000

Turner 1996
Jane Turner (ed), *The Dictionary of Art*, London: Macmillan, 1996 (34 vols)

Wood 1995
Christopher Wood, *The Dictionary of Victorian Painting*, Woodbridge: Antique Collectors' Club, 1995 (2 vols)

CUMULATIVE INDEX OF CATALOGUES (1991-2015)

Cushing, Howard Gardiner: 1999
Cusick, Jonathan: 2010, 2011, 2012, 2014, 2015

D

Dadd, Frank: 2015
Dadd, Philip: 1997
Dadd, Richard: 1997
Daley, Mike: 1992
Davidson, Victoria: **2003**, 2011, 2014
Davis, Jon: 1991, 1992, 1993
Dawson, Eric: 1993
de Grineau, Bryan: 1992
De La Bere, Stephen Baghot: 1991, 1992, 1997, 2001, 2008
Dennis, Ada: 1996
Dickens, Frank: 1993, 1997, 1999, 2003, 2011, 2014
Dickinson, Geoffrey: 2011
Dighton, Richard: 2014
Dighton, Robert: 2014
Disney, Walt (and the Disney Studio): 1991, 1993, 1999, 2000, 2002, 2003
Dixon, Charles: 1992
Dobson, Austin: 1996
Donnison, Thomas Edward: 2011
Doré, Gustave: 1997, 1999, 2009
Douglas (Thomas Douglas England): 1992, 1993
Doyle, Charles: 1991, 1992, 1997, 1999, 2002, 2003, 2007, 2009, 2011, 2012
Doyle, Richard: 1991, 1993, 1996, 1997, 1999, 2002, 2010, 2011
Draner, Jules-Renard: 1993
Drew, Simon: 1991, 1992, 1993, 1997, 1999, 2001, 2002, 2003, 2007, 2008, 2010
Du Cane, Ella: 1997
Dulac, Edmund: 1991, 1993, 1996, 1997, 2001, **2003**, 2007, 2009, 2010, 2012, 2014, 2015
Du Maurier, George: 1991, 1992, **1996**, 1997, 1999, 2003, 2007, 2009, 2010, **2011**, 2012, 2015
Duncan, John: 1991
Duncan, Walter: 1996
Dyson, Will: 1993, 1997, 1999

E

Earnshaw, Harold: 1996
East, Alfred: 1997
Edwards, Lionel: 1992
Egan, Beresford: 1997
Elgood, George Samuel: 1997
Elliott, James: 1999
Embleton, Ron: 2012
Emett, Rowland: 1991, 1992, 1993, 1996, 1997, 1999, 2000, 2001, 2003, 2007, 2008, 2009, 2011, 2014
Emmwood (John Musgrave Wood): 1991, 1993, 1997, 2002, 2007, 2010, 2011, 2014
Evans, Treyer: 2007

F

Fantoni, Barry: **2014, 2015**
Ferguson, Norman: 1993, 1999, 2003
ffolkes, Michael: 1991, 1993, 1997, 1999, 2014
Fitzgerald, John Anster: 1991, 1997, 1999, 2012
Flagg, James Montgomery: 2015
Flanders, Dennis: 1992
Flather, Lisa: 1991
Fletcher, Geoffrey Scowcroft: 1993
Flint, Francis Russell: 1992
Flint, William Russell: 1993
Folkard, Charles: 1991, 1992, 1997, 2003, 2010
Ford, Henry Justice: 2002, 2003, 2007, 2008, 2009
Ford, Noel: 1993
Foreman, Michael: 1991, 1992, 1993, 1997, 1999, 2001, 2003, 2007, 2008, **2009**, 2010, 2011, **2012**, 2014
Foster, Myles Birket: 1991, 1999
Fougasse (Cyril Kenneth Bird): 1991, **1992**, 1993, **1996**, 1999, 2003, **2009**, 2014, 2015
François, André: 2009, 2014
Fraser, Claude Lovat: 1993
Fraser, Eric: 1991, **1992**, 1993, 1997, 2001, 2002, 2003, 2007, 2008, **2009**, **2010**, **2011**, **2012**
Fraser, Gordon: 2015
French, Annie: 1991, 1992, 1997, 2003

Frith, Michael: 2010
Frost, William Edward: 1997, 2011
Fulleylove, John: 1996, 1997
Fullwood, John: 1997
Furniss, Harry: 1991, 1992, 1996, 1999, **2003**, 2009, 2012

G

Gaffney, Michael: 1991
Gardiner, Gerald: 1992, 1997, 2011
Garstin, Norman: 2003
Gaze, Harold: 1999, 2007
Gerrard, Roy: 2010, 2014, **2015**
Gibbard, Les: 2011
Gibson, Charles Dana: 1991, 1999
Gilbert, John: 1993, 1996
Giles, (Carl Ronald Giles): 1991, 1992, 1993, **1996**, 1997, 1999, 2001, 2002, 2007, 2008, 2009, 2011
Gilliam, Terry: 1992
Gilroy, John: 1997
Ginger, Phyllis: 1991, 1992, 1993
Glaser, Milton: 2015
Glashan, John: 1993, 2014
Goble, Warwick: 1997, 2002, 2007, 2008, 2010, 2011
Godfrey, Bob: 1993
Goldsmith, Beatrice May: 1996
Goodall, John Strickland: 1991, **1996**, 1997
Goodwin, Harry: 1992
Gould, Francis Carruthers: 1992, 1996, 1999, 2003, 2009, 2010, 2012
Gould, Rupert Thomas: 1996
Granville, Walter: 1992
Greeley, Valerie: 1992
Green, Charles: 1991, 1997, 1999, 2012
Green, John Kenneth: 1993
Green, Winifred: 1996, 1999
Greenaway, Kate: 1991, 1992, **1996**, 1997, 1999, 2000, **2001**, 2003, 2007, 2010, 2012
Gruelle, Johnny: 2015
Guthrie, Thomas Anstey: 1997

H

I C H: 1997
Haité, George: 1997
Hale, Kathleen: 1991, 1996, 2003,

2007, 2008, **2009**, 2010, **2011**
Hall, Amanda: **2011**, **2012**, 2014, 2015
Hall, Sidney Prior: 1991
Halswelle, Keeley: 1997
Hampson, Frank: 2002, 2003, 2008
Hancock, John: 1999
Hankey, William Lee: 1992, 1999
Hardy, Dorothy: 1991
Hardy, Dudley: 1991, 1992, 1997, 1999, 2014
Hardy, Evelyn Stuart: 1993
Hargreaves, Harry : **2015**
Haro (Haro Hodson): 1991
Harris, Herbert H: 2003
Harrison, Florence: 2007, 2008, 2011, **2014**, **2015**
Harrold, John: 1993
Hartrick, Archibald Standish: 1999
Harvey, William: 2014
Haselden, William Kerridge: 2010
Hassall, Ian: 1992, 1997
Hassall, Joan: 1992, 2011
Hassall, John: 1991, 1992, 1993, 1997, 1999, 2003, 2011
Hatherell, William: 1991, 2003
Hawkins, Colin: 1999
Hay, James Hamilton: 1997
Hayes, Claude: 1997
Haywood, Leslie: 1992
Heath, Michael: 1993
Henderson, Keith: 1992, **2015**
Hennell, Thomas: 1991
Henry, Thomas: 1999
Herbert, Susan: 1996
Hergé (Georges Remi): 1991
Hewison, Bill: 2007
Hickson, Joan: 1993
Hilder, Rowland: 1997
Hirschfeld, Al: **2007**, 2015
Hodges, Cyril Walter: 1991, 1993, 1997, 2011
Hoffnung, Gerard: 1991, **1992**, 1996, 1997, 1999, 2007, 2009, 2010, 2011, **2014**, 2015
Honeysett, Martin: 1999
Hopkins, Arthur: 1996
Hopwood, Henry: 1997
Houghton, Arthur Boyd: 2002
Housman, Laurence: 1991, 2010
Howitt, Samuel: 1993

347

348

INDEX